Praise for *Columbine: A True Crime Story*
a victim, the killers and the nation's search for answers

"Jeff Kass comes closer than anyone in explaining this national tragedy that is Columbine. His discussions with Hunter S. Thompson in the kitchen over the years revealed his depth of research and wisdom of this complex story, which he finally unmasks, a decade later in *Columbine: A True Crime Story*."
—**Anita Thompson**, wife of the late Hunter S. Thompson, and author of *The Gonzo Way*.

"It was the kind of tragedy that defined a genuine breakdown of social cohesion in the late nineties. America and guns go back a long way, as Hunter used to remind me, and demonstrate. But this was a lack of imagination, a cold assessment of cause and effect, devoid of compassion and the action of severely damaged psyches which could never have been introduced to the ramifications of consequence. Unfortunately, these kids have had many role models, filmic but very real demonstrations from *A Clockwork Orange* onwards on which to base their ideas. I reckon that the senseless motive for violence heightens the sick thrill of the act."
—**Ralph Steadman**, artist, cultural satirist, and author of *The Joke's Over: Bruised Memories: Gonzo, Hunter S. Thompson, and Me.*

"'Could this happen here?' The day after Columbine I was asked that question from parents, faculty, school administrators, students and police officers in Aspen. *Columbine: A True Crime Story* answers all questions about the killers, the families, and victims of one of the most iconic school shootings in this nation's history and more."
— **Pitkin County Sheriff Bob Braudis**

"Kass has created a tour-de-force explaining not just Columbine, but the roots of all teen violence – not just an accounting of facts, but a sordid, painful, and in the end, hopeful tale that draws us in and won't let go. It will remain with you long after the pages become dog-eared and weathered."
—**Paul Dobransky**, M.D., Psychiatrist and first responder to Columbine.

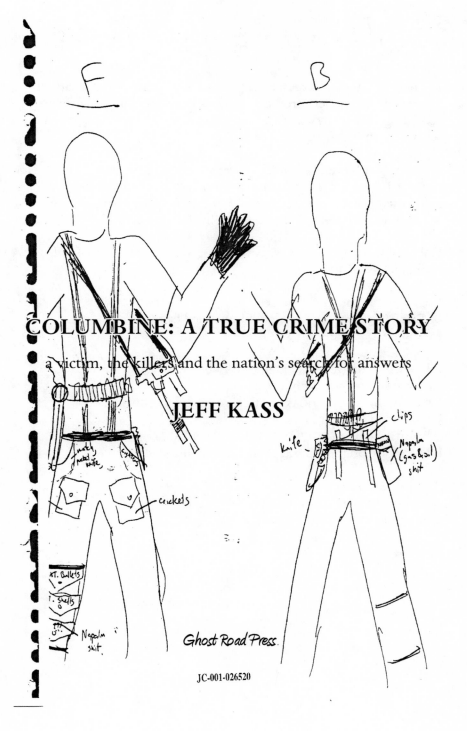

COLUMBINE: A TRUE CRIME STORY

a victim, the killers and the nation's search for answers

JEFF KASS

Ghost Road Press

Case study/profile of "Sandra" excerpted from *Your Inner Conflicts-How
to Solve Them* (Simon and Schuster, 1974) Written by Hugh Missildine
and Lawrence Galton. Used with the generous permission of Dan
Missildine and Jeremy Galton. All Rights Reserved.

Columbine photos used with the generous permission of the *Rocky
Mountain News.*

Drawings and notebook pages
of Eric Harris and Dylan Klebold obtained from
Jefferson County Sheriff's Office.

Library of Congress Cataloging-in-Publication Data.
Columbine: A True Crime Story
a victim, the killers and the nation's search for answers
Ghost Road Press
ISBN (Trade pbk.) 978-0-9816525-6-6; 0-9816525-6-5
Library of Congress Control Number: 2008937329

Editorial: Evan Lee
Cover and interior design: Matthew Davis
Cover illustration: Ralph Steadman

Ghost Road Press
Denver, Colorado
www.ghostroadpress.com

To George and Judi Kass:

My superlative editors, advisers, supporters, and of course, loving mom and dad

MAY

SUNDAY	MONDAY	TUESDAY	WEDNESDAY	THURSDAY	FRIDAY	S
25	26	27	28	29	30	

APRIL

JUNE

LUNAR CYCLE
- NEW MOON
- FIRST QUARTER
- FULL MOON
- LAST QUARTER

Cinco de Mayo (Mexico)

Mother's Day

"good wombs have born Bad sons,"
—Shakespeare

Victoria Day (Canada)

Memorial Day

FOREWORD

Jefferson County, Colorado entered our collective consciousness in a horrific way back in April 1999. A couple Holden Caulfields run amok stormed into Columbine High School and killed twelve classmates and a teacher and injured twenty-four others.

Suddenly the names of murderers Eric Harris and Dylan Klebold became synonymous with derangement. Grotesquely, these two mass murderers had videotaped their plot to raid the school brandishing two shotguns, a rifle, and a semi-automatic pistol. A huge public debate erupted over everything from gun control to Goth culture, violence in films to the use of anti-depressants for young people. Columbine became a one-word banner for American dysfunctionalism. Perhaps because Columbine was so disgusting to contemplate, few reporters probed deeply into the meaning of the debacle. After all, America had previously experienced two even more deadly school killings than Columbine.

The Bath School bombings in 1927 left forty-five, including the bomber, dead. The University of Texas shooter in 1966 killed fourteen. An even worse shooting spree occurred at Virginia Tech in 2007, but that is getting ahead of our story.

For only Columbine seemed to stab into the dark underbelly of the American psyche like a knife that kept being twisted. It remains a stain on our culture which can't be rubbed out. All murders sicken the heart but Columbine continues to haunt the soul. Had our society gone completely wrong? Was Columbine a wake-up call to parents to start being more hands-on? Or were Harris and Klebold simply two bad seeds?

Out of all the reporters covering the Colorado disaster, only Jeff Kass of the *Rocky Mountain News* kept the big picture constantly in focus. While the TV media milked Columbine for its ghastly week of soap-opera-ish drama Kass, with gumshoe persistence, stayed on the case like Sherlock Holmes.

When the national TV trucks left Colorado for another tragedy he continued on the job with his trusty laptop and a jolt of coffee.

The result is this fine work of narrative storytelling and muckraking journalism. Modeling *Columbine: A True Crime Story* after Truman Capote's *In Cold Blood*, Kass expertly probes the far-reaching consequences of the 1999 tragedy for a country where guns can be bought as if baseball cards at the Five-and-Dime store. Much like Norman Mailer in *The Executioner's Song*, Kass captures the flatness of Colorado life, the mundaneness of small town living, and how two miscreants decided to spice things up.

The writing is rhythmic, sparse, and paced. The La-Z-Boy chair becomes as important to the narrative as the two sawed-off shotguns. Like any journalist worth his salt, Kass provides lots of minute detail which adds immeasurably to the saga: "Jesus Christ Superstar" on the stereo, Blackjack Pizza for the paycheck, Apocalypse Now in the VCR, and on and on.

To produce this book Kass had to overcome numerous obstacles, including an uncooperative sheriff's office and the killers' parents who tried to block information.

But if we make the leap that Columbine was a collective tragedy – a high school bloodbath that stained all our sensibilities – then only full disclosure can heal our gaping wound. Kass has delivered the goods in this important regard. This objective, honest, and eye-opening book sheds light on the warped phenomena of school shootings in general, which Kass believes are more prevalent in the South and West than anywhere else.

Dealing with insanity is no easy matter. Trying to get into the head of Hannibal Lecter-types is a crucifixion in its own right for an aspiring writer. It takes a steady hand to paddle through the muck: Emotional swings. Zombie behavior. Anti-social personality disorder. It's all a hard pill to swallow. How much more fun it is to cover Barack Obama at the Democratic National Convention. Add to the mix reams of legal documents and you understand why the typical reporter runs for the sun after the news cycle of an event like Columbine fades from the cable scroll.

But Kass stayed with the story, in all its ugly turns of gloom and misery, and the result is truly impressive. For ten years Kass worked on this book, sniffing out ledes and procuring exclusives. So read it and weep. But also be glad that in our short-attention span society there is one old-fashioned reporter at the *Rocky Mountain News* who treats his journalistic oath seriously.

—Douglas Brinkley,
January 6, 2009

ACKNOWLEDGMENTS

They got the dedication, but it's still not enough. There was no stronger, nor better, force behind this book than my parents. I still remember my mother challenging me, nearly ten years ago in Denver, to write this book. And my brother, Brian, has always been there for me.

Sadly, there is even some breaking news in the acknowledgements. My main home as a reporter for nearly ten years has been the *Rocky Mountain News*. But as this book goes to print, the nearly 150-year-old paper has been put up for sale. Many are writing its obit. Without the *Rocky's* reporting on Columbine, there would be a hole in history. At the *Rocky*, I worked Columbine stories side by side with Kevin Vaughan and Lynn Bartels – as the many shared bylines will attest. I always thought that if one of us angered a source, the source wouldn't talk to any of us. But Kevin and Lynn are great reporters and teammates.

I thank Editor John Temple for the generous use of the *Rocky's* photos – among the finest in journalism. I also appreciate the support and wise counsel from John each time a difficult decision came across his desk. *Rocky* Managing Editor Deb Goeken granted me the leave of absence to finish this book and I also thank Deb for shepherding through - and deftly editing - many of the biggest stories I have worked on at the *Rocky*. John, Deb, and all the other editors have also been extremely kind over the years in granting me a flexible schedule that allowed me to work on the book. *Rocky* photo editor Janet Reeves was also gracious with the photos, while columnist Penny Parker stepped in for a last-minute assist, as did the photog phenom Barry Gutierrez, who did the author photo. Other *Rocky* photographers whose powerful work has come to symbolize Columbine and is in this book are: Rodolfo Gonzalez, Ellen Jaskol, George Kochaniec Jr., Matt McClain, and Chris Schneider.

The magnificent, and now departed, Hunter S. Thompson had long been an inspiration. I was lucky enough to not only meet him, but write about him and his legacy for over five years. (Surely, one of the most unusual beats in the history of journalism.) The blurb from Hunter comes from one of the many conversations I had with him about Columbine over the years in which he encouraged me to write the book and offered his contacts.

Through Hunter I met Ralph Steadman, artist extraordinaire. Among the most memorable moments is interviewing Ralph for

C-SPAN and having him take control of the show. It was all great fun. I approached Ralph for a drawing because he and Hunter were expert in plumbing the dark depths of the American psyche through their previous collaborations (exhibit one being *Fear and Loathing in Las Vegas*).

In examining Columbine, Ralph drew inspiration from the classic Edgar Allen Poe short story *Imp of the Perverse*. A passage from the story reads: "With certain minds, under certain conditions, it becomes absolutely irresistible. I am not more certain that I breathe, than that the assurance of the wrong or error of any action is often the one unconquerable force which impels us, and alone impels us to its prosecution." Ralph sent me the drawing that now graces the cover with the note, "I thought of a picture that quantifies exactly the sum-total of a deprived kid's mind...."

Curtis Robinson introduced me to Hunter. Curtis was my first editor, and remains my mentor. He's not sure what that means – and as he notes, there's no money in it – but it entails sage advice and a job recommendation at any time of the day or night. Curtis' wife, Donna, died much too young. But she was an inspirational person, and editor, for all who knew her.

Enormous thanks to Ghost Road Press publisher Matt Davis and editor Evan Lee for making this ten-year project real, standing behind the journalism, and being patient while I pushed deadline.

They say a reporter is only as good as his sources. So thank you to everyone who talked to me. You never know when the phone will be slammed down, or a door shut in your face. Psychologists Dwayne Fuselier and Aubrey Immelman were especially patient, and thorough. Sam Riddle has been exemplary. Kevin Vaughan aided with fact-checking.

Those among the Columbine families who have been especially helpful were Randy and Judy Brown, Brian Rohrbough, and Michael and Vonda Shoels. Thanks to Bobbi Kass for excellent advice, and Gail Kass for world-class legal help. They stepped in on more than one occasion. Hope Hamashige jumped in at the last minute to help with fact-checking. Jaime Aguilar at the *Rocky* wrangled the photo files and *Rocky* design director Kathy Bogan found the art files that always seemed on the verge of being lost forever. I am greatly appreciative for the blurbs from everyone, especially Anita Thompson, who offered to go above and beyond the call of duty at the last minute. Douglas Brinkley did a wonderful foreword.

Two stalwart friends who I consider blood brothers are Mike Gellman and Adam Newman. They and others have always stood by my side, criticized me when necessary, and been great travel partners, from Vegas to Vietnam: David Benlolo, Charlie Brennan, Joel Cherdack, Andy Fine, Brian Frenkel, James Gilbert, Josh Hanfling, David Kesmodel, fellow Hunter veteran Matt Moseley, Ean Seeb, Nevin Shrage, and Holly Yettick. Sorry for anyone I missed, but deadline calls.

My patient girlfriend Jolie Coursen kept me fed and sane as I locked myself in the treehouse office and Matt Davis' basement.

W.H. Auden called murder a unique crime because the victim is dead and society is left to speak up on their behalf. But Columbine tells a more specific story: It was victims families who stood up for their loved ones, who fought for a new library, and who so often pushed for information.

AUTHOR'S NOTE

When Columbine hit I was a part-time reporter in Denver at the Rocky Mountain News and stringing for a number of national publications. On Tuesday April 20, 1999, I was scheduled to take the test to work at the Associated Press because I had long wanted to be a foreign correspondent, and the AP has a multitude of overseas bureaus. At about 11:30 a.m., ten minutes after Columbine started, the deputy national editor I worked with at the Boston Globe, Dean Inouye, called me at home. He said there had been reports of a shooting at Columbine High School, a place I had never heard of. Dean said a student might be shot in the leg — the reports were sketchy, and just coming in. Dean wasn't sure he wanted me to go to the scene, but it was a possibility.

This might not be a big story, I thought. But I double-checked the local news. Wham. The wall to wall local coverage made clear that a full-blown school shooting had come to a Denver suburb. I called Dean back and said it was huge. I was going out to the school. As I was getting ready editors at the other publications I free-lanced for, the Christian Science Monitor, Newsday, and US News & World Report, called in rapid succession in the breathless, desperate voice of journalists on deadline: Can you cover the story for us? Yes, yes, yes, I said, figuring I would sort it all out later.

I have never covered a war zone. But Columbine seemed to be a close approximation. Clement Park, which rubs up against the school, was the staging area for police, reporters, and grief. That first day, before the international hordes of media and the general public arrived, friends and family gathered in the park hoping to connect with missing Columbine students and faculty. Students who did not know if their classmates were dead would find them amidst the mass, and burst into hugs and tears. On that first day, then Sheriff John Stone said the death toll might reach twenty-five. As a reporter kneeling in front of Stone at that impromptu press conference on the park grass when he uttered those words, the news was so stunning it seemed improper to immediately ask a follow up question. Stone, it turns out, was wrong. But the final number of dead, fifteen, remains no less mind-numbing.

In the following days, the park continued as a town square.

Grief was translated into clumps of teddy bears, flowers, and every manner of knick knack that twisted through the grass like a lumpy snake and stretched the equivalent of several city blocks. By the Friday after Columbine, spring snow turned Clement Park into a mud pit. War zone, I thought.

As the crowds filtered out of Columbine in the following months one fundamental question, which became the genesis for this book, remained. That was why school shootings seemed to suddenly be occurring across the country with greater frequency. It was a trend Columbine now cemented in the national psyche. But where did this come from? And when the shootings seemed to taper off, that just begged the question as to why. Then they exploded all over again.

Traditional theories of juvenile delinquency would not do. School shooters did not come from abusive homes, or bad neighborhoods. In fact, it was just the opposite.

An editor once called me "pathologically optimistic." I think it's a good trait. And armed with it, I believed that if I got to the right people, read the right stories, and uncovered the right documents, I could find the answers. I hope I got some of them.

When faced with a list of names, a sort of journalistic trick is to go in alphabetical order so that no one person is considered first. As if the random order of the alphabet conveys equality. At Columbine, there was a different random order: the one in which thirteen innocent victims were shot before they died:

Rachel Scott
Dan Rohrbough
Dave Sanders
Kyle Velasquez
Steven Curnow
Cassie Bernall
Isaiah Shoels
Matt Kechter
Lauren Townsend
John Tomlin
Kelly Flemming
Daniel Mauser
Corey DePooter

"The hardest part to understand was kids killing kids."
—**Student**

"A kid my age isn't supposed to go to that many funerals."
—**Student**

*"I hope people come here to this place to think about how they themselves
can be better people rather than come here to reflect on death."*
—**Parent**

—**Among the quotes inscribed on the Columbine Memorial**

PART ONE: 'Cause That's What We Do

ONE

Day One

On the day of Columbine seventeen-year-old Dylan Bennet Klebold is wearing a black T-shirt with "Wrath" printed in red letters across the chest. The red matches the blood that will later gurgle out of his head to form a jagged halo when he lies dead on the floor of the high school library.

Under Klebold's black trench coat is an Intratec Tec-DC9, semi-automatic pistol attached to his body with a shoulder strap. Around noon, Klebold will place the gun to his left temple and fire a 9mm bullet through his skull, exiting the right temple. Tucked away in his black cargo pants is a Stevens 12-gauge side-by-side double-barrel shotgun cut down to about twenty-three inches, which Klebold will have to reload after every two rounds.

Klebold wears his beloved black baseball cap, with the Boston Red Sox logo, backwards. His long, puffy brown hair flares out below the cap and one student thinks he looks like a clown. Klebold has also grown a goatee and mustache. On his left hand is a black, fingerless glove, while his left ring finger has a silver-colored ring with a black stone. The rest of Klebold's wardrobe consists of white socks, black boots and blue-green plaid boxer shorts. On his left boot is a red star medallion containing a hammer and sickle.

Eric David Harris, eighteen, is wearing black cargo pants and a white T-shirt that reads "Natural Selection." Under his black trench coat is a Hi-Point 9mm carbine rifle on a strap. He also carries a Savage Springfield 12-gauge shotgun with the stock and barrel cut off. It is twenty-six inches long, and Harris can cycle and fire five rounds before having to reload. Later in the day Harris will wrap his teeth around the shotgun's single barrel and pull the trigger.

Harris completes his outfit much like Klebold: fingerless black glove on his right hand, white socks, black combat boots and green plaid underwear.

Harris and Klebold have hand signals, and one imagines them jotting down the gestures before the massacre with a mixture of excitement and exactitude; serious about the carnage, but giddy to kill. The signals include:

Bombing—wave fist

Cops sighted—wave hand

Suicide—point to head with gun

Like children overloaded with candy, Harris and Klebold fill their cargo pants with CO2 bomblets, but save space in their pockets and utility belts for shotgun shells, and 9 mm cartridge magazines. A backpack and a duffel bag hold more bombs.

They carry at least four knives. Two are small, including one that resembles a dagger and has an 'R' scratched into the black handle, assumedly for Harris's nickname, Reb. Another, hulking knife looks to be about a foot long. A fourth is a contraption like brass knuckles but with spikes jutting out, and a wedge-shaped knife attached to one end. The sheriff concludes Harris and Klebold do not use their knives, but they discuss it, saying "I've always wanted to use a knife."

Their cars match their persons. Harris's dream car is a Hummer, but he calls his 1986 gray Honda Prelude the best gift he has ever received. He fills it with a pipe bomb, gas cans, and a twenty-pound propane tank. The trunk holds two large, black containers police believe are full of gasoline. One cop suspects a white plastic gallon jug labeled kitchen degreaser is homemade napalm. A pint bottle of bleach and a metal can of charcoal lighter round out the collection. Klebold's 1982 black BMW holds similar booty, along with a newsletter from the Firearms Coalition of Colorado: "Dear Firearms Activist: The Firearms Coalition of Colorado is working for you!" The newsletter urges people to make a contribution, or contact state legislators to lobby for pro-gun legislation: "When you call or write, be polite and respectful, we want to win friends, not make enemies."

The sheriff figures the car bombs, which never detonate, are set to blow up the officers and paramedics responding to Columbine.

Around 11:15 a.m. investigators believe Harris and Klebold carry two duffle bags into the cafeteria and place them beside lunch tables. Each duffle contains a twenty-pound propane bomb set to explode at 11:17 a.m., when Harris and Klebold figure "500+" will be in the cafeteria. They return to their cars and wait for the bombs to explode so they can mow down surviving students and staff who try to flee.

Peter Horvath, the dean who had once busted Harris and Klebold for stealing locker combinations, had lunch duty that day. It was his job to patrol the cafeteria. But he was late. He wonders: if he had been on time, if he would have noticed Harris and Klebold setting down the duffle bags. If he would have said something. If he would have prevented Columbine.

Brooks Brown is the on-again, off-again friend of Harris and Klebold, and says he comes across Harris minutes before the shooting. "Brooks, I like you now," Harris says. "Get out of here. Go home." Brooks leaves with the uneasy feeling that Harris is going to pull a prank. He walks down the street contemplating whether to skip fifth period and hears "a loud crack."

***

The twenty-pound duffle bag bombs don't go off. So Harris and Klebold are standing above the school, preparing to fill in the blanks. Their shooting gallery is approximately 2,000 students, and 140 teachers and staff. A number of students have taken advantage of the warm, sunny Tuesday – April 20, 1999 – to eat lunch outside on the grass. The sheriff's official timeline reads 11:19 a.m.

"Go, go!" one of them yells.

Harris and Klebold take their shotguns out from a bag, but probably just to put them in their large cargo pants pockets. For later.

Columbine students Rachel Scott and Richard Castaldo are sitting on the grass eating lunch outside the cafeteria, near the west side of the school that faces the Rocky Mountains. Rachel Scott is a cute seventeen-year-old with brown hair and a cheeky smile. She is known for her love of drama, Christianity and an occasional cigarette. She is killed with shots to the head, chest, arm, and thigh. Castaldo, a seventeen-year-old budding musician, is shot and paralyzed. From then on, he will use a wheelchair.

Harris takes off his trench coat and puts it on the ground. Maybe it is too restrictive. Or maybe he is too hot. He rests one of his guns on a chain link fence at the top of a stairway and fires at the students below.

Daniel Rohrbough is a freshman who enjoys street hockey, Nintendo, and visits his grandparents on their Kansas farm every summer. Harris quickly ends that. Using his carbine, he shoots Rohrbough in the left leg, chest, and abdomen—probably in that order. But it will take police three years to figure that out.

Around the time of Rohrbough's shooting Lance Kirklin is laying on the grass outside the school, already bleeding. Klebold stands above him.

"Help me," Kirklin moans. "Help me."

"You want help?" Klebold says. "I'll help you."

He then fires a shotgun at the left side of Kirklin's face. Kirklin will live, but require multiple reconstructive surgeries.

Students in the cafeteria begin to stand up and look around, wondering what is happening. Some think it's a senior prank, others a movie because they know Harris and Klebold are in video class. But teacher Dave Sanders, and school custodians Jon Curtis and Jay Gallatine, sense the danger. They tell students to get down. Some hide under lunch room tables, while others flee up the cafeteria stairway or head to the kitchen.

Klebold briefly charges into the cafeteria and holds his weapon in a "ready-to-fire" sweeping motion. He doesn't shoot but looks around and walks back outside. Klebold then steps over injured student Sean Graves, playing dead, and rejoins Harris at the top of the stairs.

The two shoot toward the ball fields at students fleeing the school. Harris hits Anne Marie Hochhalter with the bullets that will paralyze her, and a friend drags her away. Harris and Klebold toss bombs into the nearby, senior parking lot and onto the school roof. One explodes where Hochhalter had been.

The gunmen banter: "This is what we always wanted to do." "This is awesome!"

At 11:22 a.m. Jefferson County Sheriff's Deputy Neil Gardner, the school's community resource officer, has finished lunch in his patrol car while monitoring the "Smoker's Pit" in Clement Park adjacent the school. A panicked custodian radios him saying, "Neil, I need you in the back lot!" Gardner figures he means the south student parking lot, which is on the opposite end of the school. As Gardner heads over, his dispatch radio relays that a female is down in the south lot. Gardner flips on his lights and siren.

Meanwhile, art teacher Patricia Nielson is heading outside to tell Harris to cut it out. He is the only gunman in her line of sight. She thinks it is just a video production with a cap gun, but still not a good idea. She is at a set of glass doors facing the mountains when Harris smiles at her, levels one of his guns, and fires. The first shot snaps through the glass and hits a student who is alongside her, Brian Anderson. The shot seems to slap his necklace chain, bounce off his sternum, and does nothing more than leave scrape and burn marks on his chest.

"Dear God. Dear God. Dear God," Nielson says. She turns to run and a bullet grazes her shoulder. She drops to the ground and skins her knee as she crawls back inside the hall. Nielson and Anderson flee, but end up where the greatest carnage will occur: the library.

Gardner, wearing a yellow polo shirt, arrives in the south parking lot in about two minutes, at 11:24 a.m., and gets out of his car. Harris greets him with about ten rifle shots before his gun jams. Gardner gets off four shots while Harris fiddles with the weapon. Harris spins to the right and returns fire. Jefferson County motorcycle officer Paul Smoker, who minutes earlier was writing a speeding ticket, has driven across Clement Park through the grass and is now on scene. He pops off three shots at Harris once the teen goes into the school. Klebold fires his Tec-9 and shots ping off the lockers. Harris and Klebold will now have free reign inside. It is 11:26 a.m. Seven minutes into Columbine.

At 11:27 a.m. two pipe bombs are thrown from the second story hallway into the cafeteria. Dave Sanders, forty-seven, is dressed in a T-shirt, blue and white dress shirt, gray slacks and brown shoes. He is herding students into classrooms when a bullet tears into his neck and out his upper lip, damaging an artery. Another shot enters his upper back, right side and exits his chest, right side. It damages a vein.

The question of who shot Sanders remains unanswered. But two students will keep him alive for hours. Sanders is the third person mortally wounded at Columbine. Shot in the first minutes, he dies in the last.

Harris and Klebold continue to pace the hallway outside the library, "randomly shooting and detonating explosives," according to the sheriff's official report. A 911 call indicates they continue like this for three minutes.

Eric and Dylan's targets eventually disappear. Students and teachers have either fled the school, or barricaded themselves in classrooms, locking doors and blocking them with uprighted tables.

By the time Harris and Klebold enter the library, fifty-six people will be inside. Fifty-two are students, and four are female faculty or staff. Twelve of the fifteen who die at Columbine, including Harris and Klebold, will expire in this place dedicated to quiet contemplation. The library also sees twelve injured—half the total number.

★★★

The names of the Columbine killers and the dead are as clear as their gravestone etchings. The murdered include four girls, a black boy and a Hispanic boy. They are football, volleyball and soccer players. One wants to be a Marine, just like Eric Harris. Another yearns for a career as a wildlife biologist. Every future equation of work, school, family and success beckons.

The shooting is mostly random. Harris and Klebold single out Isaiah Shoels, who is black, but only after they happen upon him by chance. Harris and Klebold have "shit lists," and Harris has a "girls' list," yet it does not appear that anyone on the lists is specifically targeted the day of Columbine.

So we think we know what happened at Columbine, or at least the tick-tock of actual events. A decade after the shootings 30,000 or more pages of police and other official documents have been released. Add to that videos, 911 tapes, lawsuits, and extensive media coverage.

But Colorado's largest criminal investigation comes with a disclaimer. Information has been hidden, held back, and proved plain wrong. As quickly as Jefferson County Sheriff John Stone would report a detail, questions and contradictions arose.

Who shot student Daniel Rohrbough? Depending on eyewitness statements, which are often problematic, Sheriff Stone wrongly reported that Klebold was the killer. An outside investigation found it was Harris.

When did teacher Dave Sanders die? Police interviews of the two students who tended to Sanders – whose death remains among the most controversial – are among the briefest.

What did police know in the years before the shooting? The draft affidavit for a search warrant to enter Harris's home a year before Columbine was not fully acknowledged and released until 2001, after CBS News and victim families sued.

Could more lives have been saved?

Basic investigative details, such as witness names, are constantly misspelled. English grammar and spelling are a foreign language to some police reports. The shortcomings are matched only by the Jefferson County Sheriff's frequent inability to concede, or repair, the errors. Yet it is impossible to reinvestigate the shooting. So the public is forced to accept many official conclusions based on little more than intuition. What seems right or logical is taken at face value. But only after the sheriff's words are mixed with news accounts, outside investigations, and other documents does a more accurate truth begin to emerge.

Where the sheriff's investigation does appear honest and thorough, there are still gaps common to all crime investigations. In the library, for example, witnesses often give different accounts of Harris and Klebold's exact words and movements. Stress is probably one factor, along with the crouching position students took under library tables that hindered their view. Some were too distant from the atrocities to fully capture words, or movements. Smoke made it difficult to see. The fire alarm made it difficult to hear.

★★★

Six minutes into Columbine, around 11:25 a.m., Patti Nielson runs into the library. "Help," she yells, "there's a kid with a gun. We've been shot."

She repeats the warning, and asks if librarian Liz Keating is in the room. She has, in fact, gone home for lunch.

Computer teacher Rich Long, who is in the second-floor library to repair a computer, sees his former students: Klebold looks back at Harris, the same way he always looked to others before taking something on. But now Klebold is narrow-eyed and concentrating. Long recognizes him only in his physical form. "I saw and felt evil," he says.

To stay or go from the library is a life or death decision. Long pushes students into the hall and he himself leaves.

Nielson, who is at the service counter, tells students to get under the tables. Library Assistant Lois Kean and library tech Carole Weld leave the main reading area where students are crouching under tables, and flee to a side television studio and sound booth. Teacher Peggy Dodd tells kids to get out, as if it is a fire drill. Then she sees teacher Dave Sanders running down the hallway, motioning for people to get back, as if they should stay in the library. Dodd goes into the magazine room with three students, including the injured Brian Anderson, and locks the door.

Bree Pasquale makes eye contact with Isaiah Shoels.

"What's goin' on?" he asks.

"Someone's outside with a pipe bomb," she replies.

There has been no training, Nielson says, on what to do during a school shooting. She goes on instinct and tells the kids to get under the tables. A dispatcher will later repeat the advice to keep the kids down as Nielson gets on the phone with 911.

"I am a teacher at Columbine High School, there is a student here with a gun," Nielson first explains. "He has shot out a window."

Dispatch: "Has anyone been injured ma'am?"

Nielson: "I am, yes.... And the school is in a panic and I'm in the library, I've got... Students down! Under the tables kids, heads under the table! Kids are screaming, and the teachers are trying to take control of things. We need police here."

Dispatch: "OK, we're getting them there."

The dispatcher asks if Nielson can lock the library doors, but she doesn't want to move closer to the gunmen in the hallway. The pop pop pop of gunshots, like banging on metal, taps through the 911 tape. Near the end of the four minutes that have been released to the public, the dispatcher asks Nielson her name. Patti, she says quietly. Then suddenly, "He's in the library, he's shooting at everybody."

Nielson holds the phone line open, but doesn't talk. She stays on the floor and whispers the Lord's Prayer: "Our Father, which art in heaven, hallowed be thy name; thy kingdom come." She thinks she is going to die.

Harris enters the library, then Klebold. It is 11:29 a.m. A moment of doubt. "Are you still with me?" one of them says. "We're still gonna do this, right?"

They are presented with a sea of tabletops since their quarry are crouching underneath. As Nielson's phone line remains electric for twenty-two more minutes it picks up gunfire and random words as Harris and Klebold begin a real game of hide and seek. At one point, they walk right in front of Nielson.

"Get up!" one of the gunmen yells. "Everyone with a white cap or baseball cap, stand up." They want the "jocks."

They banter some more:

"So this is a library."

"We're going to burn this place up."

"This is for all these years of shit we've had to go through."

"Everyone's afraid. Look at the scared people under the tables."

"Who wants to be killed next?"

Byron Kirkland believes Harris and Klebold want students to flee, maybe so they can more easily open fire. But it doesn't work. So Harris and Klebold themselves begin ducking under tables.

The first shots appear to come from Harris, who blasts two rounds of shotgun pellets down the front counter. Evan Todd, hiding behind a copier, is injured by "flying wood splinters" according to the sheriff's official report.

Harris and Klebold then approach the first person they will kill in the library: Special needs student Kyle Velasquez. The sixteen-year-old sophomore is six feet tall has been dubbed a "gentle giant." He wears glasses, and loves homemade tortillas and cats. The official report says he is the only student not hiding under a desk or table. Others, including Kyle's parents, say he is hidden. Two shots. Ten shotgun pellets pepper Velasquez's head and shoulder.

"Harris and Klebold set down their backpacks, filled with ammunition and Molotov cocktails, on one of the computer tables," according to the sheriff's official report. Harris gets down on one knee and shoots through the west library windows toward police and fleeing students. Klebold gets next to him, takes off his trench coat, and joins him in firing out the window.

"The pigs are here," they say. "OK, let's go kill some cops now."
There will be destruction all around. Shrapnel from an explosive sizzles on the carpet. Eric shakes a bookshelf but cannot knock it over and kicks some books. Klebold shoots out the display cabinet near the front door of the library.

Columbine freshman Steven Curnow, fourteen, is a Star Wars fan. Soccer, and becoming a Navy pilot, maybe on an F-14, are among his other passions. Curnow is hiding under a computer table when Harris kills him with a shotgun slug that goes through his right shoulder and neck.

Harris then turns to Kacey Ruegsegger. She is covering her ears with her hands when Harris sends a shotgun slug through her right shoulder. Her arm floats up in the air, and comes back down. She thinks it is shot off.

"Oh," she says.

"Stop your bitching," one of the gunmen tells her.

Klebold shoots Patrick Ireland. Still, Ireland's head rises above a desk as he tries to administer first aid. He is hit a second time with shotgun pellets. His injuries are to the head, and right foot. He will not die.

Harris walks to another table. He slaps the table top twice with his left hand and says, "Peek-a-boo."

He bends down, and sees Cassie Bernall. She is a seventeen-year-old junior with blond hair who traded her fascination with witchcraft for religion. Holding the shotgun in his right hand, Harris kills her with pellets that pass through her right middle finger—possibly because she is covering her face—and into the right side of her head. The wound is smoking.

After he shoots Bernall, the shotgun recoil throws the gun rearward into his face, breaking his nose and giving him a bloody milk mustache.

"Oh man, I shot my nose," Harris says.

"Why'd you do that?" Klebold replies.

Harris makes his way to Bree Pasquale, who is sitting on the floor because there was not enough room under a nearby table. He stares her in the face and repeatedly asks if she wants to die. She repeatedly says no. Harris laughs. "Everyone's going to die," he says.

Klebold tells Harris to shoot her. "No, we're gonna blow up the school anyway," Harris says, still pointing his shotgun at her.

Aaron Cohn says he is laying face down on the floor, with Bree on top of him. Klebold says, "How about you big boy, you want to get shot today?"

Cohn looks left and sees a shotgun barrel twelve inches from his face. "Why don't you get up?" Klebold says.

Cohn doesn't move. Klebold walks on.

Harris and Klebold are hooting, hollering, and laughing. Their joy floats through the room:

"This is so much fun."

"Isn't this the best time of your life?"

"It was like the gunmen thought what they were doing was [a] game and they had scored a touchdown," Joshua Lapp told police. "They would shoot someone and then tell them to stop screaming. They seemed to be shooting people until they stopped screaming or making noises."

Next to die is Isaiah Shoels. A few minutes earlier, he had been telling jokes to a group of people in the library. The eighteen-year-old senior is only 4'11", but quick to lift weights, play football and joke around. Harris and Klebold get on opposite sides of the table with Isaiah underneath. Klebold unsuccessfully tries to pull Isaiah out by his arm.

"Get up, nigger," Klebold says.

"Nah, nah," says Isaiah.

Enough talk. A slug from Harris' shotgun travels through Isaiah's left arm, chest, and out his right armpit. It shreds part of his heart.

Who's next?

It is sixteen-year-old sophomore Matt Kechter, a junior varsity lineman on the football team who has a chubby face and wavy brown hair. He lifts weights, gets straight A's, and hopes to join the varsity line up in the fall. Klebold launches a shotgun slug through Kechter's chest. As with Bernall, student Craig Scott recalls smoke coming out of Kechter's wound. Shoels and Kechter are now leaning against each other, moaning. Soon they will die together.

Dan Steepleton's left knee is warm and he realizes Klebold has shot him. Harris tosses a CO_2 cartridge under the table and it lands on Steepleton's right thigh. The fuse is burning but Steepleton doesn't want to move it for fear he will get shot again. Makai Hall throws it out of the way, and it explodes in mid-air, about four feet away. The explosion shakes the floor.

Valeen Schnurr is crouching under the table with Lauren Townsend, both with their knees to their chest. Townsend tells her everything will be OK, and puts her right arm around Schnurr. Klebold sprays Schnurr with a round of shotgun pellets that hit her chest, abdomen, and left arm. She crawls out from under the table.

"Oh my God, help," Schnurr says.

"Do you believe in God?" Klebold asks.

Valeen says no, then yes. She is searching for the answer the gunman wants. She doesn't want to be shot again.

A second question: Why does she believe in God?

"My parents taught me and I believe," she responds.

"God is gay," says one of the gunmen.

Eighteen-year-old senior Lauren Townsend is a slim, long-haired brunette who can deftly spike a volleyball and hopes to become a wildlife biologist. Klebold rapid-fires six TEC-DC9 shots into her. Townsend is gasping and another girl holds her before she dies.

Harris walks to a table, bends down, and sees two girls. "Pathetic," he says, and walks on.

John Tomlin, a sixteen-year-old sophomore, is the all-American type. He pines after Chevy trucks and four-wheeling through the mud, along with baseball caps and Bible study. He wants to join the U.S. Army.

Tomlin spends his last minutes with Nicole Nowlen. She has ducked under one table, but thinks it too vulnerable. She asks Tomlin if she can come over to his table. He waves her over. They pull chairs around themselves, and she tells John she is worried. He motions for her to be quiet, and holds her hand. She starts talking again. He motions again for her to stay silent.

Harris points a gun under their table. He fires two rounds of pellets. Nowlen is injured, and a shotgun pellet grazes Tomlin's chest. Nowlen thinks Tomlin jumps out from under the table to avoid being hit by a second gunshot. He lands on his stomach. Klebold stands over him and finishes off his life with four shots from the TEC-DC9. Nowlen's legs are now touching Tomlin's. His legs shake, then stop a moment later.

Quiet Kelly Fleming has pale skin and long brown hair. She is a sixteen-year-old sophomore already working on her autobiography who also writes poetry and short stories. Harris kills her with a shotgun blast to her lower back. He sprays pellets under another table. Lauren Townsend is hit again.

Harris sticks his head under a table and points a gun, maybe the carbine rifle, at John Savage. Savage scoots away. Harris points the gun again. Savage scoots. Harris stands up.

"Who is under the table?" Harris asks. "Identify yourself."

"It's me, John," says Savage, who knows Harris and Klebold from classes, but considers them more acquaintances than friends.

"John Savage?" Klebold says.

"Yes," Savage replies.

"Hi," Klebold says.

"Hi Dylan," says Savage. "What are you doing?"

"Oh, killing people," Klebold says, shrugging.

"Are you going to kill me?" Savage asks.

Klebold looks at him a second. "No dude, just run," he says. "Just get out of here."

He runs outside, sprinting at top speed.

But fifteen-year-old Daniel Mauser will die. The sophomore runs cross country and aces his classes. Shortly before the shootings, he asks his parents about gun control. Harris shoots him with the carbine rifle. Daniel pushes a chair toward him. Harris stops that with a second shot.

"Did he try to jump you?" Klebold asks.

"Yeah," Harris replies.

Seventeen-year-old Corey DePooter, saving to buy his first car, is the library's last murder victim. The junior enjoys fishing, and wants to join the Marines—they will make him an honorary one over a year after the shooting. At 11:35 a.m., a 9mm bullet from Klebold's TEC-9 chops through him. Three more bullets from Harris' carbine are next.

DePooter is moaning, with bullet wounds in his neck, chest, back and arm. Before fleeing the library DePooter's best friend, Stephen "Austin" Eubanks, will take his pulse. It has stopped.

Evan Todd watches Klebold walk by the main library counter and check the door to the magazine room, where teacher Peggy Dodd is hiding. He turns the knob, but it is locked. Klebold checks the door to an adjacent room, which is open. He sweeps the room with his TEC-9, turns around, and walks toward Todd. Klebold holds the gun in his left hand and points it at Todd's face.

"Oh, look what we have here," Klebold says.

"What?" asks Harris. He is dizzy and wobbly, and his nose pushed to the side of his face.

"Just some fat fuck," Klebold replies, still pointing the TEC-9. "Are you a jock?"

"No," says Todd.

"Well, that's good," Klebold says, "we don't like jocks."

There is a pause. "Let me see your face," Klebold asks.

Todd removes his hat and tilts his face upward. Klebold looks him in the eye and says, "Give me one good reason why I shouldn't kill you."

"I don't want to get in trouble," Todd responds.

"Trouble?" says Klebold, who seems to get angry and leans in closer. "You don't even know what fucking trouble is."

"That's not what I meant. I mean, I don't have a problem with you guys, I never will and I never did," Todd says.

Klebold stares at him for a moment then looks away. "I'm gonna let this fat fuck live, you can have at him if you want to."

They walk away and Klebold shoots a 9mm round into a television.

Harris isn't paying attention. "Let's go to the commons," he says.

Klebold picks up a chair and slams it onto a computer. He walks backward, sweeping with his gun. Harris does the same. Klebold follows him out.

The moaning in the library continues. But the shots and bombs stop. The students sense it is safe to flee.

Lindsay Elmore hears someone say, "Let's get out." She runs out the library's back door.

Injured students are saying, "Help me." But Patricia Blair says, "Those who could ran."

Heidi Johnson remembers running outside and seeing two officers.

"Come on kids!" they yell. They are behind a patrol car with their guns drawn.

Art teacher Patti Nielson moves into the library break room and curls into a cupboard. She will stay there until SWAT evacuates her about four hours later.

The library rampage has lasted seven and a half minutes, but life and death will dart through the room for a few more hours.

Patrick Ireland, shot in the head and blacked out, regains consciousness. He looks at the library windows and thinks, "That's my way out." He pushes himself through a broken, second-story window on live television and falls into the arms of officers waiting atop an armored car at 2:38 p.m.

SWAT will not enter the library until 3:22 p.m., four hours and three minutes after the shooting began.

***

Dave Sanders is still dying.

After being shot, he had stumbled in a hallway and fell. An explosion went off nearby.

"Dave, you've got to get up," yells teacher Richard Long.

Long shoulders Sanders to an open doorway at Science Room Three. Sanders is bleeding profusely from his mouth onto Long's arm and pants.

"Rich, I think they shot me through the mouth," Sanders says. "Rich, I'm losing a lot of blood. I think I'm going to pass out."

Students and teachers hiding in Science Room Three cover Sanders with wool blankets. Eagle Scout Kevin Hancey and classmate Kevin Starkey put pressure on the bullet holes to stanch the bleeding. They pull out a photo from Sanders' wallet and ask about his wife. They are on the phone with 911. Dispatchers indicate the doorknob may be marked with a blue and white shirt. Famously, a white plastic board is placed in the window. It reads: "1 bleeding to death."

Hours pass. Although the number is open to question.

"I'm not going to make it," Sanders says. "Tell my girls I love them."

SWAT arrives: "We are here for the living and the walking."

Sanders is in a science room storage area, bare-chested and laying on his back. He is alive.

The sheriff says it is 2:42 p.m., and SWAT calls for medical help. A lawsuit filed by Sanders' daughter says it is "nearly 4 p.m."

At 4:45 p.m. the sheriff says Sanders is pronounced dead. He is still in the school.

***

While students and teachers are tending to Sanders, Harris and Klebold enter the science area. They shoot into empty rooms and tape a Molotov cocktail on the door of the chemical storage room. They look through the windows of locked classroom doors. They make eye contact with students inside, but do not shoot and move on.

Twenty-five minutes into Columbine, Harris walks into the cafeteria at 11:44 a.m. It is a disaster area, with overturned chairs, and food and drink left on the tables. Harris fires a few shots, maybe trying to explode one of the 20-pound propane bombs that would at this point send him skyward too. But it doesn't work.

Klebold walks across the cafeteria floor and takes a gander at a propane bomb. Harris, thirsty, drinks from a cup left on a lunch table. Klebold tosses something, maybe a CO_2 cartridge or pipe bomb. But the big bang still eludes them.

They walk up the stairs to the main office area and fire some shots, then back down to the cafeteria, where the floor is on fire in spots. They return up the stairs to the library – their comfortable killing field – and take more shots through the windows at police and paramedics. It is just after noon.

Their final count for the day will be 188 shots; Harris 124 and Klebold 64. But they save the last two for themselves. Harris and Klebold place a Molotov cocktail on a table and light it. A tiny blaze triggers a library fire alarm above their bodies at 12:08 p.m. Harris and Klebold are already dead.

***

The sheriff's department has withheld some 10,000 Columbine crime scene photos from the public, but images of Harris and Klebold as they lay dead in the library are among those that have leaked out. In one, Klebold lies on the floor on his back, his legs crossed over one another. Klebold's shotgun is at his feet, and his Boston Red Sox baseball cap is nearby. His left arm rests diagonally across his stomach. His TEC-9, attached to his body with a strap, is barely visible under his right knee. Klebold was left-handed, but one scenario is that the gun swung across his body after he shot himself through the left temple and he fell on it.

Eight "explosive devices," including a pipe bomb wrapped in gray duct tape, are removed from his left pants pocket. The blood from his skull has now seeped into the carpet and surrounds his head. Red rivulets run across his face. A coroner believes Klebold may have been capable of some "involuntary movement" after he shot himself.

Clam-digging amidst this muck is Jefferson County sheriff's deputy Mike Guerra, who had unsuccessfully sought a search warrant for Harris' home the year before. Harris' name has been ringing in Guerra's ear since earlier in the day when he staged at the Columbine parking lot. He says he was asked by lead Columbine investigator Kate Battan, "Weren't you working on a warrant for this guy?"

"Yeah," is all he can muster.

Guerra and another officer now collect a pipe bomb and seven CO_2 cartridges from Klebold's cargo pants.

Then comes Harris. Guerra finds five, unexploded CO_2 cartridges near his feet. The right cargo pocket on Harris' pants is buttoned, and Guerra cuts along the top edge. He fishes out four more CO_2 cartridges. Five CO_2 cartridge bombs are in Harris' left pants pocket.

Harris was sitting next to a bookshelf when he put his shotgun in his mouth and pulled the trigger. His body then slumped onto the floor, and his face became instantly unrecognizable. Harris' blood and pieces of his skull splattered nearby books. As police put him in a body bag, a "mass of blood" plopped out of his head.

TWO

The Wild West

Dylan Klebold lived in the Jefferson County foothills where towering slabs of red rock frame homes fed by winding dirt driveways. His modernist wood home built in 1978 has peaked roofs and multiple windows, some cut at an angle to match the roofline. When his parents purchased the gray, two-story home and surrounding ten acres for $250,000 in 1989 it had mice in the walls and needed plenty of fixing up but Dylan's father, who grew up with carpentry, welcomed the task.

Tom and Sue Klebold told their real estate agent they felt the location amid deer and frogs would be a good influence on Dylan and his older brother, Byron, because it was "closer to nature and away from the hustle and bustle of the street." It indeed seems like a quiet, scenic place for finding inspiration. Through the years, the home came to be valued at $900,000.

Dylan's bedroom was on the second floor, where he had posters of the bands Nine Inch Nails, Marilyn Manson, and Chemical Brothers, along with a poster of different liquors, and a woman in a leopard bikini, according to various accounts. There were also street signs, baseball photos, and a "PG-13" sign stolen from a movie theater. Dylan wanted to paint his whole room black but Sue vetoed the idea, so he had to settle for one black area near a window.

But Dylan did keep a shotgun in his room. He first tried to hide it in the bottom drawer of his dresser, but it was too long. He tried the bathroom, but the hole in the wall behind the wooden toilet paper dispenser was too small. Dylan didn't think his parents would find the gun if he buried it under the pile of dirty clothes in his closet, but he eventually cut down the barrel and fit it in the dresser's bottom drawer.

Dylan was a reflection of that house, rambling, distinctive, emotional, brainy; the more artistic type. He also seemed funny and harmless. He was smart and liked learning, but the formulaic nature of the classroom and oppressive school cliques turned him away from the classroom. He challenged himself and took more advanced courses, although his grades suffered because of it. Over six feet tall, he favored jeans and T-shirts and wore his light brown, wavy hair below the ears. He had a long face and his John Lennon sunglasses sat atop a goofy grin. With those sunglasses, and his hair pulled back in a ponytail, he looks like the blazing gunman in his favorite movie, *Natural Born Killers*.

After the shootings, Dylan's home became the place for reporters and police to look for answers. But few got past the Klebold gate. It guards the driveway, along with an intercom, and a dark blue newspaper box. Years after Columbine, no numbers marked the 9351 Cougar Road address, although maybe the digits were never there. The police were among those who got inside, but refuse to release any photos or videos they have of the house.

When he was alive Dylan would turn his BMW left out of the driveway. A right on West Deer Creek Canyon Road emptied him out onto the Jefferson County plains. In winter, the few stone buildings seem to float on the snowy whiteness that stretches to the horizon as if a helicopter had dropped them on the sea. The odds eventually shift as the tract homes become more common than bare land. Although whether it was raw land, or raw housing, the views were equally numbing. The number of humans walking around was about zero.

***

Jefferson County, shaped like a jagged knife blade, has a split personality. The western half where Dylan lived cuts into the Rocky Mountain foothills and creates a scenic backdrop for an eclectic mix of residents ranging from hillbillies in ramshackle homes to yuppies in multi-million dollar mansions. Denver – contrary to its reputation for blizzards – is essentially a high altitude desert where winters are softened by over 300 days of sunshine. But the Jefferson County foothills show glimmers of the massive snow and deep cold found in the heart of the Rockies.

The foothills also harbor many of Jefferson County's "Open Space" parks full of popular hiking and mountain biking trails. Paragliders jump off Lookout Mountain and swoop down to earth on the air currents, while bison graze near Interstate 70 as the highway blazes West into the mountains. Red Rocks, the scenic natural amphitheater, is known the world over for its outdoor concerts. The mountainous terrain also contains dinosaur fossils that include Triceratops footprints and ancient palm imprints on the 12th green at the city of Golden's Fossil Trace Golf Club.

The county flatlands where Eric lived spread east towards Denver and include Columbine. This is typical suburbia, with unremarkable cities like Lakewood, Littleton, and Westminster. This is also the heart of the county economy. Southwest Plaza sprawls on the plain and gets as upscale as Macy's before dropping down to Sears and JCPenney. In a county that is eighty-seven percent white, chain stores represent most of the ethnicity: Heidi's Brooklyn Deli, Qdoba Mexican Grill, Einstein Bros. Bagels.

Jefferson County's most prominent building, the courthouse, is known as the "Taj Mahal" for its approximately $60 million price tag and central, domed building flanked by two rectangular wings. The sheriff and district attorney offices sit nearby as the Taj robustly skirts the edge of the Rocky Mountains, looking to guard the terrain. Yet the Taj illustrates a suburban quandary as officers must patrol both wilderness and suburban sprawl with no downtown or center of crime to focus their attention. The county's signature building could not stop its signature crime.

★★★

Law enforcement was historically sparse in the West. The frontiersman would take the law into his own hands, and there was no better equalizer against nature, Indians and the common criminal than the gun. Churches were seen as a civilizing influence, but even they could be warlike. In Colorado, most of the early miners were Protestant, yet crusading Presbyterians stood out for moving "against Mormons, Catholics, and others regarded as species of infidels," according to the book *The Coloradans*. "These 'Christian soldiers' talked in terms of fighting battles, occupying strategic points, posting pickets, establishing outposts, and the like."

The strife is said to continue in Jefferson County today, with believers against non-believers, and sect versus sect. "The churches have very little to do with each other," says Reverend Don Marxhausen, who presided over Dylan Klebold's funeral. "There's two separate groups. The evangelicals and the mainliners."

The violent individualist who stood up for himself not only survived, but was glorified, and came to symbolize the West.

William "Buffalo Bill" Cody first came to Colorado territory in 1859 at the young age of thirteen, like many migrants, looking for gold. But after the Iowa native did not find enough nuggets to punch his ticket he was recruited by the Pony Express, according to some accounts, which was looking for "skinny, expert riders willing to risk death daily." Cody earned his nickname in 1867 while hunting buffalo to feed railroad workers. He said he killed 4,280 of the animals in seventeen months, but was also known for hyperbole.

In 1872, at age twenty-six, Cody popped into show business by portraying the Wild West. One of his trademark stories, "Buffalo Bill's First Scalp for Custer," has him shooting Cheyenne chief Yellow Hair in the midst of battle, stabbing him in the heart, and scalping him "in about five seconds."

Buffalo Bill performed in Colorado thirty-five times, and endorsed horse halters from the Gates Tire and Leather Company in Denver, helping boost the company that still keeps worldwide headquarters in a curved and shiny building full of glass in downtown. Cody's sister also lived in Denver, and that was where he died in 1917 while visiting her.

There was some controversy over whether Cody wanted to be buried in Wyoming, where the town of Cody was named after him. But close friends and the priest who administered the last rites said he wanted to be interred on Lookout Mountain in Jefferson County. His state funeral, according to one account, is "still perhaps the largest in Colorado history." He was buried per his wishes on "a promontory with spectacular views of both the mountains and plains, places where he had spent the happiest times of his life," according to the Buffalo Bill Museum & Grave, which re-enacts his burial every few years.

Col. John Milton Chivington was among those who came to Colorado to save souls. A beefy man - over six feet tall and 250 pounds - with a burly, dark beard and jutting chest, he was balding on top but two sturdy tufts of hair jutted out over each ear. In his military uniform with gold buttons up the front, he looked the part of a no-nonsense, 19th Century soldier.

Chivington was also an ordained Methodist minister and in 1860 brought his family to Colorado as the presiding elder of the Rocky Mountain District of the Methodist Church. But he would die as one of the West's most controversial figures for his gruesomely superb job of killing. At dawn on November 29, 1864 Chivington seems to have nearly taken it upon himself to lead a charge on the Sand Creek Indian Reservation. Historian Joe Frantz gives a compelling account of the incident and seems to imply 450 dead, but the National Park Service, which oversees the National Historic Site of the massacre, says 160 died. Frantz wrote:

"At dawn Chivington's militia charged through the camp of 500 peaceful Indians, despite Black Kettle's raising an American and then a white flag. Not just warriors were killed. Women and children were dragged out, shot, knifed, scalped, clubbed, mutilated, their brains knocked out, bosoms ripped open. Four hundred and fifty Indians in varying stages of insensate slaughter lay about the campground. There is no defense whatsoever for the action. It was bloodier than Chicago or Detroit or Harlem ever thought of being. Chivington and his cohorts were widely hailed as heroes by many of their fellow Americans."

Indeed, two weeks later Chivington was honored in a Denver parade. But questions soon arose about what exactly occurred at Sand Creek and Chivington arrested six of his own men for cowardice. Those men, however, said that they had held back and refused to participate in a massacre. The U.S. Secretary of War had the six men released although one of them, a longtime friend and colleague of Chivington, Capt. Silas Soule, was shot and killed from behind days later in the streets of Denver.

Chivington faced court martial charges for Sand Creek, but was no longer in the U.S. Army, and escaped that punishment. A Congressional investigation still condemned him for having "deliberately planned and executed a foul and dastardly massacre which would have disgraced the veriest savage among those who were the victims of his cruelty."

Chivington left Colorado and lived in other states but returned to Denver and worked as a deputy sheriff. He died in 1892 and was buried after what the *Rocky Mountain News* called "still the biggest, best attended funeral in the city's history."

The Sand Creek Massacre, confirming the fears of the Eastern establishment, most likely delayed Colorado's bid to become a state and enter the union. "Do not allow Colorado in, with its roving, unsettled horde of adventurers with no settled home, here or elsewhere," one Eastern newspaper wrote. "They are in Colorado solely because a state of semi-barbarism prevalent in that wild country suits their vagrant habits."

A dozen years after the Sand Creek Massacre Colorado did enter the Union and took the name of the Centennial State for being founded 100 years after the signing of the Declaration of Independence. The next year the state's premiere institution of higher learning, the University of Colorado at Boulder, admitted its first forty-four students. Nearly

125 years later, Dylan Klebold would apply there. He was neither accepted, nor rejected. His application was not complete, and he put a bullet in his head before the shortcoming could be reconciled.

★★★

Dylan was not alone. Colorado, and the West, have some of the nation's highest suicide rates. Population booms here overrun mental health resources on the new suburban frontier, and people feel compelled to pull themselves up by their own bootstraps. Wide expanses wall people off from one another, and a lack of close family for new settlers keeps people isolated. What is left is the gun. So valued for self-protection, it becomes a weapon for healing thyself: Guns are the most common method of youth and adult suicide.

★★★

While Columbine united Eric and Dylan, it does not exist. It is an unincorporated swath anchored in south Jefferson County fifteen miles southwest of Denver. It is full of middle-class families. But there is no town or city, mayor or municipality. It is a tiny dot of sprawl.

"There's no parade. Where would you have it?" explains Rev. Marxhausen, who once worked in Chicago. "There's no community center. You come from the Midwest, every area has its own downtown. There's no downtown here. The first thing clergy people who move here say is, 'Where is the community?' There is no community."

The closest anyone comes to officially recognizing Columbine is the U.S. Census, which calls it a "Census designated place": Nothing more than a group of people who live in an area with a recognized name. Just over twenty-four thousand people live in this area, which is rectangular in shape except for a triangular appendage at the southern end. About ninety-five percent of residents are white. But the population is, by many measures, above average. About forty-two percent have a bachelor's degree or higher (the national average is twenty-four percent). The median household income is $71,319, compared to about $42,000 for the rest of the country.

The heart, and horror, of Columbine is the high school. It is named for the state flower, the white and lavender Columbine, but visitors often expect an evil fortress with black clouds.

Columbine High looks perfectly normal, if outdated. Heavy on the concrete and composed of a series of nondescript wings, the large school's most prominent feature – and the only nod to any architectural flair – is the cafeteria wing and its windows that bulge out in a semi-circle.

The public library sits on the same block, connected to the school by sprawling Clement Park, which features a lake, picnic tables, and athletic fields.

The park also holds a memorial to the thirteen killed at the school. Visitors descend into an outdoor oval and are enveloped by a wall of red stone. Oversized, smooth, smoky stone plaques are embedded in the wall and engraved with quotes from Columbine students, parents, teachers, and former President Bill Clinton. An inner circle contains tributes to those who have been dubbed the thirteen innocent victims. Matthew Kechter's parents remember his broad grin after catching his first trout. Kyle Albert Velasquez's parents say he was – and is – very much loved. Daniel Lee Rohrbough's parents note that the killings happened in a country where the authorities could lie and cover-up what they did. There are references to God throughout. On the ground of the inner circle is a ribbon, also made of smooth, smoky stone. It reads: "Never Forgotten."

★★★

To arrive at his best friend Eric's house Dylan might turn left onto South Wadsworth Boulevard, the type of major thoroughfare Eric wanted to set aflame. Then right on West Chatfield Avenue. A few more turns and onto South Reed Street. Follow the road past a few houses to the cul-de-sac. 8276. Eric's house. Five miles, ten minutes. A white Ford Explorer sits in the driveway.

Eric's house is picture-perfect suburbia, the flatlands Antichrist to Dylan's mountain retreat. Eric's cul-de-sac of middle-class homes might be Ohio, or Southern California. Unremarkably, the neighborhood had a block party about five months after Columbine. Remarkably, the Harrises attended.

It is a solid neighborhood, although hardly elegant. The Harrises bought their tidy, stone two-story home for $180,000 in 1996. Inside are four modest bedrooms and four baths. The house is framed by gray trim, wood shingles, a two-car garage and plenty of windows, although the blinds were drawn after Columbine.

Eric was like that home. He could look normal in his jeans, flannel shirts and short brown preppy hair—Dylan's opposite. Yet he too wasn't accepted by the rest of the teenagers. He had some outlets—soccer, video games, and vandalism – but nothing satisfied. He frothed with anger.

The Harrises put their home up for sale in 2004, five years after Columbine. They asked $269,900 and exaggerated by calling it a "sharp contemporary" but added this "advisory to buyer": "The Sellers of this Property are the parents of Eric David Harris who was involved in the Columbine High School shooting. Sellers are not aware of any physical consequences to the property, but encourage Buyers to evaluate the Columbine incident so that they feel comfortable purchasing the Property."

The real estate agent was Jay Holliday, whose daughter Jessica was at Columbine the day of the shootings. But two other real estate agents with Columbine connections were barred from showing the house. One was Randy Brown, whose son Brooks was a sometimes friend of the killers and whose family first reported Eric to the Jefferson County Sheriff over two years before the shootings. After the shootings, Randy Brown became a vocal critic of police. "I'd love to get inside and see it and see Eric's room," Randy said of the house. "It is where this entire plot and tragedy began."

Rich Petrone, the stepfather of slain student Dan Rohrbough, was the other agent who was blackballed. "You know how you want to go to the scene of the crime?" Petrone said. "That's how it is for me."

This reporter, however, got a rare glimpse of the house. When it was up for sale a brass plaque engraved with three ducks on the front door of the Harris home read "Welcome." Above the door was a more militaristic, black metal eagle. (Eric's favorite animals were dogs and bald eagles.) Inside the home, ready for prospective buyers, it is immaculate. There is nothing to be gleaned about the previous residents. Apart from the disclosure notice, whoever lived here before is a ghost.

Stepping through the front door visitors enter a small living room with pinkish carpet, which leads to a modest kitchen. To the right is a dining room, where light streams in. Adjacent the dining room is another living room space, and a fireplace. The dining room also leads to an outside deck and a standard backyard with storage shed. Above the shed door is another black metal eagle.

Up the carpeted stairway are three bedrooms. The master is not large and includes a bathroom with a Jacuzzi bath and a small, walk-in closet.

It seems a home for modest people. Two more upstairs bedrooms are tiny. Also upstairs is an open loft space, which one police officer who searched the house the day of Columbine noted without elaboration "appeared to be used mostly by Eric Harris' mother."

The basement, Eric's domain, is awesomely large, and potentially quite private for a teenager. There is a living room and bathroom. The bedroom is larger than either of the two upstairs bedrooms. Two below ground windows cupped by metal half pipes funnel light in, and the window wells, filled with rocks, may have hidden homemade bombs.

Eric's basement is also where the two filmed some of their "basement tapes," or video diaries. The first loop rolls on Monday, March 15, 1999 around 1 a.m. Dylan sits in a tan La-Z-Boy with a toothpick in his mouth. Eric adjusts the camera from a few feet away, then sits in his own recliner. He takes a small swig of Jack Daniel's from a quart bottle and winces.

"I'm going to kill you all," Dylan says to the camera, but then tells Eric, "Shhh. Your mom can hear a bat breathing."

"She hears nothing," Eric answers, then adds, "Let me take you on a tour of my room."

First are plastic gloves taken from a doctor's office—good for building pipe bombs. A pile of magazines on the floor covers a white plastic box containing pipe bombs, shotgun shells, and two boxes of 9mm cartridges.

"Beautiful," says Dylan. "Oh my God."

Eric opens a desk drawer and removes a black, two-bell alarm clock – for a time bomb. A black plastic box holds CO_2 cartridges. Eric and Dylan will turn the cartridges, about three inches long, into popcorn for anarchists. They fill them with gunpowder, attach a fuse, and tape matches around the fuse. They swipe the matches on match strikers taped to their forearms. One striker still carries the warning: "keep away from children." For more deadly effect, they wrap nails and lead shot with duct tape around the cartridges so the fragments burrow into the hearts and minds of victims upon explosion.

A box for a BB gun contains a sawed-off shotgun, and another desk drawer contains a chunk of a shotgun handle. Eric displays a black-handled combat knife in a sheath, with a swastika scratched on the surface.

"What you will find on my body in April," Eric says of the arsenal.

Eric and Dylan mention a coffee can full of gunpowder, and a fifty-foot coil of green fuse hangs on the wall, along with a poster of a blond pin up girl. A receipt for thirteen, ten-round rifle clips from Green Mountain Guns is in a CD box, as if it is a treasured document.

Behind a CD case on a bookshelf are several large pipe bombs: Metal pipes about six inches long and stuffed with gunpowder. Eric and Dylan sometimes wrap these with lead shot too. A tackle box has more bomb-making equipment. Eric and Dylan talk about the time Eric's parents found the box, but only took the pipe bombs out.

"You guys will all die, and it will be fucking soon," Eric says to the viewers. "I hope you get an idea of what we're implying here. You all need to die. We need to die, too. We need to fucking kick-start a revolution here."

___ To fuck do you? no, I didn't think so. women, you will always be under men. its been seen throughout nature, males are almost always doing the dangerous shit while the women stay back. its your animal instincts, deal with it or commit suicide, just do it quick. thats all for now. - 5/20/98

If you recall your history the Nazi's came up with a "final solution" to the Jewish problem... kill them all. well incase you havent figured it out yet, I say,

"KILL MANKIND" no one
should survive. we all live in tiers. people are always saying they want to live in a perfect society, well Utopia doesnt exist. It is human to have flaws... you know what, Fuck it, why should I have to explain myself to you survivors. when half of this shit I say you shitheads wont understand and if you can then woopie fucking do. that just means you have something to say as my reason for killing. and the majority of the audience wont even understand my emotives either! they'll say "ah, hes crazy, hes insane, oh well, I wonder if the bulls won." you see! it's fucking worthless! all you fuckers should die! DIE what the fuck is the point if only some people see what I am saying, there will always be ones who dont, ones that are to dumb or naive or ignorant or just plain retarded. If I cant pound it into every single persons head then it is pointless. Fuck mercy fuck justice fuck morals fuck civilized fuck rules fuck laws... DIE manmade words... people think they apply to everything when they dont/cant. theres no such thing as True Good or True evil, its all relative to the observer. its just all nature, chemistry, and math. deal with it. but since dealing with it seems impossible for mankind, since we have to slap warning labels on nature, then ... you die. burn, melt, evaporate, decay, just go the fuck away!!!! YAAAH!!!

~ 6/12/98 ~

when in doubt, confuse the hell out of the enemy" - Fly 9/2/98

wait, mercy doesnt exist....

THREE

Family

"Philanthropist, Athlete Leo Yassenoff, 77, Dies," read the 1971, front page headline in the *Columbus Dispatch*.

The Jewish Community Center in Ohio's sleepy capital was named for Leo after his death, a crowning achievement that was also a refrain in Dylan's obituary, making Columbine a story of a boy from a prominent Jewish family gone horribly, horribly wrong.

Dylan and fellow gunman Eric Harris killed thirteen before taking their own lives.

Leo donated almost all of his $13 million-plus fortune to charity.

Dylan and Eric hated all.

Leo strove to promote all races, creeds, and colors.

Eric adored the Nazis.

Leo strove to promote Jewish causes.

The family line ran from Leo, to son Milton, to granddaughter Susan, to great grandson Dylan. But Dylan was not born until ten years after his great grandfather Leo's death and was not even related to Leo by blood. A little-known fact is that Leo's son—and Dylan's grandfather—Milton Rice Yassenoff, was taken in from the Jewish Infants home in Columbus.

Born October 15, 1893 in Dayton, Ohio discrimination taught Leo tolerance. He attended Ohio State University, beginning a close, lifelong bond with the school. A 1916 photo shows a lean and serious-looking Leo with neatly combed hair in an old-fashioned football uniform. Once he was a successful businessman, Leo continued to travel with the Ohio State football team, throwing them picnics, and giving players jobs, according to an unpublished family history by Solly Yassenoff, a cousin to the Klebolds. Leo lived at 2456 Fair Avenue in Bexley—the wealthy city of approximately thirteen thousand characterized by handsome brick homes and appendaged to Columbus, with its own, semi-smug identity.

But the bloodline, in a literal sense, stopped with Leo. In 1923, he married Betty Lupton, director of the Columbus Jewish Infants Home. (Despite her work, a family friend says she was not Jewish.) At the Infants Home Betty and Leo "fell in love" with Milton Rice. Born of Russian descent in Toledo, Ohio in 1919, Milton's mother was unable to provide for him. His death certificate lists his mother and father's names as "unknown."

"At the same Infants Home, Leo and Betty also discovered a very bright child named Abner, who they took in and possibly adopted," according to Solly's history. Solly does not indicate why Leo and Betty adopted rather than have their own children.

Leo's noble efforts to uplift society did not always apply to family members. Retired businessman Bernie Mentser, who knew the family, said Leo "could be sentimental one time and be hard as a brick another time."

Abner appeared to be an accomplished youth, and was involved in everything from football to the National Honor Society in high school. Solly thinks Abner graduated from Ohio State before taking an advertising job. Tragedy and maybe a little mystery struck the family when Solly writes that Abner committed suicide while visiting in Michigan in the early 1940's. Family friends say it occurred in Columbus. A death certificate for him cannot be located.

A 1936 photo reproduction of Milton shows a calm and earnest seventeen-year-old in a suit and tie with neatly combed hair who could be an All-American boy as much as the descendant of Jewish immigrants. He looks unafraid, and straight into the camera.

Almost smiling, Milton seems to have the same prominent nose as his grandson, Dylan Klebold. But Milton looks like a young businessman. At seventeen, his grandson was a school shooter.

Milton served in the army in World War II. Solly says he was stationed in Bora Bora in the South Pacific "and loved it there." Upon returning, he met and married Charlotte Haugh, who grew up in small-town Ohio, recalls Charles Huelsman III, who later became her stepson. Huelsman described her as "soft," "diplomatic," and "Terribly nice person. Social, charitable, loving, concerned, empathic, real giving person, really tried to raise her kids well."

She also converted to Judaism, Huelsman says. She and Milton had three children: Diane Elizabeth, Susan Frances, and Philip Leo, in that order. Their address was 74 S. Roosevelt Avenue in Bexley. Today, the house's thick, beige stone foundation gives way to smooth stucco as the walls reach the roof. The building materials, and the home's tidy and sturdy character, mirror the rest of the neighborhood. Residences here are nice, and slightly stately, but not ostentatious. Like other homes on the block, the lawn at 74 S. Roosevelt leads up to the door. Reporters from across the country have knocked on it since Columbine.

When the Yassenoffs lived there the living room contained a painting of Milton and Charlotte with the children, Huelsman recalls. "It's not a picture that has any strain in it. It's a pretty standard family portrait." He also remembers a piano in the living room, but only his father and kids playing it. "When I asked them (the Yassenoffs), 'Hey, you're so tall, why didn't you go out for basketball?'" Huelsman adds, "They described themselves as klutzes when it came to sports, even though they had impressive height."

The family belonged to the reform Temple Israel, but rarely attended, said family friend Albert Glick, who lived two doors down. The marriage between Milton and Charlotte, while good, made for some odd symmetry. Charlotte was a teetotaler. Milton liked to gamble at poker and have "maybe two" drinks after work after dealing with Leo, Glick said.

Milton worked in Leo's business, mostly managing the cinemas. The occupation on his death certificate read, "former executive-Academy Theatre." The father-son relationship, however, remained bare. "At the end, or close to the end, he [Leo] and his son weren't even speaking to each other," said Mentser.

Milton went along to get along. His grandson would do the same. And just as Dylan Klebold's parents buried their son, Milton's parents would do the same.

Milton died an early death. At forty-seven he succumbed to uremia, when a toxic amount of waste hits the bloodstream, which is typically related to kidney failure. His assets were pegged at $792,265. In his will he took care to note, "I believe minor children need the presence of a woman." His one-paragraph, 1967 obituary was tucked deep into the *Columbus Dispatch* on page 54-A. Daughter Susan was eighteen.

The obituary was a stark contrast with Leo's front-page billing, which would come four years later. In pictures of him wearing a suit and tie, Leo has a small chin and taut upper lip that make his mouth look like a bird's beak. He is portly, bald, and wears round glasses. After Leo died on August 30, 1971 of renal failure his Ohio estate tax return listed his "principal occupation" as builder and real estate developer. His probate file stretches 590 pages. One document values his estate at $14.8 million.

Leo left all of his estate for "charitable purposes with the exception of a few personal bequests." He said disbursements to the family would provide "generous economic returns which, if properly preserved, should last for generations to come." He also noted the importance of giving to Jewish causes "as a member of a minority group, as a matter of fact, the least populous of the minority groups." He added: "I should like if possible for a nominal subvention to be apportioned to each and every Jewish Temple or Jewish Synagogue in the City of Columbus." Leo listed almost fifty religious and secular organizations as candidates for charitable giving. Virtually every one was in Ohio, although two were in Denver: National Jewish Hospital, and The American Medical Center—formerly The Jewish Consumptive Relief Society of Denver. The will does not specify why Leo chose those out of state charities where his granddaughter Sue Klebold would eventually settle.

But after death, Leo still fought with family. His estate agreed to pay $300,000 "to certain of said claimants," that included Dylan's mother and Leo's other grandchildren.

★★★

Susan's mother, Charlotte, died of cardiac arrest in 1987 at age sixty-five. She was still living in Columbus. Her occupation was listed as bookkeeper; her estate at over $1 million. Her children were spread across the country. Diane Rafferty was in Palo Alto, California; Susan in Littleton; and Philip remained in Columbus.

After Columbine Solly, the unofficial family historian, will not talk about the family, declining written and other requests. "There's not much to say about it, and I really don't have the time to do it," he said in one phone conversation. His extensive family history does not mention Columbine.

★★★

In 1964 the Beatles were a hot new band. Democrat Lyndon Johnson won the presidential election. It was the '60's, but not yet the '60's revolution. One foot was still in the 1950s. It was the era the parents of both Columbine killers became teenagers.

Dylan Klebold's mother was born on March 25, 1949 and attended the private Columbus School for Girls from the first through twelfth grades. Susan, as a sophomore, was assistant art editor of the school paper, *Silhouette*, and art editor the next year. As a junior, she was also art editor of *TOPKNOT*, the yearbook. She was involved in *Scroll*, the literary magazine that included art, stories, and poetry. She was in I'Pittori-the art club, along with the Latin club. In her senior year, she took photos for the school newspaper.

Her short brown hair set off her boyish looks. Her smile appeared to come easily. With a pointy chin and high cheeks, she is a female version of Dylan.

Girls routinely wore blazers with a coat of arms on the left breast in the formal class photos of that time. They have white socks and saddle shoes, knee-high skirts and white blouses. Susan was no different. "I don't remember them personally, but I was at school at the same time," one woman says of Susan and Diane. "They were quiet girls.... They didn't make waves."

Columbus School for Girls touts its academic standards. Unless, of course, the learning involves one of its own alumni caught in the uncomfortable position of being the mother of a school shooter. Then the learning is shut out.

"We align ourselves with the families that sent their kids here," says Carolyn Thomas Christy, director of development at Columbus School for Girls, when asked for information on Susan.

"This family has been very good to this school," Christy says.

"She [Susan] is a very private person," she adds. "We know that Susan is."

★★★

Susan was in the Columbus School for Girls class of 1967, the same year her father died. She then enrolled in Knox College in Galesburg, Illinois. The private, liberal arts college touts its long-standing support of diversity, where the fifth Lincoln-Douglas debate took place in 1858. In her freshman photo Susan looks over her right shoulder and into the camera, the light forming a sort of halo around her head. Her lips are sealed, but there is a tiny smile. As in high school, Susan's short hair and demure expression continue.

Susan left Knox in 1969. Her stepbrother, Charles Huelsman III, is not sure why. Maybe more opportunity at her hometown university, Ohio State. Maybe she wanted to be with her mother, who she lived with upon returning to Columbus. But Huelsman is sure Susan sought counseling given her father's early death and landed in a book by Ohio State University professor Hugh Missildine.

Missildine's books seem to veer towards pop psychology. As he recounts patient histories he traces every problem, no matter how convoluted, to someone's childhood. But he is considered a major figure in Ohio medicine, starting the Columbus Children's Psychiatric Hospital and Residential Treatment Center.

Missildine's most famous book is probably *Your Inner Child of the Past*, published in 1963. Maybe his most famous patient, the then Susan Yassenoff, shows up in his 1974 book co-authored with Lawrence Galton, *Your Inner Conflicts—How to Solve Them*. Susan apparently appears under the pseudonym "Sandra," with some details of her bio altered to obscure her identity. "My father and she talked about it in front of me," Huelsman recalls of her case study. "I think Susan was rather proud to be part of a book at that young age."

And proud, possibly, because she successfully solved her problem. Although Susan does not seem to have felt that way post-Columbine. In a quick phone conversation, her only one with this author, I told her, "I came across your profile in the Hugh Missildine book."

"What?" she says.

"Yeah," I reply, "in the, it was a few, quite a few years ago, the profile you had as Sandra."

"I think you are way out of base here, I'm going to hang up now," Susan says.

She does just that.

Her lawyer, criminal defense attorney Gary Lozow, quickly called an intermediary. Lozow called it a matter that occurred when Susan Klebold was nineteen. But no further communication on the issue came my way.

This is the profile, narrated by Missildine:

Sandra is a twenty-year-old woman who came to see me because of a phobia. "I have a death phobia," she told me. "It underlines everything I do. I think about death all the time."

She is a music student, about to graduate from college, has been living for the past year with her fiancé and is very much in love with him, as he is with her. He too is in music.

When I asked her to talk about herself, she told me: "I'm afraid of failure. I won't even attempt something unless I'm assured of success. I think too much. I don't have a temper.

"War things and medical programs bother me. I was terrified of bugs as a child. Airplanes used to bother me, too, and storms. My mother used to cuddle me and comfort me when I was fearful. When I was afraid, my sister would call me stupid. I scold myself for being afraid. I often feel that I'm a burden to people.

I sometimes get depressed.

"*I think the fear of death will always be there. I wish I could turn off this part of my mind. I wish there were traumas to explain all this, but I've never had any traumas. When I get a headache, I'm always sure it is fatal. Then I worry that I will die, which makes the headache worse. Everything makes me think of death. I have to divert myself in the evening constantly–by eating, watching television, practicing my music or masturbating. I feel constantly that I'm coming a minute closer to death. What a waste of time to think of that all the time. But thinking this is a way of life with me.*"

Questioned about her family, Sandra told me that her father had been a sensitive, sweet person who enjoyed doing things for her and whom she adored. He had died suddenly just before she had graduated from high school. Her mother?

"*A saint–a real saint,*" *Sandra said.* "*She is kind, patient, never critical. When I was at home, my mother always enjoyed doing things for me and giving me things.*"

Here, then, is a young woman who came from a loving home, who is in love and is loved in return, who is bright, is intelligent, is attractive, has a deep interest in music and yet is an emotional cripple. Why should she suffer so much from, and devote so much of her attention to, an almost overpowering fear of death?

We had to examine closely her childhood, the parental attitudes to which she was exposed and the child of the past she carries with her now. She grew up in a good family with wonderful parents who made the mistake of catering to her. When she had fears as a youngster, her mother cuddled her and did everything possible to shield her from the fears. But, as Sandra could recall after we had talked at some length, her mother would be exasperated with her when she was fearful.

What it really came down to was that Sandra had been subjected to three principal practices as a child: overindulgence, including coddling of her fears; oversubmission to her fearful whims; and overt belittling on the part of her mother–and sister as well–shown through exasperation and resentment toward her fears.

Now, as an adult, Sandra had continued to treat herself with the same attitudes and practices. She coddled her fears, which only tended to strengthen them. She belittled herself resentfully. Her long-term pattern of being indulged, both by herself and by her mother, stood in the way of developing self-discipline. Her lack of self-discipline made it virtually impossible for her to control herself, particularly when she was fearful.

She had to face the fact that as long as she continued to treat herself indulgently, she would have fears; they and indulgence had always gone hand in hand.

There was nothing really mysterious about her phobia about death. It had grown out of her past conditioning and was being continued because she had continued to follow the conditioning. She would have to develop discipline. She would have to let the fears come, understand their origin, make sure she didn't belittle herself about them and then continue to do what she was going to do, whether she had fears or not. As an adult, she couldn't let the child inside force her to make activity decisions based on fears.

Not long afterward, Sandra decided to do what her fiancé had long urged: get married. She became so busy with the wedding plans that, she told me in some surprise, she was thinking less and less about her fears. That was a good indication that when her adult of the present took over from the child of the past, she could dispel the fears.

She is now much better. She is not driven by fears as she was before she started to treat herself with methods other than the old home methods of childhood. She still tends to slip back occasionally into old, indulgent, self-critical ways and to become a little fearful, but she can quickly abort the relapses.

***

Missildine, in his signature way, traces Susan's "death phobia" to her childhood (although, it seems odd, not to mention the fact that her father died when she was eighteen). Her fears and been "coddled," and allowed to fester. As an adult, she needed to quash them. It would come through understanding, and discipline. Missildine says she was successful, although the diversion of her marriage also seemed to help.

Death phobia, according to other experts, is generated because people fear death as painful, or the unknown – such as the mysterious quantity of the afterlife. Officially called thanatophobia, it is "one of the most universal fears, and may be the basis for many phobias," according to the *Encyclopedia of Phobias, Fears, and Anxieties.* Fear of flying, darkness, and enclosed places, for example, are death phobias via other routes.

Dylan also had a fascination with death. And he too became crestfallen no matter how large or small his failures. Both Susan and Dylan seem plagued by an overly sensitive nature. Missildine mentions depression for Susan, and Dylan's writings make clear that he was depressed. But in contrast with his mother, Dylan welcomed death as an escape from what he often saw as a miserable life.

★★★

The same time Missildine's death phobia counseling would have taken place, around 1969, was the year Susan entered Ohio State.

Charles Huelsman III's father married Charlotte after Milton's death, and Charles III got to know the Yassenoff clan. He recalls Susan making a remark about Vietnam around this time: "Why do we have to have this stupid war anyway?" But he is not sure whether it is part of the generalized, anti-war sentiment, or a much stronger conviction.

Susan was seen as a goody two shoes, and she also painted. At least one dark, oil painting sticks in Huelsman's mind. A woman sits in a chair, melting, in dark reds, dark yellows, and "black type blues." Melting the way a candle stuck in a bottle leaves wax dripping down the glass, he says. Huelsman believes the painting expressed a normal, but intense mood swing. "I would view the painting as more of an emotional outlet and a way to get around depression rather than a sign of harboring feelings of depression," he says.

Huelsman doesn't think Susan liked the painting, and she may have destroyed it. "I remember Susan's mother saying that she wanted to keep the picture," he says. "It's like a signpost of emotional growth. She was trying to give praise and encouragement to her daughter. Susan wouldn't have anything of it."

★★★

Some 145 miles away in the working class city of Toledo, William H. Klebold had two sons. One would end up raising the other. The other then raised a school shooter.

A native of Pearl, Texas William served in the army in Europe during World War I as a captain. He moved to the Toledo, Ohio area in 1919 and died as the proprietor of Klebold's Suburban Hardware. His obituary photo shows him in a coat and tie, a stern look on his slightly pudgy face, and a bald head.

William's first son was Donald, and he also had two daughters, Katherine Ann and Mary Lou. William later married Lillian Grace Rae. William was fifty-two and Lillian was thirty-nine when Tom Klebold was born on April 15, 1947 (his birthday falls five days before his son's murderous rampage). Lillian died six years later. William died six years after that at age sixty-four. Tom was twelve.

Donald, known as "Sam," was named executor. He and Tom were to split the remaining assets from William's will at about $10,500 each. And Sam, who turned twenty-nine the day after William died, took to raising Tom.

Tom, by all accounts, was in good company with Sam and his wife Janet, who eventually had five children of their own, according to neighbors. Tom, the oldest, was a surrogate six. Neighbors describe the family as intact, close, loving, and darned nice. They attended Lutheran church regularly but did not flaunt their religion.

"Nothing fantastic," said longtime neighbor Janet Oltmans. "Just average people."

Their home at 3244 Waldmar Road was ample, but neither grand, nor fashionable. It is solid middle class America. The wood siding has white trim, the roof is peaked. The curtains are white, and drawn. A pinwheel adds a flourish to the backyard.

Two months after the September 11, 2001 terrorist attacks small American flags adorn many a window and front door in the neighborhood, including the one on the Klebold home. Fall leaves trickle down to the lawns; a man and boy rake a nearby yard.

Sam Klebold walks out to his car. "We don't want to talk to you," he yells. "And that goes for my sons."

He continues, "We talked to the media once. They double-crossed us. We got two thousand calls."

As he speaks he is so wound up a red lozenge shoots out of his mouth. He is wearing a tan windbreaker, and white, button-down shirt. He jumps into an older model American car and drives away.

The calling card for Sam's carpentry business was the older model, white Ford van still in his driveway. He plied his trade for local doctors, attorneys and his church, Advent Lutheran, where he put in a ten-foot-high, solid walnut cross with a brass strip down the middle that hangs above the altar.

Sam did not attend college, according to family pastor Dennis Lauman: "You think of [him] as someone who's worked from the day he graduated high school."

★★★

Tom Klebold attended Sylvania High School and like other boys, wore a jacket and thin tie for his 1965 senior photo. His hair is short, but still longer than the flattops sported by some. His smile appears contended, with a touch of shyness. Tom is remembered in the yearbook as "Dextrous woodworker, go-kart racing fan." The yearbook also lists Tom on the track team, and in the team photo, he stands in the upper right corner, a blank look on his face. He is difficult to see, but if you look hard enough, he is recognizable by his full cheeks. Tom also seems to have been in the chess club.

After high school Tom attended Wittenberg University in Springfield, Ohio, which is affiliated with the Evangelical Lutheran Church in America. At Wittenberg Tom shows up, with a slight smile and standing tall, in the cross country team photo. He is wearing a tank top with the number thirty four on the chest. He shows up on the university's alumni website as the class of 1969, but Tom transferred to Ohio State, where he met Susan Klebold.

***

Tom and Sue married in Franklin County, Ohio on July 1, 1971, where the city of Columbus is located. She was twenty-two; Tom twenty-four. Both listed their occupations as "student," and different home addresses. Both had lost their fathers, and in Tom's case, his mother too.

They were married by Rabbi Jerome D. Folkman. Two months later Susan's grandfather, Leo Yassenoff, died. Folkman was set to officiate at the funeral.

Susan graduated in 1972 with a bachelor of science in art education, and a minor in psychology. Tom majored in sculpting.

The Klebolds quickly moved to Milwaukee, and Susan showed and interest in helping the troubled. She worked for six months at the Milwaukee Psychiatric Hospital as an art therapy intern for adults. She then became a psychiatric art therapist at St. Michael Hospital, also in Milwaukee, working with adults and adolescents.

But in 1975 Susan switched career tracks. She enrolled in Milwaukee's Cardinal Stritch College for a master's degree in reading. The title of her research paper was, "Selecting High Interest-Low Difficulty Books for the Poor Reader in Junior High School."

Susan worked while she was in graduate school, often in elementary schools. Her jobs included special education teacher's aide, and reading specialist. For about a year, she worked on a government program to help disadvantaged youths at the University of Wisconsin at Milwaukee. An idealistic zeitgeist ran through the program recalls Mark Warhus, Susan's supervisor. Students in high school and older attended a jobs program in areas including physical therapy, nursing, and other health profession occupations while teachers like Susan polished their English and math skills. They were low-income, mostly inner-city. Most were black, with a few Latinos and whites.

Tom and Susan didn't live in gritty Milwaukee, but the Whitefish Bay Townhouses, named after the pleasant suburb about ten minutes outside the city. Along the top of her resume at that time, Susan typed: "Personal: Married," and "Health: Excellent." She didn't stand out much, although Warhus recalls that the then-twenty-nine-year-old was attractive. "She had short hair, tall, thin, good-looking," he says. "Dressed maybe a little bit like a schoolteacher; sort of coordinated outfit type thing. I guess you call it women's sportswear."

Warhus remembers the call Susan made the day her first son, Byron, was born on October 23, 1978. "I'm calling you before I even called my mother to let you know that I can't, I won't be in today," Susan said, according to Warhus. "Or something like that. I remember it was fun, we were making a joke about it."

★★★

In 1979 Tom submitted his thesis at the University of Wisconsin in Milwaukee for a master of science in geological sciences: "The Paleomagnetic Characteristics of Sediments from the Cedarburg Bog, Ozaukee County, Wisconsin." The fifty-eight-page paper, with various charts, is about as dense as the title suggests. The acknowledgements page reads: "Finally, and most importantly, I wish to thank my wife, Susan, for her extreme patience and support both before this study was conceived and while it was being undertaken. Without her help, this research would not have been accomplished."

Next, it was on to Bartlesville, Oklahoma for Tom's work. The private school girl had come a long way, and Warhus remembers Susan joking about the move with a little trepidation.

"I think it was just sort of like, 'What's in Oklahoma?'" says Warhus. "More of the sort of reputation Oklahoma has being a kind of backwater, nothing place was sort of maybe what her concern was, you know, 'What are we going to do in Oklahoma?' But I know she was real excited for her husband, to get started with his career and everything."

Tom worked for Phillips Petroleum for slightly under a year, from August 27, 1979 to June 21, 1980, according to the company, as a geophysicist. Then it was on to Colorado, where the oil industry was booming.

FOUR

Growing Up (Young Guns)

Dylan Klebold was born in the Denver suburb of Lakewood on the now infamous date of September 11th in the year 1981. He was high-strung youngster, the type who would go to pieces if he lost at Candyland. But Dylan's parents saw him as a "healthy, happy child, who grew to be very bright."

At least that was what Tom and Sue Klebold, accompanied by two attorneys, said on April 30, 1999, ten days after Columbine. The Klebolds spoke with three sheriff deputies and a representative of the Jefferson County District Attorney's office in one of the most extensive interviews with them ever published. They provided a congenial portrait of Dylan. He was shy, good at math, and "well-loved by his teachers" and peers. Quiet, tolerant, even-tempered, and never talked back. The parents never had any problems with Dylan. They said he was gentle until the day he helped kill thirteen people.

Dylan attended Normandy Elementary School in Littleton for first and second grades and joined the Cub Scouts in second grade. And just as Tom was remembered in his own high school yearbook as a "go-kart racing fan," his parents remembered Dylan for winning a Pinewood Derby. Dylan and his friend Brooks Brown immersed themselves in Legos, and chasing frogs and crawdads. "I couldn't have asked for a better pal in grade school," Brooks wrote in his book, *No Easy Answers*. In the same book Brooks' father, Randy Brown, called Dylan "the sweetest, cutest kid you'd ever meet. He was really shy, though, and it would take him fifteen or twenty minutes to warm up to us every time he came over."

Dylan spent grades three through six in an accelerated program at Governor's Ranch Elementary, also in Littleton. The Klebolds felt the school provided a sheltering atmosphere, and Tom Klebold fought to keep Dylan enrolled when he was threatened with being pushed out in the name of gender balance. But kids from the other side of the intellectual tracks would "sneer" at those in the accelerated program, according to Brooks. Brooks and Dylan even got into a fight between themselves—the first time Brooks saw Dylan's temper—because of the tension at school.

"As Dylan got older, he never told his parents he was teased," according to Judy Brown. "Never. He kept it all inside."

Dylan was caring, Judy added, but "worried a lot about what other people thought—perhaps too much for his own good."

During elementary school Dylan's sports included soccer, T-ball, and baseball. His parents describe him at this time as competitive, yet sensitive, and well-adjusted. As a young boy Dylan had a hunting knife, and throwing knives. Around age ten he had a BB gun, and the family kept one around for nabbing woodpeckers. Dylan took three years of French at Columbine, and studied German in the fifth grade, although the Klebolds were unaware of any fascination with that language. An elementary school photo shows Dylan in a tan Members Only jacket and black T-shirt. He has thick, brown hair and a pudgy face. His mouth is slightly open, as if he is unsure of himself.

As a teen Dylan was deeply depressed. But Sue Klebold says she only saw him cry once. The incident seems to have occurred in elementary school, although the time is not specified in the police interview summary. Sue says Dylan came home from school, went to his room, and "took a box of stuffed toys from the closet and buried himself and fell asleep underneath the stuffed toys." Dylan did not give a reason for the episode.

***

Eric Harris' father, Wayne N. Harris, was born October 7, 1948 and grew up in the south Denver suburb of Englewood with parents Walter E. and Thelma J. He had an older sister, Sandra.

Walter Harris worked as a valet at the Brown Palace hotel, a downtown Denver landmark where fifty years after Wayne's birth the family of slain Columbine student Isaiah Shoels would hold a press conference to announce their lawsuit against the Klebolds and Harrises.

Wayne Harris graduated from Englewood High School in 1966 and classmates summarized the blond boy with freckles as shy, smart, studious, quiet and not a lot of friends, according to the *Rocky Mountain News*. He was neither leader nor troublemaker. He went on to the University of Colorado from 1966 to 1969 as a business major, transferred to Metropolitan State College in Denver, and graduated with a degree in aviation maintenance management.

Eric Harris' mother grew up in Denver. Her father, Richard K. Pool, was in the U.S. Army during World War II, and earned a Philippine Liberation Ribbon with two bronze stars. From 1972 to 1976 he was in the Air Force Reserve. He ran a Denver hardware store and later worked for the Colorado Department of Transportation as a warehouse supply officer.

Richard and wife Elaine had three daughters. The oldest, Cynthia Jane, was born on December 27, 1945. A year and a half later came the twins, Karen Ann and Katherine Ann – Eric's mom – on July 2, 1947. In Denver's George Washington High School yearbook, the photos of Karen and Katherine are side by side. The plain-looking Katherine smiles, and her brown hair flips up just before it hits her shoulders. More than thirty years later, one can still see the same, slightly broad nose and full cheekbones on display. The yearbook lists her activities as the Mogulmeisters ski club, and PTA fashion show hostess. She graduated high school in 1967 in the same manner as her future husband. "She wasn't in the 'in' crowd. She wasn't a nerd," a classmate told the *News*.

Wayne Harris and Katherine Pool married on April 17, 1970 at First Presbyterian Church in Englewood. Wayne was four years out of high school, Katherine three. Their anniversary falls three days short of Columbine.

Three years after marrying Wayne enlisted in the Air Force on September 5, 1973. It was the same year Columbine High School opened.

Their first son, Kevin D. Harris, was born on May 14, 1978. Eric came three years later in Wichita on April 9, 1981. Eric seemed normal to most of those who knew him. But he suffered as his family hop scotched across the country. The Harrises moved to the Dayton, Ohio area when he was two. At six years old, a trick or treat photo shows him in a skeleton costume. Eric has his hands on his hips and a quizzical look on his face, as if he wonders why he must stop what he is doing to take a picture. A neighbor called the Harrises a "typical American family from the outside."

When Eric was eight and in third grade his family moved to Wurtsmith Air Force Base in Oscoda, Michigan as Wayne was transferred. It was 1989.

Oscoda is located on an arc of land on Michigan's northeastern side, and fronts Lake Huron. The township population back then was about 12,000 and Eric remembered it as a "very, very small town." The family lived in what Eric called "a largely wooded area" and, "Of the three close neighbors I had, two of them had children my age. Every day we would play in the woods, or at our houses. We would make forts in the woods or make them out of snow, we would ride around on our bikes, or just explore the woods. It was probably the most fun I ever had in my childhood," he wrote in a class paper.

After living in the township, the family moved onto the base, according to Eric. He described it as "old" and having homes like "small condos." He also had lots of neighbors. But he was sad about leaving his friends "especially my best friend" in Oscoda, he wrote. "Even though we were still only a 10 minute drive away, we only saw each other maybe three times after that. We lived on the Air Force Base for about half a year. I made friends there, some were good, but none were as good as my friends at my old house."

The new friends had adventures, too. "We still lived close to a large wooded area so we would travel around in there almost every day," Eric wrote. "We were all the same age too, so that made it even more fun."

At Cedar Lake Elementary School Eric's parents attended every school conference, according to the *New York Times*. Eric's fifth-grade teacher did not foresee him as a troublemaker, and a neighbor told the paper, "We never even heard the kids cry."

The Harrises left Oscoda after a couple years. "It was real hard leaving my friends again," Eric recalled. "And that time I had to say goodbye to my first best friend for good."

★★★

An essay titled "Just a Day" and found on Dylan's school server files after Columbine is unsigned and undated. Randy Brown does not believe it is Dylan's. If it is Eric, he fondly recalls family fishing trips when he would wake up at 5 a.m. for something cool, "not school or some other bullshit." The sky was black, the coffee brewing. Eric didn't like the taste, but loved the smell. "I would dine on fancy breakfast cuisine, otherwise known as Cocoa Puffs," he wrote. "My brother would already be up, trying to impress our father by forcing down the coffee he hadn't grown to like yet. I always remember my brother trying to impress everyone, and myself thinking what a waste of time that would be."

Eric, who does not indicate his age at the time, becomes poetic when describing the drive into the mountains to go fishing in their 1974 Dodge Ram: "a certain halcyon hibernating within the tall peaks and the armies of pine trees." But he was already a nonconformist. "The lake is almost vacant, except for a few repulsive, suburbanite a$$holes," he writes. "I never liked those kind of people, they always seemed to ruin the serenity of the lake. I loved the water. I never went swimming, but the water was an escape in itself."

"Cast, Reel, etc. countless times, and my mind would wander to wherever it would want to go," Eric adds. "Time seemed to stop when I was fishing. The lake, the mountains, the trees, all the wildlife s$*t that people seemed to take for granted, was here. Now. It was if their presence was necessary for me to be content. Time to go! Done. Back to society. No regrets, though. Nature shared the secret serenity with someone who was actually observant enough to notice. Sucks for everyone else."

***

At eleven years old Eric was in sixth grade in another remote locale by another lake and living at another Air Force base - Plattsburgh, N.Y., by Lake Champlain. Again, Eric dwelled in melancholy. "At first I had no friends there, even though there was many kids my age," he wrote. "Then once school started, and even some help from my older brother, I had some friends. It took a while for our friendships to grow, but soon we were best friends and did everything together."

It was here that Eric found "the best friend I ever had." Kris Otten, who lived two blocks away. "Every day we would find something new to do," Eric wrote. "Some days we would walk along the shore of the lake and just mess around there. Sometimes we would look for old bullet shells from around 50 years ago and we even looked for Revolutionary War and Civil War era items. Kris once found the diary of a slave under some old Civil War barracks."

Eric and Kris played home-run derby, rode their bikes, and hung out at the gym. "We spent countless hours there, just hanging out and talking," Eric recalled.

Eric and Kris also had a friend, Jens, from Norway. "He was the shiest person I had ever known and he wasn't used to our American customs, but he was always there," Eric wrote. "Kris and I made it our mission to make Jens into a normal American kid."

Eric wrote that the "most noble sacrifice that I can remember" occurred with Kris when they were riding their bikes on a dirt trail in a wooded area one day. After entering a drainage pipe, a wave of water knocked them out. Kris got tangled up in some fishing wire and couldn't move. Eric got a bad cut on his right thigh that would require thirteen stitches. But first Eric rode his bike — with one leg — to a boat house and found a knife to cut Kris free. "This was my sacrifice," Eric recalled. "To save my friend in spite of my pain."

Eric at this time in his life would also become overwhelmed with emotion. "I hid in a closet," he recalled. "I hid from everyone when I wanted to be alone." Other times he recalled sitting in the back seat on the sixth grade school bus "talking about guns, sex, and people." It was, he wrote, "Our refuge from everyone else. Where we talked about personal things."

Katherine Harris at this time continued as a stay-at-home mom. Wayne directed the neighborhood association, was a scout leader and youth coach, and played basketball with his sons in the driveway. Wayne also pressured Eric not to mess up. But the biggest trouble Kris Otten could cite was he and Eric getting caught stealing lighters to set off firecrackers. They were both grounded.

In 1993 news came that the Plattsburgh base would be closing. But there was still the annual Independence Day celebration, which took place in a large field in the center of base housing. "Kris, Jesse and I (our other best friend) had the best seats in the house," Eric wrote. "We were about 100 feet away from the launch site of these fireworks. So they were exploding right over our heads. Then later that night there was a large party with bands playing and singing. A few weeks later, Kris moved to Georgia. This was hard to swallow. We had spent more time together than we did with our own families, and now he was gone. I still had Jesse though. And with what little time I had left in Plattsburgh, we did as much as we could together."

If Eric was a wreck after Oscoda, he was crestfallen after Plattsburgh. "It was the hardest moving from Plattsburgh. I have the most memories from there," he wrote four years later. "When I left Jesse, and when Kris left, I had a lot of feelings. I felt alone, lost, and even agitated that I had spent so much time with them and now I have to go because of something I can't stop. It doesn't take long to make a best friend, but it only takes 2 words to lose one. Those are, 'We're moving.'"

Eric, almost sixteen when he wrote those thoughts, added, "Losing a friend is almost the worst thing to happen to a person, especially in the childhood years. I have lived in many places, but the last three places have been the most fun and the greatest experiences of my childhood. Although memories stay with you, the actual friend doesn't. I have lost many great friends, and each and every time I lost one, I went through the worst days of my life."

It was still July 1993 when Wayne and Katherine Harris returned to their Colorado roots and settled in Littleton. For Eric, it was new territory all over again. Otten sensed he was unhappy, and not accepted.

***

But there was one key person who did accept Eric: Dylan Klebold. Eric, in turn, would accept Dylan. It appeared unconditional, and not till death did they part.

Eric and Dylan met at Ken Caryl Middle School. It is unclear what brought them together, but both may have been bullied, according to various accounts. Eric's eighth-grade science partner, Alisa Owen, said Eric was described as a "dork." He was intellectual, funny, and good at math and science. They were not however, qualities that would lend themselves to popularity.

Nathan Vanderau, who knew Dylan in junior high via a church group, says Dylan seemed naive, as if you could talk him into anything. Dylan's father worried about how Dylan would do in middle school but concluded that he did "moderately well." Tom and Sue did not feel they were absentee parents and were "always there for Dylan."

***

In 1995 Eric and Dylan, as freshmen, entered a new Columbine High. The school had undergone its first major renovation, tagged $13.4 million and a ceremony welcomed the special students.

In their first year at Columbine Eric and Dylan were as nondescript as the building. They were fourteen-years-old: shy, slightly built, and clean-cut.

Nick Baumgart was friends with them. He was in the same Cub Scout troop with Dylan, and had hung out with him, off and on, since third grade. But Baumgart says ninth grade was also the time he started to drift away from Dylan. There was no falling out, but like magnets, Dylan started forming a bond with Eric.

Dylan, tall and gangly, had not grown into himself. More emotional and less contained, his personality mirrored his awkward body. But he was funnier, more lighthearted, and more likeable than Eric. People wanted to hang out with Dylan.

Eric seemed like more of a leader because he was quieter and more serious. But he was sour.

Personal computers and the Internet were yet to infuse every corner of life, but Columbine High teacher Rich Long was ahead of the curve. He was giving computer classes in a warehouse — the former welding shop — where tables and chairs were hard to come by. Among his students were Eric and Dylan, who he described as, "wide-eyed freshmen anxious to take computer courses." The start-up conditions didn't bother Eric and Dylan, and they came in before, and after, school to get their projects done. They were "enjoyable to teach," Long said, because they were eager to learn and were "very skilled for that point in time."

Eric and Dylan enrolled in Long's "Computers A to Z," which covered technology, and "Structured Basic," for programming. Their budding mastery over computers provided them with a power they did not have within the general student body. But Long believes both saw the good they could do with technology, as Eric handled the Web pages for Columbine's physics and science departments.

Eric and Dylan were also attracted to computers, wrote Brooks Brown, because they provided "definite rules" and "logical simplicity." "For a young man in a world like ours, it was a godsend," he explained. "In the real world, things and rules change constantly—and you could be in trouble at a moment's notice."

Another explanation for what attracted Eric and Dylan to computers was found in Dylan's house after Columbine. It is a reprint of a famous, 1986 manifesto "The Conscience of a Hacker," and it is easy to imagine Eric and Dylan speaking the very same words. Parts of the manifesto include: "Mine is a world that begins with school... I'm smarter than most of the other kids, this crap they teach us bores me... Damn underachiever. They're all alike. I'm in junior high or high school. I've listened to teachers explain for the fifteenth time how to reduce a fraction. I understand it. 'No, Mrs. Smith, I didn't show my work. I did it in my head...' Damn kid. Probably copied it. They're all alike. I made a discovery today. I found a computer. Wait a second, this is cool. It does what I want it to. If it makes a mistake, it's because I screwed it up. Not because it doesn't like me... Or feels threatened by me... Or thinks I'm a smart ass... Or doesn't like teaching and shouldn't be here... Damn kid. All he does is play games. They're all alike. And then it happened... a door opened to a world... rushing through my phone line like heroin through an addict's veins, an electronic pulse is sent out, a refuge from the day-to-day incompetencies is sought... a board is found. 'This is it... this is where I belong...' I know everyone here... even if I've never met them, never talked to them, may never hear from them again... I know you all."

Eric and Dylan would also embed themselves in violent video games. Eric came to enjoy *Postal*, named for the act of "going postal." As the *Wall Street Journal* wrote in a front page story, the game "comes in a box riddled with fake bullet holes and features a gun-toting character who goes berserk. It invites players to 'spray protesters, mow down marching bands and char-broil whole towns.' As children writhe on the ground, bleeding and screaming for mercy, the assailant must pick off police and other 'hostile' attackers. To quit the game, the lead character must put a gun in his mouth and pull the trigger."

But Eric and Dylan's favorite game was *Doom*. The main player is a "space Marine" who grapples with demons, "cyber-organic mongrels," and "undead Marines." "Take down the hell scum with an array of weapons," is one official description. Eric wrote his own description for a class paper: "Picture an Earth that has been obliterated by nuclear war and alien attacks leaving cities and military forces in ruins with only a lone marine as humanity's last fighting force. Picture holographic walls, crushing ceilings, oceans of blood and lava, strange ancient artifacts, and horrible sour lemon and rotten meat stenches in the air. Imagine being trapped on an abandoned cold steel base floating in space for eternity, a leathery skinned monster roaming under a strobe light waiting for a fight, and astonishing weaponry designed to your special needs. All these places and ideas have been created and recreated many times by yours truly."

Eric said that if he could live anywhere it would be Phobos, one of the Mars moons mentioned in *Doom*. As to whether he believed in aliens he wrote on his AOL profile, "you bet your probbed ass I do."

"To most people it may be just another silly computer game, but to me it is an outlet for my thoughts and dreams," Eric wrote in his class paper. "I have mastered changing anything that is possible to change in that game, such as the speed of weapons, the strength and mass of monsters, the textures and colors used on the floors and walls, and greatest of all, the actual levels that are used. Several times I have dreamed of a place or area one night, then thought about it for days and days. Then, I would recreate it in *Doom* using everything from places in outer space with burned-out floor lights and dusty computers to the darkest depths of the infernal regions with minotaurs and demons running at me from every dark and threatening corner. I have also created settings such as eras of ancient abandoned military installations deep in monster-infested forests with blood stained trees and unidentifiable mangled bodies covered with dead vines and others that portray to futuristic military bases on Mars overrun with zombies that lurk in every corner. These places may seem a bit on the violent side and, I assure you, some of them are. However, many times I have made levels with absolutely no monsters or guns in them. I have created worlds with beautiful, breath taking scenery that looks like something out of a science fiction movie, a fantasy movie, or even some 'eldritch' from H.P. Lovecraft."

The Browns say they were told that Eric used their own neighborhood as a *Doom* setting, and their house as the target. And a couple weeks after Columbine the Los Angeles-based Wiesenthal Center examined Harris' games as part of its mission to monitor hate crimes. The center suggested that Harris had made a version of *Doom* that turned the game from a shooting competition into a massacre because the player was invincible. Wiesenthal researchers said it was called "God mode," and dying characters would yell out, "Lord, why is this happening to me?" Investigators figure Harris spent 100 hours to create the configuration, and in one version, he thanked Klebold for his help.

Eric claimed his interest in the game was intellectual. "Even though one might think it [*Doom*] is just a game, I believe it is one of the best ways to show my creativity and intelligence," he wrote.

Video games may have given Eric and Dylan paths for their anger: *Postal* had details that previewed Columbine, and *Doom's* philosophy of the lone Marine against the rest of hell helped inform Eric and Dylan's us against them mentality. The game's tough as nails descriptions also seeped into their brains and influenced Eric's writings. Staring at the computer screen would keep Eric and Dylan from developing the social skills to merge with the rest of the world they so desperately wanted to connect with.

But Eric and Dylan were not the only ones exposed to the joysticks: In one week in 1997, sales of *Postal* hit 15,000 copies, according to the *Wall Street Journal*. The video games did not cause their anger. That came from elsewhere.

***

Eric the high school freshman was also writing poems. "I am a nice guy who hates when people open their pop can just a little," he wrote in one. "I wonder what my soccer team will be like in the Spring. I hear myself turning on the ignition of an F-15. I see myself flying above everyone else. I want to fly. I am a nice guy who hates when people open their pop can just a little."

When Eric was a freshman his older brother Kevin was a senior who kicked and played tight end for the Columbine Rebels football team. Kevin has been widely praised as a good athlete, and a good guy. Eric called him a great brother. Eric and Dylan attended Columbine High football games and Eric wrote a poem about the team that began:

The big game has finally come tonight.
The Columbine Rebels versus the Chatfield Chargers in football.
The Chargers are filled with fright,
For the Rebels will beat them like a rag-doll.

It does not appear that Eric ever played on any high school teams, but he considered himself a Renaissance man for the sports he did participate in: football, mountain biking, and baseball (outfield and second base). His favorite was soccer (offense and defense) which he played for a club soccer team not affiliated with the school, the Columbine Rush.

Eric acknowledged in a freshman school essay that he was already the type who got angry easily. He said he was kind to people and animals and tried to settle matters "in a mature, non-violent manner" but, "I usually punish people in unusual ways who steal or make me angry." He did not elaborate on the "unusual ways."

Eric liked power, control and creating new things, he wrote. "I am always asking questions or double-checking myself to be sure I completely understand something so I am in control." But Eric didn't have much power, or control, over much of anything.

In the school essay, about the similarities between him and the Greek god Zeus, Eric wrote that they both liked to lead "large groups of people" and "I usually turn out to be a great leader." But if Eric was leading anyone, it was a rag tag band of friends who could summarily be called computer nerds.

Among the first cracks in Eric's psyche was when he took Tiffany Typher to homecoming. She didn't want to go on any more dates after that, so one day he lay on the ground outside his house and covered his head and neck with fake blood. He put a "bloody" rock in his hand as if he had bashed in his own skull, and screamed as Brooks Brown and Tiffany walked by. After a few seconds, Eric burst out laughing. Brooks did too, and saw it as nothing more than a prank.

"I knew it wasn't real, I could tell it was fake blood," Typher told *The Denver Post* a couple days after Columbine. "I yelled, 'You guys are stupid!' and started running to a friend's house and crying, because it shook me up. He was doing that so maybe I'd come back to him and say I'm sorry."

Still, Eric — and Dylan — were ready to be accepted; to be part of team Columbine. But they weren't. And never would be.

Their computer skills were sharp, but could not vault them over the ruthless world of high school social popularity contests. They didn't have the right good looks, money or athletic prowess. Their social skills were hopeless.

★★★

Eric and Dylan were also being bullied, according to Brooks Brown. "At lunchtime the jocks would kick our chairs, or push us down onto the table from behind," he wrote in his book. "They would knock our food trays onto the floor, trip us, or throw food as we were walking by. When we sat down, they would pelt us with candy."

Eric, Dylan and their friends tried to ignore the battering, Brooks added, but, "Their words hurt us and we lived in constant fear and hatred of our tormenters."

Brooks concluded: "Eric and Dylan are the ones responsible for creating this tragedy. However, Columbine is responsible for creating Eric and Dylan."

Eric and Dylan were not the only ones. Isaiah Shoels, who they would later kill, was among the few blacks at Columbine, along with his brother and sister.

"They were being called nigger over and over again," the Shoels family spokesman, Sam Riddle, told the *Rocky Mountain News*.

Jewish student Jonathan Greene said jocks threatened to burn him in an oven, "and made up songs about Jewish people and talked about Hitler." (One school official has said a suspect behind the anti-Semitism was swiftly punished by both the school and sheriff.)

But in their vast diaries and videos, Eric and Dylan never mention being bullied. In her deposition, Dylan's prom date, Robyn Anderson, says Dylan and Eric never talked about being bullied. Dylan told his father that at 6'4", he was tall enough that he didn't get pushed around. But he did indicate people picked on Eric.

By other accounts, Eric and Dylan themselves could be bullies. Columbine student Anne Marie Hochhalter, told the *Rocky Mountain News* that at one point she thought Eric and Dylan were cool. She liked the look of their trench coats, which mimicked the movie *The Matrix*, but she was turned off when she saw them insulting classmates. Dylan himself alludes to being somewhat of a bully in a March 1997 diary entry when he writes of "trying not to ridicule/make fun of people at school." Although he adds, "it does nothing to help my life... my existence is shit... eternal suffering."

***

The Trench Coat Mafia clique was forming at Columbine the same year Eric and Dylan were freshmen. Joseph Stair, one of three founding members, said he would receive weekly death threats on his locker and called the Mafia a "support group." Chris Morris and Eric Dutro were the other two founders. Dutro was called a freak and faggot, and cornered in the halls. After school, other students tossed rocks, glass bottles and ice balls at group members. Dutro called Stair a fellow dork and loner, and viewed the two of them as a couple of friends who didn't care about anyone else as long as they had each other. But with their own power base, they fought back in ways big and small, refusing to move out of the jocks' way.

Then in 1996 Dutro's parents bought him a black trench coat at Sam's Club for a Halloween Dracula costume. He liked it so much he began wearing it on a regular basis, even when police interviewed him after Columbine. As the mafia clique grew to about a dozen, some didn't even wear trench coats, but other students came up with the name Trench Coat Mafia as a tease. The trenchies rolled with it and proudly adopted the name.

But the trench coat never had the power of a Batman cape. As a group, members were not picked on, but still suffered barbs when alone. Girls in the group were called sluts, or nazi lesbians.

Dutro left for another school in 1997, after three years, because of the teasing. Chris Morris eventually stopped wearing his trench coat because others had followed his lead and it was "no longer a statement of his individuality."

For Eric and Dylan, membership in the Trench Coat Mafia might be described as more concept than reality. They were friends with Morris, and Dylan told his father that the jocks called him and his friends the Trench Coat Mafia. Tom Klebold said Dylan was "kind of amused" by the whole thing. When police searched Stair's basement after Columbine, they reported finding an inscription in his 1998 yearbook – the end of Eric and Dylan's junior year – signed with Dylan's nickname: "Yo Joe Stay different, better than the norm! Jocks suck dick. TCM!! Later <<-VODKA->>. But Stair did not consider Eric and Dylan Mafia members, and the 1998 yearbook dedication and photo for the Mafia did not include Eric and Dylan:

Trenchcoat Mafia,

We are Josh, Joe, Chris, Horst, Chuck, Brian, Pauline, Nicole, Kristen, Krista, plus Tad, Alex, Cory. Who says we're different? Insanity's healthy! Remember rocking parties at Kristen's, foos-ball at Joe's, and fencing at Christopher's! Stay alive, stay different, stay crazy! Oh, and stay away from CREAM SODA!!

Love Always,

The Chicks

For many, the yearbook photo was also the farewell to the Trench Coat Mafia, and Eric and Dylan would never join it. According to Dylan's friend Devon Adams, Eric and Dylan never even sat with the Trench Coat members during lunch or breakfast. "We never really hung out with them," she says. "I don't understand how they [Eric and Dylan] were part of it when the only similarity is they wore trench coats."

But Eric and Dylan may have considered themselves part of the group, or at least aspired to it, in their own minds. And in the end, it didn't matter whether they were members. It was the lesson they learned. When they saw the Mafia, they saw power. They saw people who stood up to other students, and the school administration. And when they put on their own trench coats, they felt powerful too.

BOOK1.JPG
4/19/99 8:33:54 AM

FIVE

Rebels

Deep into their sophomore year Eric and Dylan had transformed from young and innocent freshmen to rebels. Part of it was typical and harmless. They developed small-time cigarette habits; Dylan had tried booze for the first time with his brother at their house because he was "curious to see what it was like." Within another year he would try marijuana, again with his brother and again because he was "curious." Eric first drank at age fifteen simply because he wanted to. He sometimes drank by himself—tequila, and the cinnamon liqueur After Shock.

Eric and Dylan were also into petty vandalism. Outwardly, it was typical and harmless. But analytically, it was different. It was not about fun and games, but deep-seated philosophies. Eric harbored an anarchic anger at friends, enemies, and perceived enemies. He was judge, jury, and hangman meting out his own punishment. He would brook no opposition, and was seeing how far he could push his outbursts. He still looked the normal preppy with his short, brown hair. But his smile, with his head cocked forward and his beady eyes, now showed self-satisfaction and superiority. He felt shut out of society.

Dylan was adrift in a sea of depression, holding on to Eric as a friend and anchor.

Their violence would look the same. But their characters were different. If a thermometer could measure their psyches, Eric would shoot the mercury up. He had a hot anger. Dylan's sadness would drop the mercury to negative. But they were joined at zero — touching each other in their disillusionment, and their social standing.

It doesn't seem that any one precipitating incident set Eric and Dylan off toward their extremes. But by the time they were sixteen, they were each hurtling toward violent ends. Each had their nicknames. Dylan was "Vodka," named for the alcohol he loved and appropriately enough, a depressant, albeit one that can also yank someone out of their shell. Eric was Reb, short for Rebel, although Rebel was also the mascot of Columbine High.

En route to an early death Eric and Dylan hit roadblocks — school suspensions and a juvenile diversion program. But the obstacles only caused them to redouble their efforts. And no one came down on them hard enough, or connected all their bombs.

★★★

Eric's anger first exploded around winter of 1997 as he summarized his philosophy and deeds on his Web pages.

Hellllloooooo every one. These are the words of wisdom from REB.
This page explains the various things in the world that annoy the SHIT outa me.
God I just LOVE freedom of speech. Keep in mind that these are just my point of views, and may or may not reflect on anyone else. I do swear a lot on this page, so fuck off if your a pussy who cant handle a little god damn bad language. heeeheee. And now to get started:

YOU KNOW WHAT I HATE!!!?
When there is a group of assholes standing in the middle of a hallway or walkway, and they are just STANDING there talking and blocking my fucking way!!! Get the fuck outa the way or Ill bring a friggin sawed-off shotgun to your house and blow your snotty ass head off!!

YOU KNOW WHAT I HATE!!!?
When people don't watch where THEY ARE FUCKING GOING! Then they plow into me and say 'oops, sorry,' or 'watch it!'NNNYAAAA!!! Next time that happens I will rip out 2 of your damn ribs and shove em into your fucking eye balls!!!

YOU KNOW WHAT I HATE!!!?
OOOOOOOOJAAAAAAAAAAAAAY!!!!!!!!!! GOD I F-ING HATE THAT WORTHLESS TRIAL!!! Who in their right feeeeearrrRIGIN mind would care about that trial??!? its not any different from any other murder trial! Tell those fucking reporters to get a life! And what the fuck do we have to gain by watching that stupid trial anyway!!? Its not news! its a trial! not news! trial! Trial does not = news!

YOU KNOW WHAT I LOVE!!!?
—Natural SELECTION!!!!!!!!! God damn its the best thing that ever happened to the Earth. Getting rid of all the stupid and weak orginismsbut its all natural!! YES! I wish the government would just take off every warning label. So then all the dumbasses would either severely hurt themselves or DIE! And boom, no more dumbasses. heh.

YOU KNOW WHAT I HATE!!!?
--R rated movies on CABLE! My DOG can do a better damn editing job than those dumnshits!!!

Eric is also transforming thought into action through various "missions." Although he is not alone. Dylan is around. So is Zach Heckler, who has known Eric and Dylan since eighth grade. He was known as "Kibble" or "Kibbz" because he was fond of bringing snacks to school.

"OK people, im gonna let you in on the big secret of our clan," Eric explains. "We aint no god damn stupid ass quake clan! We are more of a gang. We plan out and execute missions. Anyone pisses us off, we do a little deed to their house. Eggs, teepee, superglue, busyboxes, large amounts of fireworks, you name it and we will probly or already have done it. We have many enemies in our school, therefor we make many missions. Its sort of a night time tradition for us."

They get drunk after each mission. "Not with wimpy beer, we only use hard liquor. Aftershock, Irish Cream, Tequila, Vodka, Whiskey, Rum, and sometimes a few shots of EVERCLEAR. We also sometimes make up our own shooters. And sample others (never try a prarie fire, its killer!)."

Eric will be sixteen in April. And then, "we can drive around any place we want to. Heh heh."

For now, Eric labels six "missions." The first, which is the first known record of Eric and Dylan's mischief, is undated: "We put an entire assortment of very loud fireworks in a tunel, and lit them off at about 1:00 A.M.," he spouts off on the Web. "This mission was part of a rebellion against these assholes that shot one of our bikes one day. They were rather angry that night, and we were very happy. We will be doing another hit on their house sometime in the near future. And that one will be much closer. And louder."

Heckler says he doesn't know whose houses are being vandalized, they are people Eric doesn't like. But a timeline begins to emerge, and one-time friend Nick Baumgart is the next target: "Our second mission was against this complete and utter fag's house. Everyone in our school hates this immature little weakling. So we decided to 'hit' his house. On Friday night (2/7/97) at about 12:15 AM we arrived at this queer's house. Fully equipped with 3 eggs, 2 roles of toilet paper, the cheap brand, no pretty flowers (We were disappointed to) superglue, and the proper tools to make his phone box a busy box (for those of you that are stupid, a busy box is where you set their box so that when they try to make call, they get a busy signal and when someone else calls, they get a busy signal too). We placed 2 eggs in his very large, thick bushes. We just barely cracked them open so they will be producing a rather repulsive and extremely BAD oder for sometime. We placed the last egg on his 'welcome' mat. It was very neat, I cracked the egg, put the yoke in the center, and the 2 halves on either side of the yoke. Then we teepeed his large pine tree and this... oak? tree. I don't know, Its big though. It wasn't a complete teepee but it was enough to agitate the home owner greatly. We also put the superglue on the front door and on the little red mail box flag."

★★★

Another target was another one-time friend, Brooks Brown, who was becoming Eric's worst enemy. Brooks had grown to be tall and lanky, smart and edgy, but didn't apply himself and was a mediocre student. With straight, brown hair and a hangdog look, the only things he seemed to enjoy at school were theater and debate. He calls the Christian ethos at Columbine suffocating, and enjoyed arguing with students outside the classroom when it came to religion. "I prided myself on making Christians cry," he says.

Brooks also became Eric and Dylan's most famous friend, because his parents recognized their troublemaking and reported it to police. It did little good. When the Browns pointed out the police shortcomings after Columbine, the sheriff labeled Brooks a possible accomplice. The sheriff's office later recanted, and none of the writings from Eric or Dylan indicate Brooks was in on the plan. And in fact, they state the opposite: That Eric dreamed of killing Brooks and his family, although three months before Columbine, Brooks says he and Eric patched things up. On the day of the shootings, Eric allowed him to live.

An early flashpoint for Eric's anger toward Brooks was the great backpack caper. The incident itself was minor. But Eric's anger, and attempt to cover it up, was noteworthy.

Second semester of sophomore year Brooks would pick Eric up for school, and was almost always late. But Eric kept accepting the rides, and kept getting angry. Brooks got sick of the arguments and finally said no more rides. Eric stopped talking to him.

On February 28, 1997 Brooks pulled up alongside a bus stop and Eric threw a chunk of ice at Brooks' Mercedes, leaving a little crack in the windshield.

"Fuck you!" Brooks yelled. "Fuck you, Eric! You're going to pay to fix this!"

"Kiss my ass, Brooks! I ain't paying for shit!" Eric said.

Brooks went to Eric's house and told Eric's mom what happened. He added, gratuitously, that Eric had been going on vandalism sprees and that Eric had liquor and spray paint in his room. Katherine Harris did not appear to believe Brooks, and asked him to wait until Eric got home. But Brooks didn't want to confront Eric again.

Meantime, another friend of Brooks had snagged Eric's backpack from the bus stop. He and Brooks drove back to the bus stop with Brooks' mom, Judy Brown. Judy told Eric they had his backpack, and were going to his house. Eric turned bright red, and began shrieking and pounding the car. He pulled as hard as he could on the door handle to get in. They drove away and returned to the Harris house. Judy calls Katherine Harris a "very sweet, a very nice lady," and says tears welled up in her eyes as she recounted Eric's behavior. Wayne Harris thought the whole thing was "just kids' stuff" and that Eric was actually afraid of Judy. Judy figured Wayne "didn't want to hear that his son had done anything wrong."

Brooks heard the next day that Eric was threatening him, and Judy called police. An officer came to their house, and she asked him to go to the Harrises', just a few blocks away, to talk about the windshield and let Eric know he didn't get away with it. The Browns think police contacted the Harrises because Wayne brought Eric over that night to apologize.

"I didn't mean any harm, and you know I would never do anything to hurt Brooks," Eric said.

Judy thought Eric was faking it. "You know, Eric, you can pull the wool over your dad's eyes, but you can't pull the wool over my eyes," she said.

"Are you calling me a liar?" Eric asked.

"Yes Eric, I guess I am," Judy responded.

He left mad, and joined his father, who was waiting in the car.

"Maybe he had gotten away with it for so long, manipulating people that way, that he was stunned when it didn't work," Judy thought.

***

Eric's mission number three is undated, but it was plastering model putty on a Mercedes owned by Brooks. The coda to mission number four was Eric's denial: "Brooks Brown thought I put a little nik [sic] in his windshield from a snowball........ BS? Yes." But mission number four was also "liquor free" because Brooks told Eric's mother about his liquor stash. "I had to ditch every bottle I had and lie like a fuckin salesman to my parents," Eric wrote.

Mission five illustrated an ongoing problem for Eric and Dylan: It was free of girls. "We were supposed to have a few chicks come with us, but they couldnt make it...so may be next time."

The last mission had a more direct prelude to Columbine: Dylan brought his sawed off BB gun. "So we loaded it, pumped it, and fired off a few shots at some houses and trees and stuff," Eric wrote. "We probly didnt do any damage to any houses, but we arent sure." Mission number six lasted about three hours, Eric figured, and employed a whopping 1,152 firecrackers. "We were tired as a priest after a 5 hour orgy," he concluded.

***

Eric was also writing of the first four bombs he and Dylan created "entirely from scratch": "Atlanta" is named for the 1996 Olympics bombing in that city, while "Pazzie" seems a likely play on the Italian word for lunacy. "Peltro" is Italian for pewter and "Pholus" is the centaur who offered wine to Heracles. "Now our only problem," Eric added, "is to find the place that will be 'ground zero.'"

***

On August 7, 1997 Brooks' younger brother Aaron walked into the Jefferson County sheriff's substation in the Southwest Plaza Mall around noon and reported Eric's Web site to Deputy Michael Burgess. Burgess later wrote that the tipster was an anonymous, "concerned citizen," but Aaron apparently gave Burgess his address. Within forty-five minutes Burgess requested that an officer be dispatched to the Browns' house. Deputy Dennis Huner met with one or both of Aaron's parents and left the house at 1:40 p.m. with seven Web pages recounting the night missions and Eric's "philosophies" in hand. Huner gave the pages to Burgess at the substation, and Burgess wrote a cover sheet indicating that "Dillon Klebled" was one of Harris' followers. Burgess sent it to

Investigator John Hicks, known in the department for his expertise in computer crimes. Hicks apparently files it away in the "Computer Crime Intel" binder and says he never sees, or thinks of it, again. The same goes for everyone else in the criminal justice system. Or at least that was the story that began emerging years after Columbine.

★★★

As Eric was blazing his anger on the Web, his father was recording his own thoughts in a small, spiral notebook. In this stroke of interesting timing, they both began their introspections around the same time. One wonders whether Wayne even told Eric to start a journal, hoping it might be therapeutic.

Wayne's journal is not so much a diary as brief notations. It is difficult to tell whether he is recording his own thoughts, or those of the people he is speaking to. Although it does appear to be a first attempt to manage his youngest son. His spiral steno pad marked "Eric" seems to reflect Wayne's military background as he stiffly records his son's behavior looking for clues, wrongdoing, and patterns. The first entry of "2/28"(1997) mentions the cracked windshield, and contains notes from what appears to be a conversation with Randy and possibly Judy Brown. "Believing Eric vs. wife," Wayne wrote, along with, "being little bully." While the exact context remains unclear, Wayne has also written:
aggression
disrespect
idle threats of physical harm, property damage, overreaction to minor incident

His second journal entry, March 3, 1997, continues the saga: "Plotting against friends' house - other boys involved, including Brooks."

A dean at Columbine High, Craig Place, was notified about Eric and Brooks, and apparently their troubled relationship, according to the journal.

Eric also wanted to talk it out with Brooks, Wayne notes, but "with an adult present." (Asking for the adult might seem a mature gesture on Eric's part, or confidence that he could manipulate an adult and put Brooks on the defensive.) Wayne adds that someone, "Would talk to Eric today and the other boys possibly together." But in the end, Eric and Brooks decide to "leave each other alone."

Wayne's other jottings from March 3 indicate he was "very concerned

about alcohol acquisition. Would get police involved if necessary."
Wayne notes that Eric denies having the alcohol, but jots down details of
Eric vandalizing Baumgart's home. Wayne talks to Nick's mom, Bonnie
Baumgart, on April 18. She recounts some of the vandalism - a door is
glued, toilet paper - but can't say who did it. She says she knows of no
problems between Eric and Nick.

The next day, a sheriff's deputy contacts Wayne about tree damage
(maybe to Nick's house). "We feel victimized too," Wayne seems to
write of his own feelings. "Brooks Brown is out to get Eric."

The journal adds, "We don't want to be accused every time something
supposedly happens. Eric is not at fault."

Wayne points the finger at Brooks, noting that he has issues with
other boys, and that a mediator or attorney may help sort out future
problems. Wayne repeats in his diary, "We feel victimized too," along
with "Manipulative," and "Con Artist," quite possibly referring to
Brooks.

Zach Heckler's name also pops up in the journal. And while Dylan's
does not, Wayne writes down "Sue," and the Klebold phone number.
After April 27, 1997, Wayne's journal falls silent for nine months. It
restarts when Eric and Dylan are arrested in January 1998 for breaking
into a van.

***

In another odd coincidence, at almost the exact same time Eric and
Wayne begin recording their thoughts, so does Dylan. Although different
feelings define him.

"Fact: People are so unaware...well, Ignorance is bliss I guess... that
would explain my depression," Dylan writes on the cover page of his
diary which he labels across the top, "A Virtual Book" and "Existences."

On this same cover page, Dylan is childlike as he notes the "properties"
of his diary: "This book cannot be opened by anyone except Dylan. Some
supernatural force blocks common people from entering." He signs his
name, and his nickname, "Vodka."

On page one Dylan draws a box symbolizing "existence" for the rest
of the world, but he is outside the box. "This is a weird time, weird life,
weird existence," he writes on March 31, 1997, the first entry, or what he
calls "El Thoughtzos." "As I sit here (partially drunk w/ a screwdriver) i
think a lot. Think... Think... that's all my life is, just shitloads of thinking...
all the time... my mind never stops..."

He thinks about friends, family and girls he loves but can never have. "Yet I can still dream," he writes, and adds, "as i see the people at school - some good, some bad - i see how different i am (aren't we all you'll say) yet i'm on such a greater scale of difference from everyone else (as far as I kno, or guess). I see jocks having fun, friends, women, LIVEZ. Or rather shallow existences compared to mine (maybe). Like ignorance is bliss. They don't know beyond this world.... yet we each are lacking something that other possesses. i lack the true human nature... & they lack the overdeveloped mind/imagination/knowledge tool."

Dylan figures he will find his place "wherever i go after this life -- that i'll finally not be at war w. myself, the world, the universe – my mind, body, everywhere, everything at PEACE..." He is about to finish his sophomore year and frets about going to school where he is "scared and nervous," and "hoping that people can accept me... that i can accept them."

On April 15, 1997, almost two years to the day before Columbine, Dylan writes: "Well, well, back at it, yes (you say) whoever the fuck 'you' is, but yea. My life is still fucked, in case you care... maybe,... (not?). I have just lost fuckin 45$ & Before that I lost my zippo & knife (I did get those back) Why the fuck is he being such an ASSHOLE??? (god i guess, whoever is the being which controls shit). He's fucking me over big time & it pisses me off. Oooh god i HATE my life, i want to die really bad right now -- Let's see what i have that's good: A nice family, a good house, food, a couple good friends & possessions. What's bad – no girls (friends or girlfriends), no other friends except a few, nobody accepting me even though i want to be accepted, me doing badly and being intimidated in any & all sports, me looking weird and acting shy – BIG problem, me getting bad grades, having no ambition or life, that's the big shit.

Was Dylan cutting himself?

"I was Mr. Cutter tonight -- I have 11 depressioners on my right hand... & my fav. contrasting symbol because it is so true and means so much - the battle between good and bad never ends... OK enough bitchin... well i'm not done yet. ok go. I don't know what I do wrong with people (mainly women) it's like they are set out to hate & ignore me, i never know what to say or do. [name deleted by police] is soo fucking lucky. He has no idea how I suffer."

May 1997:

"Yo... Whassup... Heehehehe... Know what's weird? Everyone knows everyone. I swear like i'm an outkast, & everyone is conspiring against me... Check it... (this isn't good, but I need to write, so here...

"Within the known limits of time...within the conceived boundaries of space... the average human thinks these are the setting of existence... Yet the ponderer, the outkast, the believer, helps out the human.

"Miles and miles of never ending grass, like a wheat, a farm, sunshine, a happy feeling in the presence. Absolutely nothing wrong, nothing ever is, contrary 180 degrees to normal life. No awareness, just pure bliss, unexplainable bliss. The only challenges are no challenge, & then... BAM!!! realization sets in, the world is the greatest punishment. Life....

"Dark. Light. God. Lucifer. Heaven. Hell. GOOD. BAD. Yes, the everlasting contrast.... HA fuckin morons. If people looked at History they would see what happens. I think too much. I understand I am GOD, compared to some of these unexistable brainless zombies. Yet, the actions of them interest me, like a kid w/ a new toy...."

On July 23, 1997 Dylan writes about a friend whose name police have blocked out, although it may be Zach Heckler based on the description of the deviancy they shared.

"It is not good for me right now (like it ever is)... but anyway... My best friend ever: the friend who shared, experimented, laughed, took chances with & appreciated me more than any friend ever did has been ordained... 'passed on'... in my book. Ever since [name deleted] (who I wouldn't mind killing) has loved him... that's the only place he's been with her... If anyone had any idea how sad I am... I mean we were the TEAM. When him & I first were friends, well I finally found someone who was like me: who appreciated me & shared my common interests. Ever since 7th grade i've felt lonely... when [name deleted] came around, I finally felt happiness (sometimes)... we did cigars, drinking, sabotage to houses, EVERYTHING for the first time together & now that he's 'moved on' i feel so lonely w/o a friend. Oh well, maybe he'll come around... I hope."

Undated:

My 1st love???... OH my God... I am almost sure I am in love w. [name deleted] hehehe... such a strange name, like mine... Yet everything about her I love. From her good body to her almost perfect face, her charm, her wit & cunning her NOT being popular, her friends (who I know)... I just hope she likes me as much as I LOVE Her. I think of her every second of every day. I want to be with her. I imagine me and her doing things together, the sound of her laugh, I picture her face, I love her. If soulmates exist, then I think I've found mine. I hope she likes Techno...

I love you

Dylan

★★★

Dylan wasn't the only one in the Klebold household with problems. Tom and Sue were dwelling on his older brother, Byron. It was minor, but on October 14, 1995, just shy of his seventeenth birthday, the Arapahoe County Sheriff's Department cited Byron for curfew violation, according to court records. It appears the time was 12:46 a.m. on a Saturday. The district attorney dismissed the case around one month later.

Byron attended Regis Jesuit High School in the suburb of Aurora, but went to Columbine as a senior and graduated in 1997, when Dylan was a sophomore. But after graduation, in July, he was kicked out of the house, possibly for using marijuana.

That story was partially told after Eric and Dylan got busted for breaking into a van and entered a juvenile diversion program. Dylan's file notes that, "Dylan's brother has a substance abuse problem, and was kicked out of the house for continued drug use. Dylan said that he has seen first hand how drugs can ruin your life, and that is why he decided to stop." The family went to counseling over the drug use.

The file does not name Byron's drug, but it was most likely marijuana given that Dylan's drug use was summarized as, "Has used mj. 2X does not like it and does not like what it has done to his brother. Has tried to help brother but doesn't have any impact. Realizes if someone wants to use he can't stop them."

Dylan also said he loves his brother, "but cannot condone his behavior," a diversion counselor concluded. Dylan himself indicated Byron was the least supportive family member. "isn't involved in my life (not a problem)," he wrote.

By the time of the shootings Byron was twenty and working at Ralph Schomp Automotive. He was a lot technician who shoveled snow and moved and washed cars, according to the *Rocky Mountain News*. "It was an entry-level job, but man, he's good," personnel director Jim Biner told the paper.

But it wasn't what the Klebolds had envisioned for their first-born. They would still try to shepherd Byron, but thought Dylan would be their star.

Class of 98,
top of the
"Should have died"
list.

SIX

Summer Dreams

Just around the corner from Columbine High is a strip mall with a couple of hair salons, a dry cleaner, a bar, sundry offices, and a Blackjack Pizza. The strip mall is tucked behind smaller streets and doesn't face a main thoroughfare. The grandest view from many of the storefronts is a massive parking lot.

Blackjack has since closed down; new tenants include Christian-themed schools. But the pizza shop hired Eric in the summer of 1997 on the recommendation of his buddy, Chris Morris. Dylan soon followed. Blackjack was more than just a job for Eric and Dylan. It gave them friends, paychecks to fund their arsenal, and a laboratory for their explosives. The strip mall is secluded enough so that if Eric and Dylan blew up a couple things with small, homemade bombs, not many people would notice. Although sometimes, they did want them to notice: Eric talked of installing a trip wire and bomb, at a hole in the fence behind Blackjack that kids popped through.

The Blackjack was basically a kitchen with a cash register. There were no dining tables, and Eric and Dylan eventually earned over $6 an hour tossing pizzas, as opposed to making deliveries. Owner Bob Kirgis, then twenty-eight, considered Eric and Dylan good employees. Kirgis would drink at work, and when he wasn't around, sometimes left Eric in charge. Eric and Dylan would drop by during school lunch break, just after 11 a.m., to smoke cigarettes and have free salad or pizza. Eric liked pepperoni and green pepper.

Kirgis remembers Eric and Dylan being "tied at the hip" and treating his six-year-old daughter well. Kirgis shot bottle rockets off the Blackjack roof with the two, but admonished Eric when he brought a shiny, one-foot long metal pipe bomb to the store so he could blow up a watermelon after work. Kirgis told him to take it away, and never heard either teen talk about pipe bombs again. By at least one account Dylan also brought in a bomb once, and went back and forth between working and leaving Blackjack. Eric, Dylan, and their friends talked of fighting with the jocks. But Kirgis never imagined anything on the scale of Columbine.

One fellow Blackjack employee said Eric was nice and went out of his way to wait on female customers, but could be angry and paranoid. Joseph Jonas said Eric "seemed to lose his temper easily while talking to customers on the telephone." One former employee didn't even know Eric's real name until after the shooting because he asked people to call him "Reb." Eric would also speak German, and once put on German polka music—until Kirgis told him to turn it off.

Dylan was different from Eric, at least according to Blackjack employee Kim Carlin. He was shy, backed off from food fights, and if she asked him something embarrassing, he would turn red and grin.

The month before Columbine Christopher Lau bought the Blackjack from Kirgis for about $15,000. At that point Eric and Dylan were working three to five nights a week, with the longest shifts running from 4:00 p.m. to 9:00 p.m. Eric was earning $7.65 an hour; Dylan $6.50. Their last night of work was four days before Columbine, on Friday April 16, 1999.

Lau also called them good employees and never had to discipline them. The only problem he could recall was catching them behind the store lighting a newspaper on fire. Eric, Lau added, was his best employee while Dylan was "hyper, loud, energetic, a good worker, punctual, no problems."

***

Dylan was intimidated by girls. He did the sound board for theater, where he liked being around other "weirdos," but in general did not know how to interact with other people. He liked learning, but not school. He had girl friends, but never a girlfriend. (Tom Klebold says Dylan would go out with a group of friends; what Tom called "group dating.")

It wasn't a romantic relationship but in the summer of 1997 Dylan met Devon Adams through friends she had at Blackjack. Devon, two years younger, would be entering Columbine as a freshman. Eric and Dylan would be juniors.

By the time school started Devon was friendly enough with Eric and Dylan to have breakfast and lunch with them. Dylan was not a morning person, and would sleep until noon or 1:00 p.m. on the weekends if he could. For breakfast he would eat donuts and orange juice, or soda pop. Sitting in the middle of the cafeteria, Eric and Dylan would do class work. Or at least pretend to. They could quote every line from the movie *Natural Born Killers* and Dylan, usually dressed in jeans and a T-shirt, preferred to talk. (Eric's AOL profile listed his favorite movie as the mysterious *Lost Highway* by David Lynch.) Devon also says she was marked for speaking with Dylan: A jock would say, "Why are talking to that faggot? Are you a dyke?"

But the Dylan that remains in Devon's mind is "Mr. Nice Guy. Mr. I'm just trying to make my way through high school." And funny Dylan. When Devon was confirmed in the Lutheran church, Dylan gave her a yellow greeting card: "Now you can become like a voodoo priestess and have a temple in Africa and cast spells and shrink heads," he wrote. Dressed in jeans, and a red Chemical Brothers T-shirt with a rainbow, he gave Devon her presents before the party started because a couple girls he didn't like were going to be there.

At Devon's sixteenth birthday in July 1998, Dylan wore a gray Chemical Brothers T-shirt and baseball cap with the Boston Red Sox symbol sewn on the front. (Dylan was obsessed with baseball.) The cover of the pre-printed birthday card Dylan gave her reads, "What are the chances you're getting a birthday present?" Inside, the card says, "Between slim and nun." A tall, slim cowboy is next to a nun.

"Ahh a nice dab of mildly distasteful prewritten, pointless humor to brighten yer day AAAA?!!," Dylan wrote. And because Devon had totaled her 1973 Pontiac Ventura one week before her birthday Dylan added, "Happy B-Day. Don't run me over or you'll lose yer license and ill be pissed he he he."

Devon recounts, without any irony, how she had a murder mystery party at her house called "Lethal Luau." Her mom made fried rice, and caramelized onions. Devon pushed Dylan to wear a Hawaiian shirt; he would otherwise think he's too cool for that, but wore one out of respect for her. He played a tourist named "Les Baggs," and had a good time.

Devon thought Tom Klebold was "very fair-minded." "Like one time, Dylan came in two hours past curfew and Dylan had promised to be in on curfew – it may have been midnight – and his dad got really angry at him and I think he took away Dylan's keyboard for two days, to his computer, and Dylan loved that computer. Just made it totally not possible to use the computer for two days, but it was fair punishment. I can't remember his parents ever grounding him. They just said you have to be in an hour early or something like that cause I think his parents knew how important Dylan's friends were to him."

His senior year Dylan gave Devon rides home at least once a week when her boyfriend couldn't do it. Devon paid Dylan $5 out of her own pocket but told him the money was from her mom because Dylan wouldn't want to take her money. On those drives home, they talked about school, teachers and the swamp man toy that hung from his rear view mirror and spurted water out the mouth if you pressed the stomach.

Six months before Columbine, Dylan and Devon were at a friend's house watching a movie when kids next door shined a laser light on them. Dylan, Devon, and their friend snuck up on the kids and flashed a halogen lamp in the window. "So we were proud of ourselves because we conquered over the little fifth graders," Devon recounts. They rounded out the night "spaze dancing," jumping up and down and listening to KMFDM or Nine Inch Nails. "He's either really hyper or really kicked back," Devon adds. In a photo, Dylan looks stoned as he flashes two thumbs up, but Devon assures that was not the case. "I'm straight-edge [drug-free] and he knew it, so he didn't do anything around me," she explains.

Dylan by that time had long hair that dropped below his ears and streamed out of his baseball cap, about the same way he looked the day of Columbine. His favorite shirt was dark green with white lettering that read, "AOL: WheRe KewLz HaXORz ArE." Translation: "AOL: Where Cool Hackers Are." Explanation: It's a joke because it's so easy to hack on AOL.

One of Dylan's favorite gifts to Devon was $10 cash. One time, Devon fell in love with an anteater Beanie Baby. Dylan hated Beanie Babies but for Christmas 1998, four months before Columbine, he bought her one that was gray, white and black. "Needless to say, I've collected anteaters ever since," she says. After Columbine, she toted the Beanie Baby across the country when she spoke on gun control alongside Tom Mauser, whose son Daniel was killed at Columbine.

Devon thinks the anteater is good luck because it gives her confidence. "You know, 'cause, in the line of what I do, the gun control stuff, I get discouraged, because there's a lot of opposition, there's a lot of people who aren't willing to listen. And I'm remembering just why I'm doing it. To keep those guns out of the hands of another kid like Dylan who, I don't know, feels he has no other way out, or something. Just keep him from having access to that deadly weapon."

But Devon never saw the violence when Dylan was alive. When they whacked each other with foam noodles in the pool, it was all fun and games. Other guys tackled her when they played football, but not Dylan. And when she cut her leg on the field, Dylan flipped out. He called a time out and washed her leg off. He didn't like dogs and was scared of

Devon's Siberian Husky, but dealt with the animal, again, out of respect for her.

"He didn't want to disrupt anything, you know?" Devon says. "He was always very respectful of everything."

Devon did see flashes of anger in Dylan. It might be a "dumb" occasion like getting a bad test grade. Or a spat over something inconsequential. At first, Dylan suppressed the anger. "I remember one time when he and I got in a fight cause I said something I shouldn't have to him; I was just was really, really angry at him, I don't remember why, I was just mad at him, and he just walked away, and I don't know if he ever got really mad about it. But he just walked away, and he just stayed away from me for about a week. And then it was fine. We talked about it. It was fine. But he was really, really upset for a while."

She heard about Eric and Dylan blowing things up on the nighttime, "rebel missions," or launching "tons of fireworks." She knew Eric named a bomb "Pazzie," and another "Anasazi," after an ancient people who inhabited southwest Colorado and who some believe practiced cannibalism. But she says, "Half of the student population knows how to build pipe bombs and stuff. And everyone likes playing with fireworks. I had no idea. No clue at all."

The biggest gun Devon knew Eric and Dylan shot was a BB gun at targets in Zach Heckler's backyard. But she believes easy access to weapons pushed Eric and Dylan to follow through with their plan. And guns appealed to them because, "You've got more power than anyone else in that building."

Eric, Devon believes, was the live wire who helped Dylan get from Mr. Nice Guy to Columbine killer. "He [Dylan] was entirely one person around Eric and then someone else around everyone else," Devon says. With Eric, Dylan was "Crazy Dylan," she adds. "Crazy videotapes in the basement. Crazy go shoot people. Make bombs Dylan. You know?"

Eric was the tough guy filled with aggression, she says. Scary and intimidating, he dressed commando and was never happy. He might get a CD he liked, but would then get angry and kick something. Eric was the lurker who tried to be like everyone else, but couldn't connect. The jerk who ticked people off, even Dylan. It showed in Eric's death when almost everyone who knew him said they weren't really friends with him, or had had a falling out.

"He [Eric] just kind of hung out and was a pain in everyone's bum,"

Devon says.

Dylan was the leader when it came to everything else in life. "If Dylan liked something, Eric automatically liked it," Devon says. "Bands, clothing, all the different stuff."

It wasn't so much that Dylan's parents "missed" Columbine, Devon says. They didn't even see it. He kept it hidden. When Devon realized what was happening the day of Columbine, she knew it was Eric, although it's still hard for her to believe Dylan was there too. She can only conclude, "It was the two of them against everybody else."

★★★

Eric and Dylan both followed the throbbing bass of techno, electronica and industrial, whether the beats were melodic or hard-driving. Eric called his favorites – Rammstein, KMFDM, 242, Orbital, and Loreena McKennitt – "fairly unique" although in truth they were still plenty popular. (His wingnut attraction to New Agey Loreena McKennitt probably came from her song on the soundtrack for *Soldier*, a sci-fi, shoot 'em up film Eric must have enjoyed for its *Doom*-like overtones.)

And there were other reasons behind Eric's favorite music. He said he enjoyed Rammstein because they were German and he could understand their words. But in his own mind, any German band, no matter the band's actual beliefs, probably made him feel closer to the Nazis.

KMFDM takes the initials from the German phrase *Kein Mehrheit Fur Die Mitleid*, or No Pity for the Majority. The band does not give permission to reprint its lyrics, but Eric wrote that he liked them "because of the points they are trying to get across." He listened to the song "Son of a Gun," before he played soccer, and noted that it, "shows the way I feel about myself." The song's fast, tough, and overdone beats talk of explosions, apocalypse, and through it all, a superhero.

Eric, in true fashion, also pontificated about the bands he hated: 311, Aquabats, Blink 182 Less Than Jake, Pietasters, Reel Big Fish, and "Puff freakin daddy!!! He sucks! He can absolutely NOT rap!!! No one can, because rap is GAY," he wrote in one of his Web diaries.

And he didn't like rap videos: "They are all the same!! 5 stupid cheerleaders in color coordinated nylon outfits dancing around infront of a curved orblike camera with a dumbass guy walkin around swingin his arms sayin 'uh huh yeyah werd up you know what im sayin uh huh mmmmhm yeya babey.'"

Dylan wasn't so much into lyrics. When it came to techno, says Devon, "Like, the more bass he could get in that music, like subwoofers and stuff, the better. He really liked that. A lot of it is mostly instrumental, which he liked a lot. He didn't have to deal with all the lyrics and stuff. He wanted to make up his own mind what the music was about. He did not like to be told what to be feeling. He was an individual. He always strove to be an individual. He didn't always succeed. You can just lose yourself in techno music. I remember nights staying up with him and he just drifted off. Music shuts off the outside world."

Sue Klebold says she once asked Dylan about a poster of shock rocker Marilyn Manson in his room and he replied that he didn't really listen to the lyrics, but the music. Another one of his favorite bands was the Chemical Brothers. And at one point, he talked with Devon about going to one of their upcoming concerts. But Devon notes, "He obviously never ended up going to it because it came in summer of 1999."

★★★

Eric and Dylan made videos that showcased both their goofy humor, and violence. One short shows Eric and fellow film student Eric Veik beating up a dummy, getting chased by police, and arrested. In another, Harris pretends to be teacher Rich Long, and is asked about the technology he uses to keep the school computers safe.

"I use a shotgun, I keep the old shotgun under the desk," he says.

How does he keep up with growing technology?

"I use drugs," he says.

In one skit students wax a girl's yellow, ten speed bicycle as it leans against a wall. The bike is then pelted with dirt. Eric and Dylan smash it with a hammer, and sledgehammer.

"After all this, it still retains its shine," a salesman says.

"What the hell are you doing with my sister's bike?" Dylan screams, chasing the salesman off.

In "Radioactive Clothing," Eric and Dylan are government agents trying to stop radioactive clothing from taking over the world. The film opens with Eric and Dylan sitting in the back seat of a red Pontiac wearing sunglasses. Dylan, trying to showcase his humor, laughs as he tries to say his lines. Eric, his typical violent self, says they may need more weaponry. They park the car and get out.

Dylan wears a trench coat, and his AOL T-shirt. Eric has on black pants, a white T-shirt, and black KMFDM baseball cap, backwards. They pull some fake guns out of the trunk. "Keep your eyes open, keep your fuckin fingers on the triggers," Dylan says.

With their guns drawn, two each, as it will be at Columbine, Eric and Dylan enter a house. Radioactive clothes are tossed at them from off camera, and they fire back. It's a bit comic, and the film appears to end. Afterward, in an off-screen moment, they kick back with a cigarette outside the house.

★★★

The other side of Dylan, which no one professes to have known about, was Depressive Dylan. At the top of his diary on September 5, 1997, six days before his sixteenth birthday, he wrote "Life sux."

"oooh god I want to die sooo bad.... such a sad, desolate, lonely, unsalvageable I feel I am... not fair, NOT FAIR!!!...," he continued. "I wanted happiness!! I never got it... Let's sum up my life... the most miserable existence in the history of time.... my best friend has ditched me forever, lost in bettering himself and having/enjoying/taking for granted his love.... He NEVER knew this... not 100 times near this... they look at me [name deleted] like I'm, a stranger.... I helped them both out thru life, & they left me in the abyss of suffering.... The one who I thought was my true love, [name deleted] is not.... The meanest trick was played on me - a fake love.... She in reality doesn't give a good fuck about me... doesn't even know me...... I have no happiness, no ambitions, no friends, & no LOVE!!!"

Dylan contemplates using a gun on himself. "What else can I do given i stopped the pornography. I try not to pick on people. Obviously at least one power is against me. [name deleted]... funny how I've been thinking about her over the last few days... giving myself fake realities that she, others MIGHT have liked me just a bit...."

On the edge of the paper he writes, "A dark time, infinite sadness. I want to find love."

In one poem he notes, "people are alike/I am different."

He seems to leave a suicide note: "Goodbye, sorry to everyone. I just can't take it, all the thoughts... too many... make my head twist... I must have happiness, love, peace. Goodbye."

October 14, 1997. Dylan writes his name at the top of his diary entry, then crosses it out. He draws an arrow at his own name. "Fuck that," he writes, and continues (referring to the jocks and others as zombies): "hell & back... I've been to the zombie bliss side... & I hate it as much if not more than the awareness part. I'm back now... A taste of what I thought I want... wrong. Possible girlfriends are coming... I'll give the phony shit up in a second. Want TRUE love.... I just want something i can never have.... true true I hate everything. Why can't I die... not fair. I want pure bliss... to be cuddling with [name deleted], who I think I love deeper than ever... I was hollow, thought I was right. Another form of the Downward Spiral.. deeper & deeper it goes.... This is a weird entry... I should feel happy, but shit brought me down. I feel terrible.... [name deleted] lucky bastard gets a perfect soulmate, who he can admit FUCKIN SUICIDE to & I get rejected for being honest about fuckin hate for jocks.... Why is it that the zombies achieve something me wants (overdeveloped me). They can love, why can't I?... How tragic for my... DUMASS SHITHEAD... MOTHERFUCKIN... FUCK!"

This is the postscript: "No emotions. Not caring. Yet another stage in this shit life. Suicide.... Dylan Klebold."

Guns in

Schools

By:

Eric Harris

period 4

12/10/97

Mr. Webb

SEVEN

Junior Criminals

There was no more extraordinary time to trap Eric and Dylan than during a nine-month period when they were high school juniors. Police and school authorities tracked them for a string of crimes and misdemeanors from September 1997 to May 1998. But no one added it up. The authorities cross-referenced the crimes, but no one came down hard enough. Then the police simply gave up.

The punishment that was meted out didn't deter Eric and Dylan. In fact, it spurred them — not to do a better crime, but a bigger one. They were now pushing back against the cops, and their classmates. Their vengeance grew.

★★★

As Eric and Dylan became juniors in the fall of 1997 Columbine's longtime boys and girls soccer coach, Peter Horvath, was beginning his two-year stint as a dean of students. It would be Horvath's first, and last, tour of duty, in part because the job was hardly uplifting. "You were in charge of discipline and attendance. Basically all you did is bust kids every day, suspend kids, track kids' attendance and you know, have kids come in every day and lie to your face about things and, you know, that gets old after a while," Horvath says, in his first media interview.

Horvath, tall and thin with short hair, was thirty-seven when Columbine hit and seems to get jittery when discussing Eric and Dylan, among his first clients, and no doubt his most infamous. Horvath first came across Eric and Dylan when one student reported a couple missing items from a locker, including a camera, and another student said he got a threatening note in his locker warning him to back off Devon Adams.

Horvath described Eric and Dylan as "brilliant" but ended up suspending them along with Devon and her boyfriend, Zach Heckler on October 2 for hacking into the school's computer system to get locker combinations. Zach, considered the mastermind, got five days, Horvath recalls. Eric and Dylan each got three days (although another document indicates Dylan got five).

Devon says they did it because Columbine did not challenge them. "Because we were all just bored. When you get bored, you act out."

After serving their suspensions Horvath met with Eric, Dylan and their parents. "You know, in front of your parents you're agreeing to you're going to start walking a fine line now," Horvath explains.

Horvath sensed that Tom Klebold, in general, opposed the idea of suspensions, and the Harrises did not agree with Eric's three days. But the parents also accepted the punishments. On the bottom page of Eric's suspension sheet, it appears one of his parents made notations: "called Mr. Horvath. What will be on Eric's records? In-house only because police were not involved. Destroyed upon graduation."

Eric and Dylan's ability to hack into the lockers was a result of their special access granted through Rich Long's computer class. The incident soured the teacher, who had been trying to get Eric an internship with a computer company. It not only ended Long's respect for Eric, but apparently any respect Wayne Harris had for Long.

Long had met Eric and Dylan's parents seven to eight times over the years at back to school nights, and he was typically full of compliments for the boys. As a U.S. Army vet himself, Long picked up on Wayne Harris' posture, mannerisms, and stark sense of right and wrong that denoted a military background. He saw the Harrises as strict, but caring. He felt they wanted Eric to have more extracurricular activities, but let him slip into a more secret existence. But after the hacking incident, Wayne blamed Long. "You trusted my son too much," he said, according to Long.

***

One month after the suspensions, on November 3, 1997, the first mention of a killing spree comes in Dylan's diary:

All people I ever might have loved have abandoned me. My parents piss me off & hate me... want me to have fuckin ambition!! How can I when I get screwed & destroyed By everything?!!! I have no money, no happiness, no friends... Eric will be getting further away soon... I'll have less than nothing... how normal. I wanted to love.... I wanted to be happy and ambitious and free & nice & good & ignorant.... everyone abandoned me... I have small stupid pleasures.... my so called hobbies & doings.... those are all that's left for me.... nobody will help me... only exist w/ me if it suits them. i helped, why can't they? [name blocked out] will get me a gun, I'll go on my killing spree against anyone I want. more crazy... the meak are trampled on, the assholes prevail, the gods are decieving, lost in my little insane asylum w/ the nuthouse redneck music playing... wanna die & be free w/ my love.... if she even exists. She probably hates me... finds a redneck or a jock who treats her like shit... I have lost my emotions... People eventually find happiness. I never will. Does that make me a nonhuman? YES. The god of sadness....

Eric was channeling school shootings at almost the same time. Although it was in an eerie, albeit uncharacteristically low key manner. A class paper dated December 10, 1997 came one month after Dylan's journal entry. "In the past few weeks there has been news of several shootings in high schools," Eric begins.

The research paper is about two pages and titled "Guns in Schools." Eric notes that, "it is just as easy to bring a loaded handgun to school as it is to bring a calculator." He never hints that the essay might be autobiographical, but adds, "Students bring guns to school for many reasons. Some for protection, some for attacking, and even some to show off. However, a school is no place for a gun. Solutions for this problem are hard to come by and often too expensive for most schools to even consider. However metal detectors and more police officers are two very good solutions."

★★★

Eric and Dylan rang in 1998 by landing in their most documented trouble ever (aside from Columbine), although it seems more to do with boredom than violence.

On Friday January 30 Eric, Dylan and Zach were in a car at a local church listening to music, according to written statements Eric and Dylan later gave police. Around 8:30 p.m. Eric and Dylan left in Eric's gray Honda Prelude to go home but stopped on a gravel road near a white van and red truck.

Dylan says Eric set off some fireworks. Eric says, "We got out of my car and looked around for something to do. We found some beer bottles and we broke those for about 15 minutes."

The two went back to Eric's car. Eric, possibly showing a psychopathic trait, tries to displace blame and says it was Dylan's idea to break into the white van belonging to Denver-based Westover Mechanical Services and loot the equipment inside. "At first I was very uncomfortable and questioning with the thought," Eric magnanimously wrote. "I became more interested within about 5 minutes and we then decided to break the passenger window with our fists."

Dylan put it like this: "Then, almost at the same time, we both got the idea of breaking into this white van. We hoped to get the stuff inside."

A white car came to the area, someone got out, went in the red truck, and both the car and truck drove away. Eric looked out for more cars, and at one point got in his Honda in case they had to make a quick getaway. Dylan slipped a ski glove on his left hand, and punched the van's passenger side window three times. Nothing gave. So Eric took the right ski glove – foreshadowing how the two would split a pair of gloves the day of Columbine – and gave the same window a punch. Still nothing.

They decided to try a rock. Dylan lifted one that was about ten to twelve inches around, so large he had to use both hands, according to Eric. Dylan broke the window after about six tries, and the rock fell into the front seat. Eric helped clear the rest of the glass off the window.

They took gauges, a meter, a calculator, a socket tool set, black sunglasses, a mini flashlight, a checkbook, and other items. It took about fifteen minutes as Dylan placed the loot in the back seat of the Honda, Eric said. Total value was $1,719. The two drove to nearby Deer Creek Canyon Park. Deputy Timothy S. Walsh saw the car when he drove into the park at about 9:20 p.m. The park had closed one hour after sunset, or around 6:15 p.m.

Walsh got out of his patrol car, and stood behind the Honda. The dome light was on. Eric and Dylan appeared to be listening to music and looking for a CD. Walsh saw Dylan, in the passenger seat, take a yellow meter, later identified as a stolen item, and push the buttons. Eric looked on, intently. The meter lit up, and they became excited, yelling "cool." Dylan grabbed a small, black flashlight, also identified as a stolen item, and flicked it on. "Wow! That is really bright," Eric said.

It appears Eric then grabbed the stolen video control pad, and said, "Hey, we've got a Nintendo game pad." As the two continued looking at the items in the back seat, Eric said, "Hey, we better put this stuff in the trunk." He released the trunk door from the inside and got out of the car. Walsh introduced himself.

Eric told Walsh they were "messing around" where the van had been parked when they found the items neatly stacked in the grass. Walsh asked to see the items, and Eric said, "Sure."

Eric and Dylan took eleven items out of the car and put them on the trunk. Walsh asked again how they found the stuff. Klebold said the same thing: They found it in the grass near Deer Creek Canyon Road. Walsh told the boys he would send a deputy to the area to see if any cars were broken into. Someone leaving this much property around was suspicious. Walsh asked them to be honest.

Eric looked at Dylan, and a short silence followed. Dylan told the officer what they had done. Walsh took them into custody, and separated them. Eric went with Walsh, who called another car for Dylan. Police dispatch contacted the parents and had them meet the kids at the sheriff's south substation.

Walsh met with Wayne and Kathy Harris, and read Eric his Miranda rights in front of them. Eric waived his rights, and talked. According to Eric's account, Dylan spotted the property inside the van and said, "Should we break into it and steal it? It would be nice to steal some stuff in there. Should we do it?"

"Hell no," Eric claims he replied.

They then discussed it, and Eric agreed to do the break-in. "Yeah, we'll try it," Eric concluded.

The Klebolds first consulted with an attorney, who is not named in the police report, before allowing Dylan to talk. Walsh took Eric and Dylan to the Jefferson County jail, where they were "booked through" and released to their parents. The kids had no prior records. Eric's father, Wayne, later returned to the sheriff's department to get a movie rental that had been collected as evidence, *Event Horizon*, about a spaceship in danger of being sucked into a black hole.

★★★

After the van break-in Eric said his family was "shocked" and "All trust is lost." Eric felt he could turn to friends and co-workers for help, and outwardly he was the tough anarchist. But he also confided that he was having problems with anger, depression, and suicidal thoughts. He would blow up, lash out and punch walls, especially if people he didn't respect, which seemed to be almost everyone, told him what to do. His head was filled with disorganized thoughts and too many inside jokes. He was anxious, stressed, suspicious, jealous, and moody. He hated too many things to have many friends. He wanted to kill people.

In February 1998 he started seeing psychologist Kevin Albert at the Colorado Family Center in Littleton. Albert has declined all interview requests but a rare view into Eric's treatment is provided by a somewhat obscure court filing written by psychiatrist Peter Breggin, a critic of psychiatric drugs and maybe best-known for his 1995 book *Talking Back to Prozac*. Breggin, as might be expected, blames the drug Eric was on by the time of Columbine, Luvox, for the shootings. Breggin says Eric suffered from "Mood Disorder with Depressive and Manic Features that reached a psychotic level of violence and suicide."

The vast majority of the medical establishment stands behind such drugs for improving peoples' lives and allowing them to function in society. Yet part of Breggin's analysis, citing Eric's pharmacy and medical records, also appears to be a straightforward retelling of Eric's treatment. The visits were once or twice a month, and sometimes Eric's family met with Albert. Albert initially recommended that Eric be put on an antidepressant. In a visit to his general physician Eric's medical records indicate "possible depression" and "mild/minimal depressive symptoms." But he was "not suicidal/homicidal."

Eric was prescribed the antidepressant Zoloft, although a notation also indicates it was for ADD, apparently attention deficit disorder. Zoloft is an SSRI, or "selective serotonin reuptake inhibitor." It increases the amount of serotonin, sometimes called the "feel good" chemical, in the brain.

But as of April 15, 1998 Albert had a message for Eric's medical doctor, Jon Cram, who was able to prescribe medicine: "Eric's depression leads to negative thinking and he cannot stop this process–his thinking is a bit obsessional," according to Breggin's report. Eric was taken off Zoloft, and put on Luvox, another SSRI, which is indicated for obsessive compulsive disorder. The first Luvox prescription listed by Breggin comes on April 25, 1998 for twenty-five milligrams. It was doubled to fifty milligrams just over a month later, and doubled again another month later, in early July. Breggin writes that three and a half months before Columbine, the prescriptions indicate Eric's dose was increased. Breggin also writes that on March 13, 1999, just over one month before Columbine, the medical record notes "it's 'OK' to increase the dose to 200 mg. per day."

Breggin's report does not make clear whether Cram or Albert thought the medication and therapy were working. In a law enforcement evaluation shortly after beginning therapy Eric wrote that his treatment was "nice" and "It helps me realize things." But he wrote in his diary on April 21, 1998:

"My doctor wants to put me on medication to stop thinking about so many things and to stop getting angry. well, I think that anyone who doesnt think like me is just bullshitting themselves. try it sometime if you think you are worthy, which you probly will you little shits, drop all your beliefs and views and ideas that have been burned into your head and try to think about why your here. but I bet most of you fuckers cant even think that deep, so that is why you must die. how dare you think that I and you are part of the same species when we are sooooooo different. you arent human you are a Robot. you dont take advantage of your capabilites given to you at birth. you just drop them and hop onto the boat and head down the stream of life with all the other fuckers of your type. well god damit I wont be a part of it! I have thought to much, realized to much, found out to much, and I am to self aware to just stop what I am thinking and go back to society because what I do and think isnt "right" or "morally accepted" NO, NO, NO, God Fucking damit NO! I will sooner die than betray my own thoughts. but before I leave this worthless place, I will kill who ever I deam unfit..."

***

Dylan called the van break-in the most traumatic experience of his life. He wrote that the impact on his family of the "unethical" act was "a bad one." He was grounded for a month, and prohibited from seeing Eric. "My parents were devastated as well as I," he added.

Days later, on February 2, 1998, he used for the first time in his diary NBK, the initials of one of his and Eric's favorite movies, *Natural Born Killers*, which became a code for the shootings. The 1994 Oliver Stone film was a natural fit for Eric and Dylan given its murderous rampages imbued with irony and social commentary. The film follows the over the top violence of an escaped criminal and his highly charged girlfriend. Woody Harrelson and Juliette Lewis play the hell-bent lovebirds. This is the end-game, the film seems to say, when America becomes fascinated with violence.

As in the movie, Dylan lists a partner in crime in his diary. And as in the movie, it may be a girl. "Either I'll commit suicide, or i'll get w/ [name deleted] & it will be NBK for us," Dylan wrote that February. "My hapiness, her hapiness, NOTHING else matters. I've been caught w/ most of my crimes – xcpt drinking, smoking, & the house vandalism, & the pipe bombs."

But unlike the boyfriend and girlfriend pair in the movie, Eric and Dylan never had any girlfriends. Sequestered in their own dark friendship, they molt into the NBK couple.

On February 2 Dylan also writes about a suicide bombing if a certain girl doesn't love him: "id slit my wrist & blow up [the homemade pipe bomb] atlanta strapped to my neck."

"Society is tightening its grip on me," he later adds, and he "will snap." "I didn't want to be a jock... I hated the happiness that they have & I will have something infinitely better...," he writes on the side of the page, and then, "By the way, some zombies are smarter than others, some manipulative... like my parents... I am GOD. zombies will pay for their arrogance, hate, fear, abandonment, & distrust."

To an unnamed girl he says: "My mind sometimes gets stuck on its own things, I think about human things – all I try to do is imagine the happiness between us. That is something we cannot even conceive in this toilet earth."

There is an undated letter, maybe to the same girl:

(Please don't skip to the back: read the note as it was written)

You don't consciously know who I am, & doubtedly unconsciously too. I, who write this, love you beyond infinince. I think about you all the time, how this world would be a better place If you loved me as I do you. I know what you're thinking: "(some psycho wrote me this harrassing letter)." I hoped we would have been together... you seem a lot like me. Pensive, quiet, an observer, not wanting what is offered here. (School, life, etc.) You almost seem lonely, like me. You probably have a boyfriend though, & might not have given this note another thought. I have thought you my true love for a long time now, but .... well... there was hesitation. You see I can't tell if you think of anyone as I do you & if you did who that would be. Fate put me in need of you, yet this earth blocked that with uncertainties. I will go away soon, but I just had to write this to you, the one I truly loved. Please, for my sake, don't tell anybody about this, as it was only meant for you. Also, please don't feel any guilt about my soon-to-be "absence" of this world. It is solely my decision: nobody else's.... the thoughts of us... doing everything together, not necessarily anything, just to be together would have been pure heaven. I guess it's time to tell you who I am. I was in a class with you 1st semester, & was blessed w. being with you in a report. I still remember your laugh. Innocent, beautiful, pure. This semester I still see you - rarely.... To most people, I appear... well... almost scary, but that's who I appear to be as people are afraid of what they don't understand. Anyway, you have noticed me a few times. I catch every one of these gazes w/ an open heart.... Even if you did like me ever the slightest bit, you would hate me if you knew who I was. I am a criminal, I have done things that almost nobody would even think about condoning. The reason that I'm writing you now is that I have been caught for the crimes I comitted, & I want to go to a new existence. You know what I mean. (Suicide) I have nothing to live for, & I won't be able to survive in this world after this legal conviction. However, if it was true that you loved me as I do you... I would find a way to survive. Anything to be with you. I would enjoy life knowing that you loved me. 99/100 chances you prob. think I'm crazy, & want to stay as far away as possible. If that's the case, then I'm very sorry for involving an innocent person in my problems, & please don't think twice. However, If you are who I hoped for in my dreams & realities, then do me a favor: Leave a piece of paper in my locker, saying anything that comes to you. Well, I guess this is it – goobdbye, & I love(d) you.

The note, signed by Dylan, is in block letters with misspellings and crossed-out words. He gives the girl his locker number and the combo, and draws two hearts, one with DK inside. The name or initials in the other heart are blocked out, per the sheriff's department. It is unknown if he ever passed on the note, and if so, the girl's reaction.

★★★

About one month after the van break-in, Dylan scratched something into another student's locker. Peter Horvath, the dean, doesn't know why Dylan chose the locker, and doesn't recall the student's name, only that the student felt threatened when he saw Dylan scratching with a paper clip. Because Dylan didn't finish, the design he was scratching was unclear, Horvath says.

Dylan was detained, and Horvath was with him for about forty minutes while they waited for Tom Klebold to arrive and deal with the incident. "Dylan became very agitated," according to a summary of Horvath's interview with police. Horvath tried to calm him down, and Dylan cussed at him, although it wasn't personal. Dylan was "very upset with the school system and the way CHS handled people, to include the people that picked on him and others," according to the police interview. Horvath thought Dylan was a "pretty angry kid" who also had anger issues with his dad and was upset with "stuff at home," the police report continued.

Yet in an interview with this author Horvath doesn't recall Dylan being upset with his father, but at "being suspended for what he felt was a pretty minor incident." Dylan, Horvath adds, "understands the politics of how like a school system works. He was smart around that. And he was angry at the system; not angry at me, but angry at the system; that the system would be established that it would allow for what he did to be a suspendable offense, if that makes any sense to you. He was mad at the world because he was being suspended, but he was mad at the system because the system that was designed was allowing him to be suspended."

Horvath continued: "Talking to Dylan was like talking to a very intellectual person. He wasn't a stupid kid. He's not a thug kid that's getting suspended. He's a smart, intelligent kid. I just remember the conversation being at a level; that would you know, you'd sit there and you'd think, 'Wow, this is a pretty high level conversation for a kid like this.' You could just tell his feelings around, I'm going to use the word politics again but again, he was too intelligent sometimes I felt for his age. You know, he knew too much about certain things and he spoke too eloquently about knowing the law and why he was being suspended and knowing, just you know, speaking about how society is this way towards people."

Tom Klebold, who Horvath thought of as an "Einstein" eventually arrived. With his glasses, and salt and pepper hair, he was proper, eloquent, and astute. He also had serious problems with this second suspension, and asked Dylan to leave the room—an unusual move in Horvath's experience. "He [Tom] felt as though it was too severe for what had happened," Horvath said of the standard, three-day suspension for essentially a vandalism charge.

"Can't we do anything else? Can't he [Dylan] just do, you know, twenty-five hours of community service, thirty hours of community service?" Tom Klebold asked.

Nope. Horvath didn't budge.

***

The next month, on March 17, 1998, Brooks Brown says Dylan walked up to him at school and gave him a piece of paper with Eric's Web site address. Don't tell Eric I told you, Dylan said. But look it up tonight. Brooks did. Some stuff from the 1997 riffs was still there. But Eric had also done some updating; he had found a ground zero for his beloved bombs: "Mother fucker blew BIG. Pazzie was a complete success and it blew dee fuck outa a little creek bed. Flipping thing was heart-pounding gut-wrenching brain-twiching ground-moving insanely cool! His brothers havent found a target yet though."

Eric also expanded on his thoughts regarding Brooks.

My belief is that if I say something, it goes. I am the law, if you don't like it, you die. If I don't like you or I don't like what you want me to do, you die. If I do something incorrect, oh fucking well, you die. Dead people cant do many things, like argue, whine, bitch, complain, narc, rat out, criticize, or even fucking talk. So that's the only way to solve arguments with all you fuckheads out there, I just kill! God I cant wait till I can kill you people. Ill just go to some downtown area in some big ass city and blow up and shoot everything I can. Feel no remorse, no shame. Ich sage FICKT DU! I will rig up explosives all over a town and detonate each one of them at will after I mow down a whole fucking area full of you snotty ass rich mother fucking high strung godlike attitude having worthless pieces of shit whores. i don't care if I live or die in the shootout, all I want to do is kill and injure as many of you pricks as I can, especially a few people. Like brooks brown.

"I sat there staring at the screen for a moment," Brooks wrote in his book. "It was unexpected, to say the least."

Brooks told his parents. Randy suggested telling the Harrises or maybe faxing the pages to them anonymously. Judy Brown wasn't impressed with how the Harrises handled the windshield incident. They settled on the police.

The Browns called the Jefferson County Sheriff on March 18, and Deputy Mark Miller was dispatched to their home. Randy talked about the other run-ins with Eric, and said the family feared for Brooks' safety. Brooks says he did not mention Dylan but the Browns gave police his name anyway because he was such close friends with Eric, and Eric's Web site mentioned Dylan taking part in the "Rebel Missions."

Deputy Miller examined the Web pages but said he didn't know much about computers and that other officers were more expert. Miller submitted a report to the records department and recommended that copies be forwarded to the investigations division, and the Columbine High School resource officer - Jefferson County Sheriff's Deputy Neil Gardner. A notation on the bottom of Miller's report reads: "Copies to: Dep. Gardner Columbine S.R.O."

The report, however, would harm the Jefferson County Sheriff more than Eric and Dylan.

★★★

Eric and Dylan still faced charges of theft, criminal mischief, and first-degree criminal trespass in the van break-in, but were working out a deal with the District Attorney to plead guilty and enter a diversion program. For one year they would participate in activities ranging from community service to anger management. The District Attorney would then dismiss all charges upon successful completion.

The District Attorney also ran the diversion program but no one, including Eric and Dylan, ever seems to have heard about the Browns' March 18 report. And on March 19, diversion counselor Andrea Sanchez filled out the one-page intake forms for Eric and Dylan to determine their eligibility for the program.

Eric and Dylan would not only be accepted into the program but allowed to leave early for a job well done. Yet diversion hardly stopped them. If anything, it inflamed them.

★★★

Sanchez indicated on the boilerplate intake forms that Eric and Dylan had not been physically or sexually abused, and did not have problems at school with discipline, truancy, or "success." Their suspension for hacking into the school computer for locker combinations was noted, but the two teens were not in a gang, and did not carry weapons. They did not have girlfriends and said they had never been sexually active, but were educated on sexually transmitted diseases and birth control. Neither said they had experienced a significant loss.

Dylan said Eric was his only friend with a criminal history. Eric said Dylan was, "Best friend past and current," and his only friend with a criminal history. They both took responsibility for breaking into the van and neither had any prior police contact.

Written notes on Eric say, "Quick temper—punch objects." Eric himself checked off the litany of problems he was having after the break-in, including homicidal thoughts.

The families had no criminal histories. Both sets of parents said they knew the names, ages, addresses, and phone numbers of Eric and Dylan's friends. Eric and Dylan said they checked in with their parents every three hours.

★★★

The intake forms also include an eight-page "parent information" section. For Dylan, there is no clear indication which parent filled out the form, but the handwriting appears feminine. One or both of the parents, with staccato answers, indicated the following: Dylan often stayed around the house and "stays in his room constantly." He was typically disciplined for "disrespect, failure to do what's been asked." Punishments included grounding, loss of privileges, additional chores, and being yelled at. Family feuds were characterized by "loud but controlled discussion." Conflicts ended when "People communicate, spend time together." Although it would not be mandated for Dylan, the parental attitude toward mental health treatment was, "I support it but need more info." "Significant loss" for the Klebolds was Tom Klebold's recent diagnosis of rheumatoid arthritis. Over the last ten years, the family had had "episodic financial difficulties." On a morbidly upbeat note, the parents were glad Dylan was caught, and thought diversion would help. "Grateful!" they wrote when asked about the program.

Assuming Susan filled out the questionnaire, she had notable way of addressing some of Dylan's behavior, often crossing out phrases or words that seemed to make him more culpable. Of Dylan's suspension at school, she explained: "He and two friends gained access to school's computer figured out how to find old locker combination."

She then crossed out "gained access" and wrote: "He and two friends who had access to school's computer figured out how to find old locker combination."

She said Dylan "opened a locker or two" to see if the combinations were "current", as if he was only trying to help the school. Dylan himself explained the situation as, "Hacking and possessing important documents."

Susan also noted another suspension Dylan had for scratching a school locker, and when it came to Dylan's ticket for running a red light Susan first wrote that he slowed down then kept going "when he thought no one was around." She then wrote that he had actually come to a full stop before going through the light. Dylan himself said it was "running a red light when no one was around."

Susan said the van "allegedly had a parking ticket on it which made the boys think it was abandoned." She did not quite finish writing the word "parking," then crossed it out altogether. Eric and Dylan never mentioned any ticket. Nor did any police report.

The Klebolds indicated they had not seen any sudden behavior changes in Dylan and were surprised when he admitted to occasional use of marijuana and alcohol. "Was not aware of it at all until [counselor] Andrea Sanchez asked the question a few moments ago," the parent, or parents, wrote.

The parental attitude towards alcohol and drugs was oddly written in the third person. "Vehemently opposed to drug use. Dylan's father is more tolerant to limited/reasonable alcohol use than Dylan's mother is." The family had no history of alcohol or drug addiction (although that does not appear to be completely true given Byron's case). Tom and Sue indicated they were proud of Dylan's accomplishments. One list filled out by Sanchez reviewed "family problems" and included a section labeled: "psychiatric history." Sanchez marked that in the affirmative, and circled "father, mother, sibs."

Contradicting the normalcy Dylan's parents channeled to police and the public after Columbine, they told the diversion program he had issues related to anger, authority figures, jobs, and loneliness. "Dylan is introverted and has grown up isolated from those who are different in age, culture, or other factors," Susan explained. "He is often angry or sullen, and behaviors seem disrespectful to others. He seems intolerant of those in authority and intolerant of others." She then crossed out the phrase, "He seems intolerant of those in authority."

Still, Susan had pegged Dylan's core problems. And outlined the profile of many school shooters.

★★★

Dylan also answered questions for intake. When he fought with his parents or brother they would yell at each other. It would end, "When we are aware of each others' arguments & understand them." His punishment included being grounded and not being able to use the computer.

Dylan's attitude toward diversion was, "I'm hoping I can get the best I can out of it & am optimistic about it." He did not think he needed mental health treatment but wrote, "I will do it if diversion deems it necessary or desirable."

Dylan characterized his classroom behavior as "good," and Sanchez concluded, in stark contrast to what his own parents said, "Dylan gets along well with teachers and administrators, and has many friends."

Regular classes did not challenge Dylan, Sanchez noted. He mostly took honors courses, but struggled with them. Dylan said he made a "good" effort at schoolwork, but acknowledged he could try harder.

His past jobs included a courtesy clerk at Albertson's supermarket, which he left because he didn't want to join the union. He had worked there twenty hours a week earning $5.45 an hour. He also worked at Blackjack Pizza about ten hours a week for $5.15 an hour as a cook. He left, he said, to find a better job. The longest he had ever held a job was three months.

Dylan indicated he had problems with finances, and jobs. "Kind of difficult to find a technician job when I am only sixteen years," he added, apparently referring to a computers. Dylan said his spare time was spent on: "computers & networks, shooting pool, movies, electronics, reading, going to start working on a car soon." He had three friends; two were sixteen, one seventeen. Dylan said he had broken the law "quite a few times," and also indicated he had been in trouble with the law–maybe a reference to the van break-in itself.

He said he felt in control of his life, and got along equally well with men and women. Gangs were "pointless," and he had no interest in them.

Dylan said he never drank or used drugs with a family member, despite the drinking he claims to have done with his brother. Dylan summarized his drinking habits as a couple times by himself but indicated his past and present drinking was "light." He had not had a drink for about two months; the last time was when he had had some vodka at his house. He said he was "careful" with booze. According to Dylan, a few of his friends occasionally drank, and he himself had passed out one to three times from "drugs" (maybe he meant alcohol). He concluded that booze was OK in moderation.

In different places Dylan indicated that "maybe yes" he wanted to stop drinking, but also that he had stopped drinking because it "wasn't worth it." He also said he didn't like the taste or effect of alcohol. When asked how his parents felt about drugs and alcohol, he simply drew a question mark.

Dylan said he had not used marijuana for several months and characterized his past use as "light." "It is a waste of everything," he wrote of the drug, "definitely not worth it."

Dylan said harder drugs were "devastating." He had never been offered, or used, them. Likewise, his friends did not use them.

When asked if the family had any history of drug or alcohol addiction Dylan wrote, "None that I know of." Yet the file goes on to note his brother's drug struggles.

As for Dylan's relationship with his parents Sanchez wrote, "Dylan had a difficult time communicating with them, but he is getting better." Dylan said he got along with his parents "better than most kids." Dylan was comfortable bringing friends over to his house. When he had problems, which generally meant his grades, he turned to his parents. Dylan felt Tom and Sue were loving, dependable and trustworthy. Both were equally supportive because they "encourage me to succeed."

"Dylan was cooperative and open during his intake," Sanchez wrote. He felt diversion was the appropriate solution, and the tasks he would have to pursue were fair. But Sanchez concluded, "It is my belief that even though Dylan knows what he did was wrong, he still lessens the seriousness of his offense."

★★★

Eric, his parents, and counselor Sanchez filled out the same diversion forms. Eric had considered suicide more than twice, but Sanchez's notes indicate it was "never seriously, mostly out of anger." She also wrote of his suicidal thoughts that he, "didn't plan or think much about it."

Sanchez affirmatively marked the spot for "psychiatric history: father, mother, sibs." In the margin, she wrote, "Marriage/Fam. Therapy." The parents said their attitude toward mental health treatment was, "Can be effective. Worth a try." As with Dylan, it is unclear which Harris filled out the parental form, although the printing is somewhat blocky, and masculine.

In his Web pages, Eric boasted of his drinking. But here, he said he had drank a total of three times, and had never been drunk. He said he did not like the taste, nor effects, of alcohol. His current attitude toward drinking was "don't want to anymore, don't need it." He said he had not had a drink since July, 1997, about eight months before filling out the diversion forms. That time, he had tequila.

Eric's AOL profile indicated his favorite class in school was bowling, and his favorite thing to do on the weekend was to bowl and get stoned. But he told Sanchez he had never used illegal drugs. They were "trouble," and mirroring Dylan's statement, a "waste of time and of life." Yet Eric also indicated he had passed out one to three times as a result of using drugs. Like Dylan, he was probably referring to alcohol, but the passing out did not seem to raise any eyebrows. His friends, he said, did not use drugs or alcohol.

His parents' attitude toward alcohol and drugs was, "Won't tolerate it, don't ever use anything." Wayne and Katherine Harris agreed that their philosophy was, "Discourage abuse of alcohol, no illegal use of drugs or alcohol." Brooks Brown had told Katherine Harris about Eric's alcohol stash after the backpack fight. Yet the parents wrote they were not aware of his using any drugs or alcohol. Eric and his parents agreed there was no drug or alcohol addiction in the family.

Eric said his parents were supportive, dependable, loving, and "strict, but fair." They might yell at him, but would also discuss his problems and make him accept responsibility. He got grounded for poor grades, too much time on the computer, and car offenses.

The Harrises marked "no" as for any financial difficulties. Were Eric's friends a positive, or negative influence? "Was involved in this incident with his best friend," the parents wrote. "One other friend has had some problems. Other friends seem mostly positive." No names were specified.

At the time of diversion, the Harrises said they had not seen any sudden behavioral changes in Eric. He could often be found at home, and checked in with them once a day, after school. Yet Eric wrote that he was often away from home, either at school or work. He classified the most traumatic experiences in his life as "moving from Plattsburgh, New York and this incident."

Eric's attitude toward diversion was: "Looking forward to it, hopefully it will set me strait [sic]." The parents said of diversion: "Good alternative to confinement, fines."

The parents termed Eric's grades as B's and C's. They mentioned the suspension for breaking into the school computer. Eric and his parents classified his attendance and classroom as "good."

Sanchez indicated that he got along well with teachers and administrators, but contradicted Eric's own words and wrote that he had many friends. She concluded Eric had been cooperative, open and honest during intake. "He feels Diversion is appropriate for his actions, but feels Dylan is more responsible since it was his idea." Eric thought about the van owner while taking the equipment, but it did not stop him.

It appears Sanchez filled out the "Action Plan" for Eric and wrote that his "presenting problems" were "Anger/Stress." Managing them became the program goals. Dylan's action plan had no goals.

★★★

Six days later, on March 25, Eric and Dylan appeared in court to finalize the plea agreement so they could formally enter diversion. But first Jefferson County Magistrate John DeVita probed the kids and their fathers. One thing that struck DeVita was that both boys were accompanied by their fathers. Usually, it was the mothers who showed up. The hearing began with the Klebolds.

"This has been a rather traumatic experience, I think," Tom Klebold told DeVita. "It's probably a good, a good thing, a good experience that he did get caught the first time. As far as I can tell, this was the first time."

DeVita: "Would he tell you if there were any more?"

Tom: "Yes, he would, actually."

DeVita: "It means you got a good relationship?"

Tom: "Yes."

But Dylan worried DeVita because his grades were C's and B's.

"I bet you're an A student if you put your brain power to the paper work," DeVita said.

"I don't know, sir," Dylan said, mumbling the rest of his response.

"When the hell you going to find out?" DeVita demanded back.

"You've got one year of school left," DeVita said. "When are you going to get with the program? Look at your dad and make him a promise. You look him right in the eye and you make him a promise about whatever you are going to do to get the kind of grades you are capable of."

Eric was next and irked DeVita when he said the van break-in was his first illegal act.

"Why don't I believe that?" DeVita said. He added: "First time out of the box and you get caught. I don't believe it. And if I did believe it, then you got to think real seriously about getting another line of income, because you have no future as a thief. It's a real rare occurrence when somebody gets caught the first time."

"We think this was the first time," Wayne Harris said. "We are glad he got caught the first time. We haven't had any indication of any other prior problems."

Eric said he got A's and B's. His curfew was 10:00 p.m. on the weekends, and 6:00 p.m. on weekdays.

"Good for you, dad," DeVita said. "So, dad, I think your curfew is appropriate. It sounds to me like you got the circumstances and situation under control just by ratcheting back his curfew."

DeVita was pleased Eric had a job, and asked, "Do you have any chores around the home?"

Eric: "Yes, your honor."

DeVita: "What are they?"

Eric: "Laundry, pick up the trash, vacuum, sweep the floors."

DeVita: "Do you do that without being told?"

Eric: "Yes, your honor."

DeVita signed off on Eric and Dylan after five minutes each. The teens were sandwiched between other cases considered more serious and DeVita, who lives in the Columbine area, says he was fooled by the polite youngsters.

★★★

Nate Dykeman met Eric and Dylan in the eighth grade. A lanky 6'4" and 165 pounds, Nate considered Tom and Sue Klebold a second set of parents. After Columbine, he made news for talking about Eric, Eric's parents, and a bomb. And also for selling a videotape or videotapes he and Dylan made to ABC for $10,000, or $16,000, depending on the story.

The day after Columbine, Dykeman was already talking with authorities, but a lie detector examiner concluded he was "deceptive" when asked whether he helped plan Columbine. Dykeman then said he "had not told everything he knew... because he was afraid he would get arrested and blamed for what happened," according to a report of his FBI interview. The report goes on to say, "Dykeman advised that he was aware that Harris and Klebold had been experimenting with black powder and pipe bombs for over a year. Dykeman advised that he saw them blow up several things, and he also saw pipe bombs...."

The FBI report added these details: "Dykeman advised that he saw pipe bombs at Harris' house on several occasions. Dykeman said that Harris took him into his parents' bedroom closet and showed him a pipe bomb which his parents had confiscated from his room. Harris related to Dykeman that his parents had found the pipe bomb, but didn't know what to do with it. Harris then showed him two or three other pipe bombs that he had made which he was keeping in his room. These pipe bombs were made after his parents had confiscated the one that they had in their closet."

As the allegations go, Wayne Harris was "furious" over the pipe bomb. Eric was grounded and not allowed to use his car. But the question remained: What to do with the bomb? It was even more pressing because Eric, according to one news account, had already entered diversion.

"You know, they can't turn it over to the police," Dykeman told an A&E documentary. "Eric would get arrested. They can't detonate it because it's homemade explosive. It might damage something or hurt someone. They can't throw it out, obviously, so they were kind of caught in a weird situation on what to do with it."

In a paid interview Dykeman told the tabloid National Enquirer that Wayne "took [Eric] somewhere safe and made him detonate it." Dykeman, in another account, said he didn't know what happened to the pipe bomb. But their buddy Zach Heckler also told police of a time that Eric and his dad set off a pipe bomb Eric had made.

Eric himself says in a videotape that his parents took away a bomb, and wrote a one-paragraph essay for class dated September 1998 and titled "Good to be Bad, Bad to be Good." *A time when it was bad to be good was when I had to give away all my weapons to my parents. It was after I got into serious trouble with the law, so my parents wanted to take all forms of weapons that I had away. It was bad not because I might use the weapons, just because I paid good money or spent a lot of time making them. It made me feel that all that time and money was wasted. But since weapons are dangerous and my parents didn't trust me, I suppose it was for the better.*

After Columbine, a lawsuit against the Harrises alleged that around February 1998 Wayne found one of Eric's pipe bombs at their home, took it to a vacant field, and exploded it. Wayne Harris denied it in a court filing .

But whatever happened, it did not deter Eric and Dylan. As Dykeman put it, "They just kept creating a larger bang."

★★★

The sheriff's office still had a shot at Eric and Dylan. Randy and Judy Brown made a follow up call shortly after making their police report and learned that the file was with Deputy John Hicks. The same John Hicks who had ended up with the family's other Web report on Eric and Dylan seven months earlier.

On March 31, 1998 the Browns met with Hicks at the sheriff's office. He was taken aback by the ferocity of Eric's Web pages, but concluded they did not constitute a computer crime. Eric said he wanted to kill people "like Brooks Brown" not Brooks Brown himself. But Hicks flagged the bomb-making and brought in bomb squad members Glenn Grove and Mike Guerra. (Guerra maintains he was not part of the meeting, but only popped in to quickly check something with Grove.) The Browns recall that during the meeting, Grove and Guerra found another case where a pipe bomb mirrored one of those described in Eric's Web pages. Hicks also found a record of Eric's van break-in.

The day after the meeting, Judy Brown says she saw Eric in line at a supermarket buying *Rifle* magazine. She quickly went home to call detectives and check on the progress of the case. Randy Brown also called. But in the end, as the *Rocky Mountain News* put it, "Randy and Judy Brown can't count the times they called the Jefferson County sheriff about Eric Harris. But they know how many times detectives called back: Zero."

Full accounts from the deputies themselves did not come until five years after Columbine as the Colorado Attorney General took up an investigation.

Guerra says he began working on a draft affidavit for a search warrant to enter Eric's home. He was never formally assigned the case, but a supervisor knew what he was doing. Either way, Guerra plotted the location of the similar pipe bomb found in February 1998 and calculated it was two or three miles from Eric's house. (Another check by the *Rocky Mountain News* found it to be about one and a half miles.) We may never know if Guerra made the right connection. But it seems like pretty good detective work.

Guerra also seems to have found a record of the van break-in about two months earlier but says he thought "it wasn't anything out of the ordinary." On April 9, 1998 (Eric' seventeenth birthday) Guerra went to Columbine to discuss Eric and Dylan with the school resource officer, Deputy Gardner. "I remember he said they were just kind of misfit kids; they really weren't any big deal," Guerra recalls. "They weren't a problem to anybody. I think I may have gotten the vehicle descriptions from him; if they drove, or if they didn't drive."

Guerra asked Deputy John Healy, who coincidentally had assisted with the van break-in, to try and find Eric's Web site. Healy couldn't, but he found "a domain name profile of Eric Harris" that said he wanted to join the Marines. It seems like the right Eric Harris.

Deputy Grove says he was there when Guerra showed the draft affidavit to Sgt. Jim Prichett and Lt. John Kiekbusch. Kiekbusch said Guerra still didn't have a strong enough case to bring it to the district attorney (and eventually a judge). Guerra needed to get a description of the Harris home, and an eyewitness who could link Harris to a pipe bomb.

There are also three other accounts: Prichett says he did not see the draft. Kiekbusch says he received a "verbal briefing." Guerra recalls talking to Kiekbusch about it and says he "may have" shown it to him.

Guerra at one point said he talked to someone - he can't remember who - in the district attorney's office. Then he said he hadn't done that.

Guerra went by Eric's home to get a physical description and it appears he interviewed at least one neighbor. John Voehl estimates that anywhere from six months to one and a half years before the shootings, a police officer, possibly from the Jefferson County Sheriff's Office, went around asking about teenagers in the neighborhood. The officer came back later to ask specific questions about the Harris house. Guerra worked on the draft until at least May 1 – about one month after the meeting with the Browns.

The document was never formalized. But it does exist. The undated, one and a half-page draft zeros in on Eric's alleged bombs: Atlanta, Pholus, Peitro and Pazzie. Guerra wrote that at about six inches long and one inch wide, the bombs matched the size and explosive contents of the bomb listed in the February 1998 police report. He included a description of the Harris home. If granted the warrant, Guerra wrote that he would look for "materials, components, literature, books, video tapes, and any drafts, or notes pertaining to manufacture of pyrotechnic devises [sic], improvised or commercial explosives. Electronic mail messages which were sent or received from the address to establish ownership; paper work [sic] which show's [sic] ownership of occupancy of the residence." He excerpted the Web site statement that Eric wanted to kill and injure as many people as possible, "Like brooks brown."

But the draft would die before it became a search warrant. Guerra says he was pulled away to do other assignments and, "Since this wasn't assigned to me as an open investigation, it kind of went to the bottom of the pile."

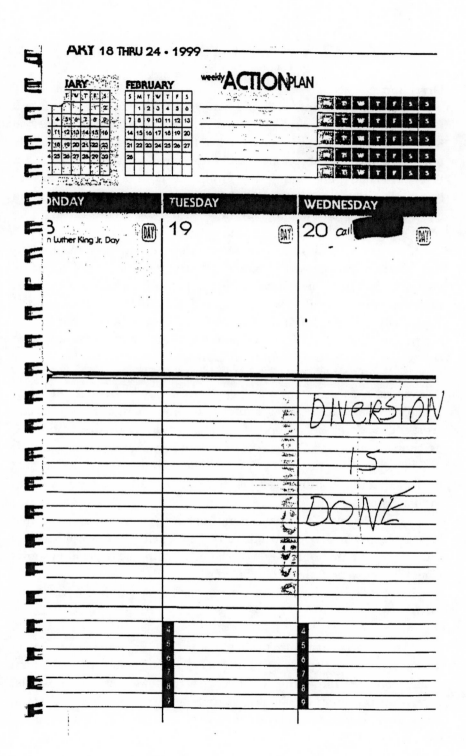

JANUARY	FEBRUARY

MONDAY **TUESDAY** **WEDNESDAY**

18
Martin Luther King Jr. Day [DAY]

19 [DAY]

20 call [DAY]

DIVERSION

IS

DONE

EIGHT

Diversion

After three months, Andrea Sanchez moved on and handed off Eric and Dylan's diversion cases to Robert Kriegshauser. In six years on the job Kriegshauser had supervised maybe five hundred clients, although only ten to fifteen were "exceptional," and allowed to leave the program early. Eric and Dylan were among that group. "In my opinion, you have to be a perfect client, pretty much," Kriegshauser said. "You have to be an exemplar example of taking care of your responsibilities through the court system. You have to try real hard, basically."

Kriegshauser and Sanchez have never spoken publicly. But in 2002 Kriegshauser was deposed as part of a lawsuit when injured Columbine victim Mark Taylor sued Solvay Pharmaceuticals, the maker of Luvox, the psychiatric drug Eric was on when he carried out the shootings. Taylor alleged that the drug did not calm Eric, as hoped, but fed his anger. Taylor dropped his suit in February of 2003 and Solvay agreed to contribute $10,000 to the American Cancer Society.

Kriegshauser's deposition has never before been made public, but it provides fodder for any number of Columbine theories. Eric and Dylan's ability to fool Kriegshauser may show them to be master con artists. That deceit also supports the popular diagnosis that Eric was a psychopath (although Dylan's deceit was also well done).

The deposition's fine grain view into the diversion program may feed the idea that the program itself was flawed given Eric and Dylan's ability to slip through.

Or maybe it was Kriegshauser and Sanchez. Their written notes that have been publicly released are full of misspellings and might show them to be not too bright. Yet, for what it's worth, the deposition shows Kriegshauser to be dedicated to his job.

The point of the lawsuit, of course, was to try and prove it was the Luvox.

★★★

After the District Attorney's office recommends a case, the diversion officer contacts the family by phone. They ask questions to see if there is any "obvious initial ineligibility." A form tells them, "If possible, determine if there is an obvious safety issue. If parents report that the juvenile's behavior remains out of control or he is an immediate threat to himself or others (continual runaway, recent attempt of suicide, assaultive, etc), his case may be more appropriately handled through court." The information kids and their parents provide is not checked for accuracy. "It's all voluntary stuff," Kriegshauser told the attorneys. "We don't go out and investigate them." Although the program, which lasts for a year, uses what leverage it can. "So we tell them up front that if we catch them in a lie, it's going to be harder going for them, so we hope they are going to be honest."

Eric and Dylan tested negative after taking the standard urine scans. Dylan, but not Eric, underwent a drug and alcohol evaluation. Kriegshauser cannot pinpoint why. It was Sanchez's decision, but the drug use by Dylan's brother may have been a factor.

Eric and Dylan had to complete forty hours of community service and like other diversion participants, were not supposed to possess weapons, including BB guns and even pocket knives. "If they say yes to [having] a knife, I say, 'Well, for the duration of this program, you don't own it,'" Kriegshauser said. "It goes to your parents, locked away."

Kriegshauser's deposition mentions an item in the diversion file that was not released when the files were made public: A letter from Sanchez to the Columbine High School dean, Peter Horvath, informing him that at least Eric was in diversion. "The intention was, basically, so that the school would know we're out there, and we would like to marry up our forces to see if we could get the kid on a better track," Kriegshauser explained. "So it would facilitate the passing of information, both attendance records, progress reports, discipline stuff, whatever that would look like, that would be happening at the school." But Kriegshauser was unaware of any follow-up with the school.

There is also the issue of the Browns' report. It would not show up on a records check because deputies did not make an arrest, or take other formal action. Kriegshauser says he was unaware of the report, but if he did find out about an added criminal complaint once someone was in diversion, he said he would want to talk with the police, the kid, and the parents, and see if they were found guilty. The kid might stay in diversion, depending on how far along they were, and if they were making progress. Or Kriegshauser might terminate them. But as far as he knew, participants were not checked once they entered the program anyway.

"We know our communication with the police and the other agencies is poor," Kriegshauser said. "It's a system-wide issue. So we put it on the juvenile, and we hope that the parents—and that's where we get a lot of our information—will tell us if they have had contact with the police. Even if it's not an arrest, even if they get stopped in a car because they had a tail light out and they got their name taken, we tell them to report that to us."

Kriegshauser added that he never caught Eric in a lie, and Eric even told him about a speeding ticket he received while in the program. "I never doubted Eric's honesty," Kriegshauser said, and noted, "He never gave me cause to."

★★★

On April 16, 1998, Sanchez wrote of her first meeting with Eric once he had formally entered diversion. "Eric has been having difficulty with his medication [Zoloft] for depression," she wrote. "A few nights ago he was unable to concentrate and felt restless." But the doctor was going to switch the medication. School and work were going well. Prom, maybe a reference to junior prom, was coming up. Eric wasn't going to the dance, but would attend the after-party. He also took a urinalysis on the 16th, and told Sanchez it would be clean.

Two weeks later, on April 30, Sanchez wrote, "After-prom party was fun," and "Grades on report card were A's, B's, and a C. Eric is feeling okay now that he isn't on medication, but knows he will feel better when he begins his new medication."

★★★

Every diversion "client" writes an apology letter to the victim, according to Kriegshauser, even if they are busted for drugs. (In that case, the letter goes to the parents.) Eric and Dylan's letters went to Ricky Lynn Becker of Westover Mechanical Services. He was apparently assigned the van the night Eric and Dylan broke in. Kriegshauser said the diversion counselor decides whether to make a copy for the file before the letter is sent to the victim. Dylan's letter has never surfaced. Eric's did not appear when his file was made public, but was first leaked to the media. A copy of the letter apparently resided in his computer and was not formally released until 2006.

Dear Mr. Ricky Becker,

Hello, my name is Eric Harris. On a Friday night in late-January my friend and I broke into your utility van and stole several items while it was parked at Deer Creek Canyon Road and Wadsworth. I am writing this letter partly *because I have been ordered to from my diversion officer, but mostly because I strongly feel I owe you an apology and explanation.*

I believe that you felt a great deal of anger and disappointment when you learned of our act. Anger because someone you did not know was in your car and rummaging through your personal belongings. Disappointment because you thought your car would have been safe at the parking lot where it was and it wasn't. If it was my car that was broken into, I would have felt extreme anger, frustration, and a sense of invasion. I would have felt uneasy driving in my car again knowing that someone else was in it without my permission. I am truly sorry for that.

The reason why I chose to do such a stupid thing is that I did not think. I did not realize the consequences of such a crime, and I let the stupid side of me take over. Maybe I thought I wouldn't be caught, or that I could get away. I realized very soon afterwards what I had done and how utterly stupid it was. At home, my parents and everyone else that knew me was shocked that I did something like that. My parents lost almost all their trust in me and I was grounded for two months. Besides that I have lost many of my privileges and freedom that I enjoyed before this happened. I am now enrolled in the diversion program for one full year. I have 45 hours of community service to complete and several courses and classes to attend over the course of my enrollment.

Once again I would like to say that I am truly sorry for what I have done and for any inconvenience I have caused you, your family, or your company.

Respectfully,
Eric Harris

Sanchez thought that Eric did a good job on the letter, which is undated. But in his personal diary on April 12, 1998 Eric wrote:

Isnt america supposed to be the land of the free? how come, If im free I cant deprive a stupid fucking dumbshit from his possessions If he leaves them sitting in the front seat of his fucking van out in plain sight and in the middle fucking nowhere on a Fri-fucking-day night. NATURAL SELECTION. fucker should be shot. same thing with all those rich snotty toadies at my school. fuckers think they are higher than me and everyone else with all their $ just because they were born into it? Ich denk NEIN. BTW, "sorry" is just a word, it doesnt mean SHIT to me. everyone should be put to a test. an ULTIMATE DOOM test, see who can survive in an environment using only smarts and military skills. put them in a doom world, no authority, no refuge, no BS copout excuses. If you *cant figure out the area of a triangle or what "cation" means, you die! if you cant take down a demon w/ a chainsaw or kill a hell prince w/ a shotgun, you die! fucking snotty rich fuckheads. [Censored by Jefferson County Sheriff] who rely on others or on sympathy or $ to get them through life should be put to this challenge. plus it would get rid of all the fat, retarded, crippled, stupid, dumb, ignorant, worthless people of this world, no one is worthy of this planet, only me and whoever I choose. there is just no respect for anything higher than your fucking boss or parent. everyone should be shot out into space and only the people I say should be left behind.*

★★★

Three months into the diversion program Dylan was failing to complete his first ten hours of community service. He started off doing work at Eldorado Canyon State Park near Boulder, known for its rock climbing routes. He claimed to have worked seven hours, from 7:40 a.m. to 2:40 p.m. on Tuesday June 2, but it was inexplicably his first, and last time there. Sanchez was miffed over his lack of hours and assigned him a two-page paper on time management.

Dylan then launched into another odd stint of community service: Just one and a half hours at St. Philip Lutheran Church. Again, according to his diversion file, he never showed up there again and there is no explanation why. The only St. Philip listed in the metro area, at the time, was headed by Rev. Don Marxhausen, the same pastor who would preside at Dylan's funeral and where Dylan's family had briefly worshipped a few years earlier. But various church workers, including Marxhausen, do not remember Dylan doing community service there.

On June 11 Dylan ended up at the Link Recreation Center in Lakewood for his community service, the same place Eric was going. Link, a former junior high school now run by the city of Lakewood in Jefferson County, has a little bit of everything: weight room, video games, and pool tables. The former cafeteria rents out for events. Eric and Dylan only worked together once, on June 23. Still, Dylan completed thirty-six and a half hours there to finish out his service requirements.

Dave Kirchoff, the Link Center coordinator, remembered watching Columbine unfold on television, "like everybody else in the world." The next day, a staffer thought the names Eric Harris and Dylan Klebold sounded familiar and they checked the paperwork.

"It's a little creepy," Kirchoff says. "The creepiest part is to realize they'd been involved in something like that and realize you had no idea; no inkling it was a possibility."

Link doesn't usually take people like Eric and Dylan with theft charges because if anything goes missing, the diversion workers are among the first suspects, Kirchoff said. (The same goes for Eldorado.) But Kirchoff does not remember anything on Eric and Dylan's paperwork indicating a theft charge, or them saying anything about it. "But we do ask," Kirchoff says. "They may not have been one hundred percent up front with us."

Community service at Link generally means custodial work like wiping down equipment. Workers make the rounds with glass cleaner, towels, and brooms. Friends often want to work together, although the center usually only needs one person at a time. Kirchoff figures Eric and Dylan ended up in just about every nook and cranny in the rec center.

Eric's final review for Link reads, "great worker," and such words are not handed out lightly to the two hundred who do community service there each year. "For me to put something like this, they were pretty dependable, somewhat competent," Kirchoff says.

Dylan may have been as good, but Kirchoff didn't sign him out. He had a vague recollection of Dylan because of his "unique face." Kirchoff did not recall any trouble from the two. Indeed, Eric and Dylan were focusing their energies elsewhere.

"My recollection of them is almost non-existent," Kirchoff said. "That was kind of the interesting thing; they came in, did their work, did it reasonably well, but there wasn't anything striking about them."

Kriegshauser did not know details of Eric and Dylan's community service, according to his deposition. The clients "never tell us what they do or what they are required to do," he said.

Kriegshauser will call a program if he thinks a kid is not really doing the community service, and he did check with Link, but doesn't think they called back. "Which is a typical thing," he says. "We leave a message, but nobody calls back." Yet, at least in the case of Eric, Kriegshauser had no reason to believe he "was anything but a great worker."

★★★

Dylan turned in his time management essay (for blowing his community service hours) to Sanchez using a font so thick and bold it almost looks like Arabic. The essay contains no capital letters, and two large paragraphs. It was, arguably, Dylan's way of being difficult and giving the finger to authority. The undated paper simply titled "time management" also showed some intellectual flair. Dylan wrote on the Seven Years War, a series of worldwide conflicts between two coalitions that included the French on one side and the English on the other; his one obvious mistake was that it occurred in the 17th rather than the 18th century.

"Time management is an essential aspect of society," he began. "Since the invention of clocks in the middle ages, people have become more productive, efficient, and have had better life styles [sic]. knowing how and when to do certain things is one key to a happy lifestyle."

The British vanquished the French in a pivotal North American battle, which is what Dylan seems to refer to when he wrote that the French general "did not know time management, as he hesitated when he should have acted. an experienced time management connoisseur would have rotated the cannons sooner, ending the british threat. in conclusion, this and other examples show the importance of time management."

Sanchez termed the paper "very creative and well-written." It was also her last day overseeing Eric and Dylan before she turned the cases over to Kriegshauser. She concluded in her final analysis Dylan was a "nice young man, kind of goofy, and a bizarre sense of humor, he makes me laugh." She added: "I sometimes see him and Eric together, I like to meet apart too so I can discuss Eric's meds and his shrink meetings. That is all I have to say, Bye Bye!!!!"

Sanchez ended her June 24 entry on Eric with an expression in Spanish, "Muy facile hombre," which might be interpreted as "An easygoing guy." A separate, final summary sheet from Sanchez had a couple more conclusions about Eric. "Really nice young man. Seems responsible and remorseful," she wrote, later adding, "I am not at all worried about drug use from Eric, pretty good head on shoulders (now watch he will get a hot UA [urinalysis] for Acid or something)."

Eric and Dylan's educational level probably did vaunt them well above the other diversion clients, and they did not come across as common criminals – indeed, their crimes were not done for material gain so much as revenge. But Sanchez may not have had the time, nor ability, to divine that. And Eric and Dylan were expertly deceitful.

***

In his first full meeting with Eric, Kriegshauser showcased his "strict, or kind of black and white" philosophy. They discussed Eric's medication, and mood. The meeting would have lasted fifteen minutes to a half-hour and Eric was, "Very receptive. He was always extremely respectful," Kriegshauser says.

Kriegshauser met that same day with Dylan for the same bureaucratic matters. But Dylan did not appear for the next appointment, on July 27. He called Kriegshauser on the 28th to say he had messed up the time. Kriegshauser was as angry as Sanchez had been when Dylan didn't meet his community service hours. Kriegshauser now demanded that Dylan use a Day-Timer. "And, typically speaking, that's how I respond when somebody says they missed an appointment," Kriegshauser said in his deposition. "They forgot the time. They had something else scheduled. Well, guess what, you're not scheduling your time appropriately. You need to be able to manage all of these obligations. So start bringing one [a Day-Timer] every time you come and see me." (Time management was never an issue with Eric, Kriegshauser said.)

If clients like Eric and Dylan were doing "really well," Kriegshauser explained, he liked to talk more intimately with them and go beyond the standard checklist stuff. So on August 24, "I brought up how do you feel about diversion, or however it came out. So the conversation basically went about or went around government, rules in society, authority versus not authority, chaos versus not chaos, that kind of stuff." Dylan sounded like the same Dylan who was critical of society with Horvath. And Eric and Dylan both railed against blind faith in law and authority. "He [Eric] was anti-government, like just about every other client I have," Kriegshauser said. "He didn't like the fact that he was in trouble. He didn't like having the man tell him what to do. But he wasn't belligerent about it. He listened to what I was trying to express to him."

Eric and Dylan asked something to the effect of, "What if we smoke pot? What if we don't agree with the rule that it's illegal?"

Kriegshauser replied, "Well, it's illegal; and I told you [you] can't do it, period."

Eric said, "Well, it figures, because you're the authority, which is real typical."

Kriegshauser has since gone over that conversation in his head "a billion times." But the details may not have mattered.

In fact the diversion program itself, meant to soothe and rectify Eric and Dylan, probably prodded them towards Columbine as they chafed against the strict guidelines and boiled inside for being caught.

***

Dylan's grades were all over the map, from an 'A' in video to two D's, which, notably, were not in slacker classes: French and honors chemistry. The common denominator was that Dylan rejected school because of the classroom strictures and because he didn't like the people. He was also channeling his energy and smarts into mass murder. Like Magistrate DeVita, Kriegshauser understood Dylan was smarter than his grades showed.

"I got the distinct impression it was lack of effort," he said. "He seemed far more capable than that in my discussions with him. He seemed articulate and intelligent, and it just—just didn't add up for him. Now, they were AP classes, advanced placement classes, but they still seemed low compared to what he should be doing."

Kriegshauser told Dylan to improve his grades and if not, he would have to come into the diversion office daily to do homework and compile a weekly homework log. At first, Dylan's grades went up, but then dropped to an F in gym. The math teacher noted that Dylan could use his class time more appropriately, and Dylan admitted reading a book during class.

"I told him that his effort needs to improve or he will face consequences here including possible termination," Kriegshauser wrote in the log. "I also confronted him on his minimizing and excuse giving. I told him to listen to himself and think about what he is saying. It all sounds like he feels like the victim although he denies this."

By contrast, Kriegshauser felt Eric's grades, As and Bs, were good throughout the program. "He's a darned good student," Kriegshauser said of Eric in his deposition. "No concerns about school."

Eric, but not Dylan, was ordered to a Mothers Against Drunk Driving panel. On the panel victims or perpetrators talk about their experiences, although it is not just about alcohol use, but giving people "victim empathy." The panel had no impact on Eric, Kriegshauser recalled.

But by September, Kriegshauser felt Eric was doing well in the program. "Eric asked if he would be allowed to go on a trip to Germany in March," Kriegshauser wrote in his notes. "I told him that I would bases [sic] my decision on his progress at that time. I told him that if he works hard I will try to ST [successfully terminate] him a little early so he can enjoy his trip with out [sic] stress about Diversion. I reminded him that his effort and progress must remain excellent for this to happen."

(Kriegshauser, in his deposition, did not recall any other details about the trip to Germany.)

The next month Kriegshauser learned Eric had received a speeding ticket. His parents grounded him for three weeks, and yanked his computer privileges for about two weeks. Kriegshauser felt that was appropriate, and didn't give Eric any additional tasks.

Eric was sent to a one-day program called Violence is Preventable. (Kriegshauser said such emotions never seemed to be a problem with Dylan). On December 1, 1998 Eric turned in his essay on what he had learned. It was exactly what Kriegshauser would want to hear:

The anger management class I took was helpful in many ways. I feel the instructors were well qualified [sic] for this class and the class size was not too big. I learned several things about how drugs and alcohol contribute to violence, and how to avoid using drugs and alcohol. I felt like the class was focused more on people who had committed violent crimes and people who use drugs and alcohol, rather than being more broad. Nevertheless I still learned what anger is, how to recognize it, and how to deal with it. Violence is expensive, along with anger. Committing violent crimes brings forth fees, bills, and punishment that have very deep affects on that person, not to mention the emotional turmoil it causes.... I believe the most valuable part of this class was thinking up ideas for ways to control anger and for ways to release stress in a non-violent manner. Things such as writing, taking a walk, talking, lifting weights, listening to different music, and exercising are all good ways to vent anger. We also discussed the positive and negative results of anger and violence.... I feel that all of the suggestions can all be helpful, but the main part of anger management comes from the individual. If the person does not want to control his/her anger, then it can be a problem. The person must want to control his/her anger and actually want to not be violent or angry. It all starts in the person's mind. I have learned that thousands of suggestions are worthless if you still believe in violence. I am happy to say that with the help in this class, and several other diversion-related experiences, I do want to try to control my anger.

But Kriegshauser wrote a different conclusion on December 1, 1998 in Eric's diversion file. "Eric honestly reported that he felt like the class was something of a waste of time. He had heard most of it ect."

★★★

Kriegshauser struck a couple programs from Eric and Dylan's diversion menu. One was criminal justice class, which is about six hours on a

Saturday and costs $60, according to Kriegshauser. In an auditorium, maybe one hundred kids speak with youths from a juvenile detention facility. "They will talk about making more appropriate choices, and they will talk about being less destructive to themselves," Kriegshauser explained. "It's basically just kind of think before you act." Kriegshauser dropped it because "it was more gang-related and just didn't fit who they [Eric and Dylan] were."

Kriegshauser also decided Eric did not need the life skills class he had been assigned. "He demonstrated to me that he had life skills under control," Kriegshauser told the attorneys gathered round him in the deposition. "He was pretty responsible and he was respectful and he thought of consequence of action, generally. He never had a major concern with that stuff. Or at least never showed any. So I put on, instead of that class, an adult legal issues packet, which was a packet intended to get—intended to get him to start thinking about if he continued criminal behavior, what could happen to him once he was an adult, based on the fact he was getting ready to graduate."

In that exercise both Eric and Dylan were asked to explain certain crimes and penalties. It seems Columbine was on their minds. Dylan's example for disorderly conduct was, "Billy Bob sets off a smoke bomb in a library." For "complicity" he wrote, "Rashib tells Samir how to make a bomb, but only Samir detonates it."

For accessory to a crime, Eric wrote, "Bobby murders Johny [sic]. Bobby's older brother, Billy, throws the shotgun used in the murder into a lake...."

For disorderly conduct Eric wrote, "Bob and his AK-47 go downtown and he fires off a few shots while yelling 'LET'S FIGHT.'"

"It's about making appropriate choices with friends," Kriegshauser explained, and Eric thought the course was interesting because he "discovered things that he did not know."

Sanchez had required Eric to continue his psychological counseling, and Kriegshauser agreed with the move. "I figure the parent must have seen something or something occurred," he said, and added, "My thought is they are already working on those issues, the family is responsible enough to take care of that on their own. If there's a problem, right or wrong, my theory is they will let me know if there's a concern."

Kriegshauser added, "Nobody in the office in diversion is a mental health professional."

If the diversion program refers a child for counseling, Kriegshauser said he would maintain contact with the counselor, but not otherwise. Kriegshauser never initiated any contact with Eric's psychologist, Kevin Albert. Nor did Albert contact him.

But Kriegshauser did speak with Eric about his counseling. "And he [Eric] said he was doing great," Kriegshauser recalled. "He said he thought the medications were working. He had no continued real temper control problems. He felt real stable. And I said, 'Well, if you have any problems, let me know, because we want to get you—get whatever needs to be modified if you continue to have problems with that.'"

As of January 19, 1999, three months before Columbine, Eric told Kriegshauser he had one more counseling session left. If Kriegshauser felt the counseling was not going well, he said he would not have let Eric out of diversion.

Eric always maintained a steady mood, Kriegshauser says. He never seemed to be drunk or high, and never started rambling conversations with strangers. He never lost his temper, or seemed abnormally irritable. Aside from his complaints about government, Kriegshauser never knew Eric to be violent, or express hatred toward any person or group. Eric did not indicate he thought he was better than anyone else. He didn't seem obsessive compulsive. He didn't pace, shake, or tremble. He didn't appear hyperactive, or depressed.

Some things never came up in conversation with Eric and Dylan, such as Nazism, bullying, or school authority figures. They never discussed sex, a topic Kriegshauser said he would normally bring up only if it was an issue, such as a teen pregnancy. Kriegshauser did not discuss the break-in with the boys, and they did not talk about their older brothers.

Kriegshauser estimated he met with Eric and Dylan together at least five times, a practice altered since Columbine since one boy can influence the other, the theory goes, and prevent the counselor from getting a proper read on the client. Another five times he met with them separately. Kriegshauser described the interaction between Eric and Dylan as "appropriate." Once when Kriegshauser "confronted" Dylan over his grades Eric was there. "And Eric seemed absolutely appropriate in his response to that. Not that he was active in it, but he wasn't making excuses for Dylan. He wasn't—he was, like, yes, yes. And Dylan responded very appropriately. He was remorseful when he was around. Their demeanor together was just like it was when they were apart, respectful."

Kriegshauser did not believe either boy was more open with him when they were alone. "I thought I was getting good information at all times," he said. Kriegshauser was asked if he thought Dylan was shy. "No, not particularly," he answered.

Kriegshauser has difficulty pinpointing how much Eric and Dylan each paid in diversion and ledgers in the files are confusing. But Kriegshauser estimates they paid $300 in court fees alone, not including the various programs such as Eric's anger management. Kriegshauser believes Eric paid for the program himself, something he hopes every juveniles does "because they are the ones that do something wrong." But he cannot enforce that philosophy, and parents pay for their children if they want.

John DeCamp, the attorney for injured Columbine student Mark Taylor, whose lawsuit sparked the deposition, briefly chimed in during the session. While questions from the Solvay attorney took up about 140 of the 167 deposition pages, DeCamp took up only eight. After confirming that Eric was "one impressive young man," DeCamp asked Kriegshauser what may have made him "so to speak, go off the deep end."

"I have no idea," Kriegshauser said. "When he left my program, he seemed absolutely appropriate and responsible. I have not idea what made this occur."

DeCamp asked Kriegshauser if he saw any leader between the two. He didn't. DeCamp asked about Eric and Dylan's love of video games, namely *Doom*. Kriegshauser said the game came up when he mentioned he was looking for "fun things to do" on his computer, and Eric and Dylan gave him a *"Doom Bible."* Kriegshauser said he kept it for a bit, then gave it back because it was inappropriate for him to accept gifts.

DeCamp noted that no one had mentioned the medication Eric switched to after taking Zoloft. Indeed, it seems Luvox was never mentioned during questioning by Luvox attorney Andrew Efaw, which may be exactly what he wanted.

★★★

January 19, 1999. Three months and one day before Columbine. Kriegshauser met with both Eric and Dylan. He also contacted Tom and Sue Klebold because he was concerned about Dylan's looming 'D' in calculus. But the Klebolds raised another issue. They wanted Kriegshauser to tell Dylan he could get in trouble for any hijinks.

"It's an interesting conversation," Kriegshauser elaborated in his deposition.

The Klebolds said it looked like Dylan was "on track" and they were looking at colleges.

"OK. My intention is to early terminate him," Kriegshauser told the parents. "Do you feel OK with that?'"

"Yes, we feel OK with that," the Klebolds replied. "By the way, would you mention to him about high school pranks, senior pranks, because we're concerned he might do something that would mess his chances for college, or something like that, up."

"OK, sure," Kriegshauser said. "I'll talk to him."

There is no other indication in the deposition as to why the Klebolds thought Dylan might pull a senior prank.

Kriegshauser met the next day with Eric and Dylan together. Kriegshauser said he gave Eric (and we would assume Dylan) some version of the general termination speech. They talked about the paperwork, and Kriegshauser asked their thoughts on the program, good and bad, so he could improve it. "And we talk about make sure they stay focused," Kriegshauser said. "You know, they done good to get off diversion and continuing that would be beneficial. And, basically, keeping their eye on the ball."

Kriegshauser told Dylan, "to be very careful about choices in the future especially since he is nearing graduation." He talked to Eric "about making good choices in the future."

Kriegshauser did not have the final decision on letting Eric and Dylan terminate early. He had to send the case to a team of three other officers and the program director. As the forwarding officer, he said, he did not have a vote. The others depend on the file for their decision. Kriegshauser also noted that Magistrate DeVita, who had questioned the boys before they entered the program, signed off on the early release.

Kriegshauser "terminated" Eric and Dylan from diversion early on February 3, 1999. On the last day he met with them, he might have learned their nicknames, Vodka, and Rebel. "I have a bulletin board in my office," he said in his deposition. "And when I was out getting their paperwork, they individually took my—one of those plastic pin things you stick up on a thing, and they put out a V and an R. And I said, 'What's that? Well, it's just something to remember us by. Really? What does it mean?' And I recall them saying, virtual reality. But they might have said

Vodka and Rebel. Now, I don't know. But that's the only time I ever knew about it."

In terminating Dylan, Kriegshauser wrote a one-page report and noted that Dylan did "a very nice job." His attitude was "solid and he remained motivated." The most effective part of the program seemed to be the community service. "He learned a lot from having to give up free time to work for no money." Dylan struggled with staying motivated in school, but maintained a good G.P.A.

His "prognosis" read: "Good. Dylan is a bright young man who has a great deal of potential. If he is able to tap his potential and become self motivated [sic] he should do well in life." The report ended with, "He needs to strive to self motivate [sic] himself so he can remain on a positive path. He is intelligent enough to make any dream a reality but he needs to understand hard work is part of it."

Eric's "successful early termination" report was equally upbeat. "Eric did a very nice job on Diversion," Kriegshauser wrote. Eric's report continued: "PROGNOSIS: Good. Eric is a very bright young man who is likely to succeed in life. He is intelligent enough to achieve lofty goals as long as he stays on task and remains motivated."

In the deposition, Kriegshauser was asked to elaborate on those comments. "He [Eric] seemed to have some goals," Kriegshauser replied. "We talked about goals. He seemed to listen. He just seemed like a kid who was going to do pretty darn good."

Under "recommendations," Kriegshauser typed out: "Eric should seek out more education at higher levels. He impressed me as being very articulate and intelligent. These are skills that he should grow and use as frequently as possible."

In the deposition Kriegshauser also said of his termination report, "Well, these are funny, because successful terminations nobody ever reads. So this is more talking to the air. But, basically, Eric impressed me as a very, very bright kid. And we don't see an incredible amount of bright kids. Nothing personal to the other kids that aren't bright or incredibly bright. And it seems to me that when someone comes across as very articulate or intelligent, those people would benefit from striving to push themselves to higher levels."

BOOK 2: HELL ON EARTH

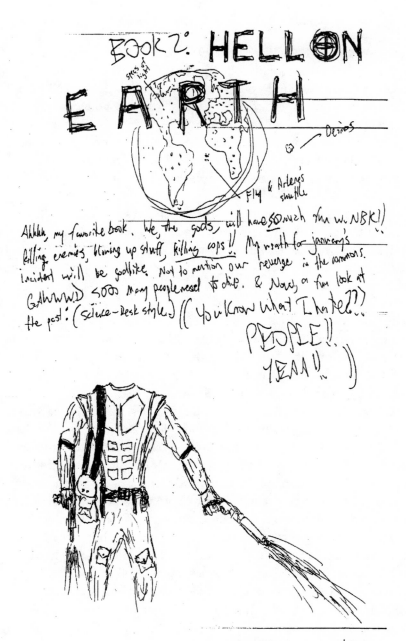

Ahhhh, my favorite book. We, the gods, will have so much fun w. NBK!) killing enemies, blowing up stuff, killing cops! My wrath for janitor's incident will be godlike. Not to mention our revenge in the commons. GAhhhh.D sooo many people need to die. & Now, a fun look at the past: (science-desk style.) ((You know what I hate?!. PEOPLE!! YEAH!.))

NINE

Gun Show

In the spring of 1998 Eric and Dylan were entering diversion. But as Dylan wrote in Eric's yearbook, "the holy April morning of NBK," was in their sights. "We, the gods, will have so much fun w. NBK!! killing enemies, blowing up stuff, killing cops!!" Dylan added. He made an apparent reference to the van break-in: "My wrath for January's incident will be godlike. Not to mention our revenge in the commons.'" The commons, or cafeteria, is where they would place 20-pound propane bombs the day of the shootings. It was still one year away, but Dylan's rage seems to have gelled.

Eric returned the favor. He wrote in Dylan's yearbook, "God I can't wait till they die. I can taste the blood now—NBK... You know what I hate? MANKIND!!!!...kill everything...kill everything" Eric wrote "die," "beat," and "worthless" - or an 'X' - on the photo of almost every student in his yearbook.

★★★

In his last summer alive Dylan quit Blackjack to take a job at Computer Renaissance that would pay over five dollars an hour. His resume listed a variety of qualifications, including "Built my personal computer & helped build those of friends & family." His sole reference was Columbine computer instructor Rich Long.

Eric took a second job at Tortilla Wraps in Littleton, where he worked with Nate Dykeman. His job references included Sue Klebold and Columbine English teacher Jason Webb, a favorite who Eric had bought a Christmas present for. On the job Eric appeared both normal, and exemplary. He dressed in jeans and tennis shoes, and never lost his temper. He was also "a really good worker and a person who was a nice guy with the customers," according to manager David Cave.

Another manager recommended a raise for Eric because he was "one of her best employees. He was always on time and worked hard."

Eric returned to school, like any senior, eager to finish. "I will experience several new subjects, review several old ones, and no doubt learn many new an useful things that will help me in life," he wrote in an essay titled "Great Senior Expectations." "In general, I am expecting to learn to express my opinions in a civilized, respectable manner." But he also noted, "I expect my senior year to be full of surprises."

In other essays Eric focused on guns, Hitler, and general mayhem. "How many people can a football stadium hold? Can it hold fifty, sixty thousand? Most stadiums can," he asked in a comprehensive, well-written, multi-page research paper. "Now, picture a stadium filled, not just seats but the field and all the air above it, with dead men, women, and children. That is just a fraction of the casualties inflicted by the Third Reich. The Third Reich almost completely wiped out the Jewish population in Europe. Now in our minds, that is utterly inhumane, immoral, and evil, but in the Nazi's minds, it was perfectly fine to exterminate an entire race."

"Sometimes twisted Nazi officers would line up prisoners and fire a rifle round into the first just to see how many chests it would go through," Eric recounted.

Eric calmly notes that "in Nazi Germany all mentally disabled people or people with 'incurable mental defectives' were killed." Months earlier, he had already translated those themes to his diary:

KILL all retards, people w/ brain fuck ups, drug adics, people cant figure out how to use a fucking lighter. Geeeawd! People spend millions of dollars on saving the lives of retards, and why I don't buy that shit like, "oh he's my son though!" so the fuck what, he aint normal, kill him. put him out his misery…. "but he is worth the time, he is human too" no he isnt, if he was then he would swallow a bullet cause he would realize what a fucking waste and burden he was.

Elsewhere, Eric privately laid out his Nazi fascination.

I love the nazis too… by the way, I fucking cant get enough of the swastika, the SS and the iron cross. Hitler and his head boys fucked up a few times and it cost them the war, but I love their beliefs and who they were, what they did, and what they wanted.

Eric was also giving his thoughts on Columbine:

someones bound to say "what where they thinking?" when we go NBK or when we were planning it, so this is what I am thinking. "I have a goal to destroy as much as possible so I must not be sidetracked by my feelings of sympathy, mercy, or any of that, so I will force myself to believe that everyone is just another monster from Doom…, so it's either me or them. I have to turn off my feelings." keep this in mind, I want to burn the world, I want to kill everyone except about 5 people, who I will name later, so if you are reading this you are lucky you escaped my rampage because I wanted to kill you.

For one class Eric's assignment was to reflect upon a variety of newspaper articles. He commented on an editorial about death: "With medical technology and thousands of safety procedures in today's society, I believe the majority of people think, 'oh, I'll talk about death some other time, it's not like I'll be dying soon.' It may be a hard topic, but oh well, it definitely needs to be discussed in case of the terrible event that a loved one slips into a coma or something of that nature."

Eric discussed a story about people who didn't move out of the way of emergency vehicles such as ambulances – something hard to read without recalling the ambulances staged outside Columbine after the shootings. "Completely ridiculous that motorists risk the lives of others that are in desperate need of medical attention because of their arrogance," Eric wrote.

One classroom piece was certainly among the dearest to his heart: The Brady Bill requiring licensed gun dealers to perform background checks on customers and the use of an FBI database. "The FBI just shot themselves in the foot," Eric opined, with a bit of humor, even though the FBI was not responsible for passing the law. "There are a few loopholes in the new Brady bill. The biggest gaping hole is that the background checks are only required for licensed dealers... not private dealers."

It was a loophole Eric and Dylan would soon exploit, and another idea Eric translated to his diary:

Fuck you Brady! all I want is a couple of guns, and thanks to your fucking bill I will probably not get any! come on, I'll have a clean record and I only want for personal protection. Its not like I'm some psycho who would go on a shooting spree.... fuckers.

In the same entry, Eric switched from aggression to melancholy, and back to aggression.

Everyone is always making fun of me because of how I look, how fucking weak I am and shit, well I will get you all back: ultimate fucking revenge here. you people could have shown more respect, treated me better, asked for knowledge or guidance more, treated me more like a senior and maybe I wouldn't have been so ready to tear your fucking heads off. Then again, I have <u>always</u> hated how I looked, I make fun of people who look like me, sometimes without even thinking sometimes just because I want to rip on myself. Thats where a lot of my hate grows from. The fact that I have practically no selfesteem, especially concerning girls and looks and such. therefore people make fun of me ... constantly... therefore I get no respect and therefore I get fucking PISSED. as of this date I have enough explosives to kill about 100 people, and then if I get a couple of bayonets, swords, axes, whatever I'll be able to kill at least 10 more and that just *isnt enough! GUNS! I <u>need</u> guns! Give me some fucking firearms!*

★★★

Robyn Anderson would ask Dylan to the senior prom. But first, he asked her to the Tanner Gun Show.

Robyn was slightly chubby with a round face and short, blond hair. Her looks were average. She was a churchgoer and straight-A student who, on a Sunday, bought three of the four guns used at Columbine. She was never prosecuted for a crime, but after the shootings, did not attend high school graduation.

Robyn thought Dylan was smart, but didn't always exert himself. He was quiet, and got along well with others — at least he tended to do what the group wanted — but he was also content to be alone and play computer games. Robyn knew Eric and Dylan didn't mesh with the jocks, but they never talked about Hitler, or killing, and never wore swastikas. Robyn did not talk politics with them, and if she had to label them with any religious belief, it was atheism. Robyn says she never knew about Dylan's infatuation with bombs and even after Columbine maintained, "He really wasn't like the person that committed this crime."

When Robyn first met Dylan in 1995 she thought he was a "rough guy," but came to call him one of the sweetest people she knew and friends say she was infatuated with him. He didn't return the spark and they never dated but she called him about three times a week and they usually went midnight bowling on Fridays. Others would join them, including Eric, but Robyn never said much to him.

Robyn had visited the Klebold home, and spoken with Dylan's parents maybe three times. "They were caring parents, from what I could tell," she said. "He—his mom would call him Dyl, you know. 'We're just going to a movie, Dyl, we'll be back.' They would—you know, they wanted to know where he was going to be and who he was with, and basic parenting rules." The Klebolds, for their part, knew Robyn as someone who studied calculus with Dylan. They called her "very sweet."

Eric and Dylan called her the ticket to the gun show. They were one year under eighteen, and could not purchase guns themselves. But Robyn could. Eighteen days earlier, she had turned eighteen.

On November 22, 1998 Eric and Dylan picked up Robyn at about 10:00 a.m. and talked about wanting a shotgun. Robyn did not want to submit to a background check, but Eric and Dylan had already scouted the gun show for "private dealers," so Robyn did not have to complete any paperwork.

At the show the trio walked over to the man Eric and Dylan had spoken with the day before, Ronald Frank Hartmann, fifty-nine. He had served twenty years in the U.S. Armed Forces and after that worked as a civilian government employee. He had a Stevens double-barrel shotgun for sale that was manufactured around 1969. The gun was almost as old as Eric and Dylan combined, but they would launch it into history.

Eric and Dylan asked Hartmann if he had anything shorter than the double barrel and he brought out a tape measure to show them how far down they could legally cut the barrel. Hartmann asked Eric and Dylan if they had "brought someone eighteen years old this time." They said they had.

Hartmann asked Anderson her age. She said she was eighteen but looked young, so Hartmann asked for ID. She produced her driver's license.

Hartmann told her the shotgun was $245, about the same price they would pay for every gun they bought that day. Robyn pulled a wallet out of her bag, brimming with Dylan's money, and counted out the cash. She paid mostly in twenties and no receipt was given. Hartmann went to hand the shotgun to Robyn but Dylan took it.

"Are you going to be a gentleman and carry it for her?" Hartmann asked.

"Yes," Dylan replied.

Anderson seemed timid and nervous but Hartmann figured it was her first gun purchase. She and Dylan both seemed clean cut. Nothing to worry about.

Hartmann then turned to his friend and fellow gun vendor James Washington, a fifty-year-old Colorado Springs resident working as a senior investigative and security specialist with the Defense Security Service. (One of the agency's jobs is performing background checks for government agencies.)

"That girl just turned eighteen," Hartmann said.

Robyn, Eric and Dylan then searched for another private dealer. Now it was Eric's turn and he negotiated for another shotgun. A large binder clip in Robyn's purse held Eric's money and Robyn can't recall if she paid for the gun, or Eric handed over the money. The dealer did not ask for any ID. Again, there was no receipt, and again, the gun was about thirty years old.

One more gun to go. One more private dealer. This time, it was a black 9mm carbine rifle in a box with two magazine clips. Robyn was asked for her ID, and the seller double-checked with someone at another table. Again, the money held together with a binder clip was produced. Again, Robyn couldn't remember if she or Eric actually handed the money over. Again, there was no receipt.

Eric and Dylan also purchased bullets, and Eric bought a folding knife. (Robyn said she played no part in those transactions.) All told, it took about an hour.

Robyn told police Eric and Dylan buying guns did not surprise her because they had jobs and didn't spend money on anything else like dating. She thought the guns might be for hunting, or a gun collection.

But Eric and Dylan never talked about hunting, and when Dylan tried to shoot a deer in his backyard with a BB gun his mom wouldn't let him. The boys also asked Robyn not to say anything about the guns. They, in turn, promised not to mention her.

So as they were leaving the gun show, a thought crossed Robyn's mind. Maybe they would shoot someone.

"You guys aren't going to do anything stupid, are you?" she asked.

"No," they said.

Robyn says that if she had known about plans for Columbine, she would have told police.

★★★

After the gun show they dropped off Eric at his house. Eric put his two guns and other merchandise in the trunk of his car.

"Well folks, today was a very important day," he wrote in his diary.

"We have GUNS! We fucking got em you sons of bitches! HA!! HA HA HA! Neener! Booga Booga. heh it's all over now."

Eric inserted a small drawing of a man sticking out his tongue, putting his thumbs in his ears, and waving his fingers to tease.

"This capped it off, the point of no return."

Despite his joy, Eric still had an empty heart. "it's really a shame," he wrote. "I had a lot of fun at that gun show, I would have loved it if you were there dad. we would have done some major bonding. would have been great."

But he quickly snapped: "If [I] have to cheat and lie to everyone then that's fine. THIS is what I am motivated for. THIS is my goal, THIS is what I want 'to do with my life.'"

Dylan went with Robyn to her house. She got in her car, and followed Dylan to his house. They were going to study calculus. Dylan drove his car into the garage, put the shotgun under his jacket, and with his other purchases in a bag, went up to his room.

★★★

As they were purchasing the guns, Eric was finalizing a proposed business project for government and economics class: "Hit-Men For Hire." Eric's two-paragraph product overview was, "In this city, protection is needed. Day by day people grow more and more agitated with one another and become less understanding and forgiving. Even though programs made by anti-hate groups and police try to keep people from being prejudiced and having stereotypes, most people are still the same.

"The so-called 'Trench Coat Mafia' is a small group of friends who generally wear dark clothes, military fatigues, and long black dusters. Most people usually just stare and whisper when they see us. We don't mind because we generally don't like people anyway. Now they have reasons to stay clear of us."

In the "map" section Eric wrote, "The locations in the Columbine area are strategically positioned so we can launch attacks in almost any neighborhood with a few minutes notice. We also have caches of weaponry and explosives located around the CHS area and in certain fields, all to serve you, the customer."

In the paper, Eric leveled with the teacher: "The business is basically to kill people who anger our clients." He added, "Several weapons, such as a sawed-off pump-action riot gun, an AB-10 machine pistol, home made rocket launchers, swords and daggers were gathered to help our business."

Eric discussed the money aspect of the business and noted, "Political contributions are the main expense."

Some five years after Columbine, police released the video for the assignment. Eric Veik, a friend of Eric and Dylan, stars as the dork. Wearing a tie and windbreaker, he tells the camera in a whiny voice: "People are always making fun of me. I don't like it. I really don't, it makes me mad."

Then Eric and Dylan, wearing sunglasses, confidently stride down an alley.

"Oooh," Veik says in awe.

"We're here to protect you, for a cost," Eric says.

"I'll pay anything," Veik replies.

Eric quotes him $20 a day but adds, "You know, we can't have weapons on school grounds."

That's OK with Veik.

"We'll protect you [at] school, then take away any bullies that are picking on you, whatever," Eric says. "Off school grounds, we can relocate this person. That would be $1,000."

"Thank you so much," Veik says.

Then a "jock," walks down the alley. Eric and Dylan surprise him, draw their guns, and shoot.

In what appear to be outtakes, or what Veik calls "intimidation scenes," Eric and Dylan yell at the supposed bully.

"No you goddamn piece of punk ass shit," screams Dylan, dressed in a trench coat and backwards baseball cap. "Do not, mess with that friggin kid. If you do, I'll rip off your god damn head and shove it so far up your friggin ass, you'll be coughing up dandruff for four, friggin months."

Eric, dressed in jeans, a black blazer, and backwards baseball cap, also does a mock dress-down of the imaginary bully. He talks like a drill sergeant, with a commanding lilt. His eyes bulge out, and he stares into the camera. "Look, I don't care what you say," Eric threatens. "If you ever touch him again, I will frickin kill you. I'm going to pull out a God damn shotgun and blow your damn head off. Do you understand? You little worthless piece of crap."

★★★

On or around December 18, almost a month after the gun show, Ronald Martin received a call at his Lakewood store, Green Mountain Guns. The caller asked about magazines for the Hi-Point rifle. Martin said he could order them, but they would have to be pre-paid. On December 18 Eric Harris walked in. Martin took the order, which he thought was unusual because of the large amount of magazines, nine, and because the Hi-Point was not considered a good gun. Eric paid $143.51 in cash. Someone from Green Mountain later called Eric's house to let him know the order had arrived. Wayne Harris took the call but said he hadn't ordered anything.

"Yes, they did have the right number," Eric would later say. He picked up the order on December 29. It was almost Happy New Year — Eric and Dylan's last.

Eric and Dylan unsuccessfully lobbied another Columbine student, and various Blackjack co-workers, to buy the fourth gun. One co-worker was Philip Duran, twenty-two at the time of Columbine. He didn't want his name on any paperwork but put them in touch with Mark Manes. Manes, twenty-one, was fascinated with guns although his mother Diann was a member of Handgun Control, the group chaired by the wife of James Brady, namesake of the Brady bill.

On January 23, 1999, Eric and Dylan were about to graduate the diversion program with flying colors. They also hit familiar ground and met Manes and Duran at the Tanner Gun Show. They looked at TEC-9s before Manes agreed to sell them one he already owned for $500.

That night, Dylan went to Manes' house and gave him $300. Two weeks later Manes, Duran, Eric and Dylan went to an informal shooting range in a forested area about an hour south of Denver known as Rampart Range. Manes forgot to ask Dylan for the other $200 he was owed, so he had Duran be the intermediary.

A week after the first shooting practice Manes went up a second time with Eric and a couple other people, but Dylan had to work. A third time Eric and Dylan were again together with Duran, Manes and Manes' girlfriend, Jessica Miklich. It is March 6, just over a month before Columbine, and Eric and Dylan have surprises: A video camera and two sawed-off shotguns. The camera is from Columbine High, but they will not say where they got the guns. Duran will film the outing.

Eric is dressed in a Denver Broncos sweatshirt while both he and Dylan wear backwards baseball caps and black trench coats. Their video has no plot, only a fifteen-minute stream of consciousness shooting gallery as Eric, Dylan and the others blast nearly two hundred rounds at whatever is around them.

"Look at the top of the thing," Dylan says of a pockmarked bowling pin.

"Lead pellets all around," someone else says.

There is laughter. Dylan fires the double-barrel shotgun into a pine tree, leaving a hole. "That's a fucking slug," he says.

The next line about a shotgun slug is the most chilling, although it is unclear who speaks it: "Imagine that in someone's fucking brain."

"It hurt my wrist like a son of a bitch," Dylan chimes in.

"You've got an entry and exit wound there," Eric says of the bowling pin. At one point, he blows on the tip of the shotgun barrel as if to clear any smoke.

Their hands are bleeding from the heavy recoil of the shotguns. "Guns are bad when you saw them off and make them illegal," someone says. "Bad things happen to you. Just say no to sawed-offs."

"Bad," says Eric, who spanks his shotgun.

"No, no, no," Klebold says to his shotgun.

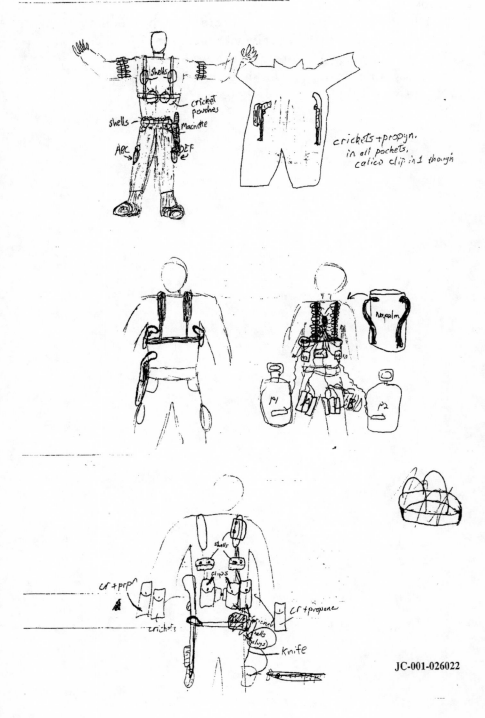

crickets+propyn.
in all pockets,
calico clip in 1 though

TEN

The Basement Tapes

Eric and Dylan hoped a big-time director would make a movie about them. Maybe Spielberg, maybe Tarantino. Their own home movies were dumb, funny and violent. Their video Bible was the so-called "basement tapes." Ghoulish, insightful, and all over the map. The basement tapes were not for class, but the whole world to see.

Eric explains that he wants to kill "niggers, spics, Jews, gays, fucking whites." Of the other school shootings in Oregon and Kentucky he says, "Do not think we're trying to copy anyone." He and Dylan had the idea, "before the first one ever happened." Their plan is better, "not like those fucks in Kentucky with camouflage and .22s. Those kids were only trying to be accepted by others."

The result of their revenge, Dylan hopes, will be "The most deaths in U.S. history."

"Hopefully," Eric adds, kissing the gun he holds in his arms and has named Arlene, in honor of a character in *Doom*.

"We're hoping, we're hoping. I hope we kill 250 of you," Dylan says.

"If you're going to go fucking psycho and kill a bunch of people like us... do it right," Dylan says.

In the lead up to the shootings, they tricked people. "I could convince them that I'm going to climb Mount Everest, or I have a twin brother growing out of my back," Eric says. "I can make you believe anything."

"People have no clue," Dylan says at one point.

The event, Dylan says, will be the most "nerve-racking fifteen minutes of my life, after the bombs are set and we're waiting to charge through the school. Seconds will be like hours. I can't wait. I'll be shaking like a leaf."

For Eric, "It's going to be like fucking *Doom*. Tick, tick, tick, tick Haa! That fucking shotgun is straight out of *Doom*!"

They turn to those who will survive the massacre.

"I hope people have flashbacks," Eric says.

Then there are those who wronged them.

"You've given us shit for years," Klebold explains. "You're fucking going to pay for all the shit. We don't give a shit because we're going to die doing it."

They envision the huge bombs for unsuspecting victims in the cafeteria.

"Isn't it fun to get the respect that we're going to deserve?" Eric says.

Indeed, the target shooting and video warm-ups are not enough. "More rage. More rage," Eric says at one point. "Keep building it on."

★ ★ ★

The first tape rolls on March 15, 1999, nine days since Eric and Dylan filmed the Rampart Range shooting spree with Mark Manes and Phil Duran. Acknowledgements are in order. Knowing their audience, Eric and Dylan also address their remarks to "you detectives."

"Oh, I'd like to make a thank you to Mark and Phil," Dylan says. "Very cool. You helped us do what we needed to do. Thank you. Hope you don't get fucked."

"Yeah, you know it's not their fault," Eric chimes in. "I mean, they had no fucking clue."

"We used them," Dylan says. "Like you use a horse to carry shit."

If it hadn't been them, it would have been someone else over twenty-one. Leave Manes and Duran alone, Dylan adds.

"We would have gone on and on," Eric says. "We would have found some way around it, 'cause that's what we do."

"Don't blame them and don't fucking arrest them for what we did," Dylan says.

"Don't arrest any of our friends, any of our co-workers, any of our family members," Eric says.

They expect stricter gun laws to be discussed after Columbine but say it will only create a black market. More laws, Dylan adds, isn't the answer.

They mention Brandon Larson, a Columbine High football player. "You will find his body," they say. (Larson was not killed and says he had no problems with Eric and Dylan, although he may have been an unwitting symbol of the social or sports hierarchy.)

"We're proving ourselves," they add.

According to *TIME*, "At one point Harris gets very quiet. His parents have probably noticed that's he's become distant, withdrawn lately, but it's been for their own good. 'I don't want to spend any more time with them,' he says. 'I wish they were out of town so I didn't have to look at them and bond more.'"

Eric recalls his mom's thoughtfulness, bringing him candy and Slim

Jims. "I really am sorry about all this," he says.

"But war's war," he adds.

"This goes to all my family: I'm sorry I have so much rage," Klebold says "You made me what I am. Actually, you just added to what I am."

Dylan says his older brother Byron, and Byron's friends, constantly "ripped" on him. Even his extended family treated him poorly. "You made me what I am," he says. "You added to the rage."

Klebold even remembers the Foothills Day Care center, where he felt the "stuck-up" kids hated him. He hated them back. "Being shy didn't help," he says. "I'm going to kill you all. You've been giving us shit for years."

Columbine High also took its toll. "If you could see all the anger I've stored over the past four fucking years," Klebold says.

Eric talks about how people made fun of his face, his shirts, and his hair when he was growing up. He complains about his father and says whenever the family moved, five times, he had to start "at the bottom of the ladder" and no chance to earn any respect.

Then it's Dylan's turn. He says of his parents, "They gave me my fucking life. It's up to me what I do with it."

Eric shrugs. "My parents might have made some mistakes that they weren't really aware of in their life with me, but they couldn't have helped it." He knows what's in store for them. "They're going to go through hell once we're finished. They're never going to see the end of it."

Eric quotes the same Shakespeare line found in his day planner on the date for Mother's Day: "Good wombs hath borne bad sons."

Dylan tells how his parents taught him self awareness, and self-reliance. "I appreciate that," he says, but adds, "I'm sorry I have so much rage."

Dylan continues: "You can't understand what we feel; you can't understand no matter how much you think you can."

Eric plays with a pair of scissors. Dylan mixes candy and whiskey in his mouth. He holds up a piece of candy and says, "Hey guys, it's a house."

"Fuck you Walsh," Dylan says, in reference to the deputy who busted them for the van break in.

Harris mentions shooting some "Christianic bitches" in the head. But they love Robyn Anderson. "Thanks to the gun show, and to Robyn," they say. "Robyn is very cool."

Eric talks of carrying his gym bag, the "terrorist bag," into the house with a gun butt sticking out. Mom assumed it was his BB gun.

Dylan backs out of the room and pretends to be Eric's mom. Eric waves at the camera. "Hi, mom," he says.

Dylan recalls his parents walking into his own room as he was trying on his trench coat to see if he could hide a shotgun. "They didn't even know it was there."

Dylan imagines how his parents will feel: "If only we could have reached them sooner, or found this tape."

"If only we would have searched their room," Eric adds. If Mom, Dad, or anyone else had asked more probing questions, "We would've been fucked," he adds.

"We wouldn't be able to do what we're going to do," Dylan says.

The camera tours Eric's bedroom arsenal. The tape is shut off.

★ ★ ★

Filming resumes on March 18, "in the middle of the night." They wonder: Should they attach nails to pipe bombs "Echo" and "Delta"?

They swerve to a different topic. "Religions are gay," and for "people who are weak and can't deal with life."

They return to time bombs, bombs with tripwires, and diversionary bombs, maybe a reference to the bombs they will actually end up dropping a short distance from Columbine the day of the shootings to distract police. The "fucking fire department is going to be busy for a month," they say.

They seem to return to Deputy Walsh, who is white, but discuss the "nigger that stopped us that day." They talk about spics, how black people speak in Ebonics, and how students in bowling class thought of the pins as particular ethnic groups to help them bowl better.

"World peace is an impossible thing," they say. Bomb-making information is on the Internet. "Mrs. X, Y, Z bought our guns."

"Only two weeks left, and one more weekend," they say, and "it is coming up fucking quick."

They discuss credit card fraud, and Eric raises his hand as if he has done it.

They wouldn't be anywhere without their "tests." They need a lot more napalm, but may just use oil and gas, a combination that is "one hell of a mental picture." People might catch fire.

Graduation, they predict, will be a "memorial service with lots of people crying," including a candlelight memorial.

Eric has 100 cartridges and ten loaded magazines but needs lasers for his rifle. "You guys are lucky it doesn't hold more ammo," they say.

There is still "a lot of shit to do." Dylan needs to get his pants, fill his magazines, and get pouches for his shells.

They talk about shopping at Radio Shack, where Harris will say the supplies are for special effects in a movie. "We are, but we aren't, psycho," they say.

★★★

Concrete details of the "basement tapes" began emerging in November 1999 when lead Columbine investigator Kate Battan read a one-minute excerpt of Eric and Dylan thanking their gun suppliers at the sentencing for Mark Manes. *The Denver Post* at that point described the videos as "visual suicide notes" and a "memorial tape." They are in fact one of the finest views into the minds of the killers. An invaluable tool for police, journalists, mental health experts, and anyone in a position to catch the warning signs of a school shooter — in other words, everyone.

Of course, the Jefferson County Sheriff's Office didn't see it like that. That November, spokesman Steve Davis said the tapes did not contain startling information. "Everybody's got this idea that there's this huge, juicy stuff," he told me for a story in the *Chicago Tribune*.

But of course, the sheriff didn't want to release the tapes. Sheriff John Stone did show them exclusively to *TIME* magazine, before he even showed them to victim families, but claimed the journalists did not have permission to mention, or quote from, the tapes. The magazine said that wasn't true, as its cover story anchored by the tapes hit newsstands in December 1999.

In maybe one of the most bizarre paths of a piece of evidence, the tapes were then shown to journalists, victim families, the Klebolds, and select others such as law enforcement officials. Their contents were extensively reported in the media, and later summarized in official police reports released by the sheriff. But lawsuits quickly put the tapes under wraps. They have never been seen publicly since.

In 2006 Jefferson County Sheriff Ted Mink was given the latitude to show the tapes but declined. Numerous school shootings have occurred since Columbine, but Mink believed the tapes could cause copycats.

***

On the basement tapes, Eric and Dylan sense what will happen to the videos: "Klebold asked Harris if he thinks the cops will listen to the whole video," according to the sheriff's own summary. "They then discuss that they believe that the video will be cut up into little pieces, and the police will just show the public what they want it to look like."

Eric and Dylan want to distribute the videos to four news stations, and Eric wants to email copies of his journal. Eric seems to refer to a book about *Doom*, describing it as his life's work, and wanting to get it published.

***

The auteurs film another tour of the guns and arsenal in Eric's basement. It is sometime before April 1. Eric will soon be eighteen. He poses, sans shirt, with his shotgun, and carbine on a sling.

"My parents are going to fucking Passover," Klebold says.

"You're Jewish?" Eric asks angrily.

Dylan now seems scared of Eric. Apparently, they had never discussed the issue.

Dylan pans to a window. "You can't see it, it's buried there," he says. "That's why it's called a bunker."

The camera stops.

***

The camera restarts from a car dashboard, and Harris appears to be driving alone. It is dark outside, and raindrops fall on the window. Amidst loud music, Eric mentions "the Blackjack crew."

"Sorry dudes, I had to do what I had to do," Eric says, and adds: "It is a weird feeling knowing you're going to be dead in two and a half weeks."

Harris isn't sure if they should do "it" before, or after prom. He wishes he could have re-visited Michigan, and old friends. He becomes silent, and appears to start crying. He reaches over to the camera and shuts it off.

***

Monday, April 11. "Reb's Tape." Eric is in the driver's seat. They are on their way to get more gear.

"Directors will be fighting over this story," Dylan says. The camera is turned off. And on again. Eric is again driving and smoking what he calls his "birthday cigar." They have purchased two large fuel containers, and three propane bottles. The camera is turned off.

The camera is turned on. Eric appears to be alone and the camera rests on something, maybe his knee, and he stares into the lens. His headboard appears behind him. He talks about the cops who may make his "parents pay." He says his mother and father are the "best parents" but he would have gotten around anything they tried to do this past year.

"There's no one else to blame but me and Vodka," he says.

Eric adds that it's been tough recently. His parents have been hard on him for putting off insurance, and the Marine Corps.

"This is my last week on earth," he says.

"To you coolios (cool people) out there still alive, sorry I hurt you or your friends," Eric adds. This is total KMFDM, and there are seven and one-third days left. Then he says, "fucking bitches" and rattles off a list of names. He's going to be one tired motherfucker come Monday then, "Boom! I'll get shot and die."

Eric films his planning book, which he describes as the "Writings of God," and a drawing of backpacks labeled "Napalm." Eric calls the pending rampage a "suicide plan."

★★★

April 17. The day of prom. Dylan's bedroom. He is wearing black army pants, and a black T-shirt with "Wrath" printed across the front in red, the same shirt he will die in. Dylan attaches a tan ammo pouch to his waist, and a green pouch to his right shin. He puts a sawed-off shotgun into a pants cargo pocket. The TEC-9 pistol is on a sling hanging over his shoulder. He talks about how he didn't want to go to prom with Robyn Anderson, but his parents are paying for it.

"Since I'm going to be dying," he adds, "I thought I might do something cool."

They talk about practicing the next couple nights. Dylan thanks "Mr. Stevens," an apparent reference to his Stevens shotgun. Dylan adds, "He knew I was fucking buying it," an apparent reference to one of the gun dealers who depended on Anderson's ID.

Dylan puts on his trench coat but says he looks fat with all the gear on. He figures he'll have to take the coat off during the shootings because it gets in the way of swinging the TEC-9, which has a shoulder strap. But he doesn't want to take off the coat because he likes it.

"Fucking snow is gay," they say, and hope the "shit" clears out by

Tuesday. Harris says he needs dry weather "for my fires." The tape goes out.

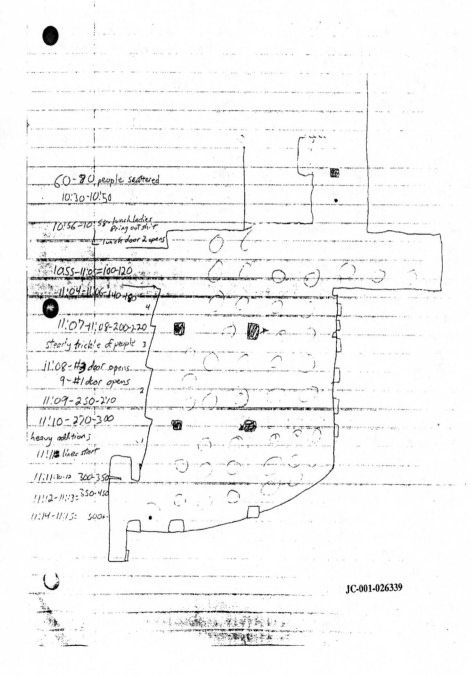

60 - 80 people scattered
10:30-10:50

10:50-10:55= lunch ladies
bring out shit
lunch door 2 opens

10:55-11:05= 100-120

11:04-11:06= 140-180

11:07-11:08= 200-270

steady trickle of people 3

11:08- #3 door opens
9 - #1 door opens

11:09 - 250-270

11:10 - 270-300

heavy additions

11:11 lines start

11:11:10-12 300-350

11:12-11:13- 350-450

11:14-11:15: 500+

ELEVEN

Senior Projects

For Eric Harris college, majoring in computers, was a maybe. The military was another option. Probably taking his cue from *Doom's* main character, Eric had long wanted to be a Marine. (He once wrote that he wanted a job to "blow up things.") And he literally dreamt of the military. Loaded with gear he walked through a deep forest one night as flares flew through the air and cast shadows. Eric emerged onto a beach full of dolphins, whales, and stars as a voice said, "Watch out for the flares and have a swell time." Then Eric himself got launched into the stars.

So Eric must have thought it was divine intervention – and a scene right out of *Doom* when the Marines found him his senior year. Specifically, it was Staff Sgt. Mark "Gonzo" Gonzales. Thirty years old at the time of Columbine, Gonzales had started out as an embarkation specialist, ensuring that planes were properly loaded before missions. Over the years, he had been based in Norfolk, Virginia; Okinawa; and Camp Pendleton, California. He had been in eighteen countries, but never seen combat.

To progress in the marines Gonzales needed to sign up for a "special assignment." His first choice was drill instructor. "Unfortunately," he says, he was chosen to be a recruiter in 1998. But he adds, "My mom was happy."

A good recruiter is like a good salesman, and Gonzales was selling the branch of the military with a reputation for gung-ho. "Every young man or woman is different," Gonzales says. "They all have different needs. You just try to relate it to what you know about the Marine Corps."

In an interview shortly after Columbine, Gonzales wears a short-sleeve khaki shirt, blue, creased dress pants, and a buzz cut. His build is firm and trim. He does not want the interview, which takes place in the conference room of a Denver recruiting office, to be tape-recorded. The room is adorned with televisions, videos, flags, black cushion chairs, and maps of Colorado.

Gonzales figures he had brought forty-seven recruits into the Marines, seven of them women. In Texas, Gonzales had lots of walk-ins who wanted to sign up. In Colorado, he had only one. Cruising malls and county fairs in uniform was part of his strategy. So was setting up tables at high schools. "We're basically just like a counselor in high school," he said of recruits. "Trying to improve their circumstances."

Gonzales focuses on those aged seventeen to twenty nine. Some recruiters will walk up to anyone and everyone, although he shies away from the overweight because they probably won't meet the fitness standards.

Gonzales is also a Columbine High School graduate, class of 1987. That was part of the reason he was recruiting in the area. As a military recruiter, he had access to a list of local high school students. That's how he called Eric Harris on Friday, April 2, 1999, eighteen days before Columbine. They had a twenty-minute phone interview as Gonzales did a pre-screening. He asked about medical background, divorce, mental health, counseling, prescription drug use, along with height, weight, and any use of glasses. Eric said he had had a broken nose and broken wrist when he was younger; Gonzales didn't recall how they happened.

Eric did not let on to seeing a psychologist, or taking prescription medication, an obstacle to joining the Marines, whether he knew it or not. "You run into that a lot of times because the kid might be embarrassed to tell you," Gonzales says. "It's kind of impersonal to give it over the phone."

Eric told Gonzales he worked at Blackjack and liked computers, soccer, and weapons. Nothing out of the ordinary, Gonzales thought. Eric said his grades were As and Bs. "He's very smart," Gonzales adds.

Gonzales asked what Eric's parents thought about him joining the Marine Corps. "They wouldn't mind," he said.

Gonzales set up a time to meet Eric three days later, on Monday April 5 at 1:00 p.m. "I felt he might be a good lead because he thought about the Marine Corps and he was interested in weapons."

★★★

Eric seemed to be on another track. After speaking with Gonzales he recorded his thoughts in his diary the next night:

Months have passed. Its the first Friday night in the final month. much shit has happened. Vodka has a Tec-9, we test fired all of our babies, we have 6 time clocks ready, 39 crickets, 24 pipe bombs, and the napalm is under construction. Right now I'm trying to get fucked and trying to finish off these time bombs. NBK came quick. Why the fuck can't I get any? I mean, I'm nice and considerate and all that shit, but nooooo. I think I try to hard. but I kinda need to considering

NBK is closing in. The amount of dramatic irony and foreshadowing is fucking amazing. Everything I see and hear I incorporate into NBK somehow. Either bombs, clocks, guns, napalm, killing people, any and everything finds some tie to it. Feels like a Goddamn movie sometimes. I wanna try to put some mines and trip bombs around this town too maybe. Get a few extra frags on the scoreboard. I hate you people for leaving me out of so many fun things. And no, don't fucking say "Well that's your fault" because it isn't, you people had my phone#, and I asked and all, but no no no no don't let the weird looking Eric KID come along, ooh fucking nooo.

★★★

On April 5 Eric was on time to meet Gonzales at the Littleton recruiting office near Columbine. He wore a black Rammstein T-shirt, black cargo pants, and tennis shoes. Following procedure, Gonzales re-screened him on the same questions to make sure his answers were consistent and there were no obvious road blocks. Eric then took the Enlistment Screening Test that measures word and math skills. Gonzales scored the twenty-two-minute, multiple choice scan-tron test on the spot. Gonzales said an average score is forty to sixty. A score over sixty allows someone to qualify for almost any division of the corps. Eric scored seventy-four out of ninety-nine. Gonzales told him he did pretty good. Then he assessed his values.

The Marines reputation is first on the battlefield, bayonets drawn. But like any wise corporation, they actually look for character traits that vault their people above the lemmings. To that end, the corps has a list of eleven traits needed for success and gathered from a survey of former Marines in the Fortune 500. The traits are presented to applicants on eleven small tiles in different colors to make them easier to see. They then pick the tiles that explain their reasons for wanting to join the Marines.

Eric's top three picks, Gonzales recalls, were physical fitness; leadership and management skills; and the triple-header called self-reliance, self-direction and self-discipline, or "self times three."

Gonzales did not recall why Eric chose the particular traits, but the "self times three" was not any sort of a red flag that a potential recruit was selfish. "I've had captains of the football teams pick this," he said.

On the battlefield, Eric was most interested in Special Forces, or infantry. Like most people, Gonzales said, "He was basically looking for the excitement."

Their meeting lasted one, to one and a half hours. Gonzales noted that Eric wasn't a bookworm, but he wasn't a jock. He just seemed down the middle, a "normal person." Eric never mentioned Dylan, nor made any remarks about shooting up his school. He did not say anything about the van break-in, which likely would have been uncovered in a background check, and raised questions. Gonzales gave him some pamphlets, and Eric asked what the Marines provided for college tuition. He seemed genuinely interested in joining up.

Next came the closing. "Are you ready to be a Marine?" Gonzales asked.

But Eric wanted to graduate high school first, which was typical enough. And Gonzales wanted Eric to talk to his parents. He figured they would have questions. Gonzales also knew that people begin to hear negative things about joining up once they tell friends and family, so he arranged a follow up meeting.

Three days later, on Thursday April 8, at 1:00 p.m., he met with Eric, one day before his eighteenth birthday. The meeting lasted fifteen to twenty minutes and Gonzales says, "He [Eric] was pretty much sold on the Marine Corps but he wanted to have the parents involved."

If a recruit is seventeen, Gonzales says he is required to meet with the parents, so Eric's case was a judgment call. But Gonzales usually sees the parents when someone is still in high school, and wanted to meet the parents the night of the eighth. Eric said he would talk with them and call Gonzales.

The next day, Friday, April 9, Eric celebrated his birthday. His friends gathered at the Draft Bar and Grill in nearby Southwest Plaza shopping mall. Chris Morris was there, along with Nicole Markham. It was the last time Cory Friesen would see Eric and Dylan, and he remembered them saying they wished the jocks were all dead. He didn't take it seriously. Dylan and Robyn finished off the night with Eric at the Rock N' Bowl bowling alley, which dimmed the lights and featured a DJ from midnight to 2:00 a.m.

Three days later, on Monday April 12, Gonzales still hadn't heard back from Eric about meeting the parents. So he went to Blackjack Pizza. It was eight days before Columbine.

"Hey Eric, how come you didn't call me, what's up?" Gonzales asked.

Eric may have said he was too busy working, Gonzales recalls. But they set a meeting with the parents for Thursday the 15th at 6:00 p.m. at the Harris house.

Gonzales and Eric's dad hit it off. They had both been to Okinawa, and reminisced about the beaches, jet skis, boats, and golf. They stayed in the living room in the front of the house, and made other small talk about work. "Their house was nice," Gonzales added. "Normal parents."

Wayne Harris wore a dress shirt and slacks, having just gotten off work. Katherine Harris dressed "casual." Gonzales believes Eric was wearing shorts and a T-shirt. Gonzales himself was in military dress, and ready to conduct business.

He said he understood the parents had questions. Indeed, they were most curious about educational opportunities and the delayed entry program, which allows high school seniors to join the Corps immediately, but go to boot camp after graduation. "Mom wasn't too keen on combat-related jobs," Gonzales said. "I explained to her it'd be his choice and there's a lot of other jobs to choose from."

There were no other questions. Gonzales was there about a half hour. He was getting ready to leave when Katherine Harris left the room and came back with a prescription drug bottle.

"What about this?" she asked.

"What's that?" Gonzales asked.

Katherine Harris said it was Luvox. Gonzales had never heard of it before. He asked if it was like Ritalin or Prozac, which he classified as mood-altering drugs and therefore a disqualifying factor for the Marines. She said it was.

"We got a problem," Gonzales said, and explained to them that recruits cannot be on any prescription drug, even penicillin. For more serious drugs such as Ritalin, recruits had to be off the drug for a year.

"After a year," Gonzales told Eric, "give us a call if you're still interested."

Gonzales isn't convinced that Katherine Harris tried to sabotage Eric's recruitment because she didn't want him in the Marines; she was supportive of the college opportunities the Marines offered.

"I just told them that was it, thanked them for their time," Gonzales said. Eric looked "disappointed, but not devastated."

The Harrises said nothing further, but "were disappointed as well." Gonzales himself was also let down.

If the meeting had gone well, the plan was for Eric to do some more screening then sign up on Saturday the 17th, take a physical exam, and be sworn in at the federal courthouse in downtown Denver (where the Columbine lawsuits would later be heard). Instead, Gonzales went to his car and called his boss on the cell phone. Eric Harris wasn't going to be a player, he said.

★★★

Eric Harris also made a call Thursday night to Mark Manes. Eric was now old enough to buy his own ammo, but asked Manes to get him some 9mm ammunition. Manes said OK, but then forgot to do it.

On Friday April 16 Eric talked at school about being rejected by the Marines. "He seemed disappointed, even though he talked like he was blowing it off," according to Brooks Brown.

"Dylan and I were the first ones Eric told about the rejection," Nate Dykeman told *The National Enquirer*. "He asked me, 'Where do I go from there?' He saw it as a last option." In a dead end sort of way at least one thing was looking up: Eric received a promotion that day at Blackjack to shift manager. But none of it really mattered.

As the shooting started at Columbine, Gonzales was on his way to the school to pick up transcripts on another student. Then he remembered he had an 11:30 a.m. appointment in the nearby suburb of Lakewood, and flipped a U-turn. He later saw Eric Harris' house on television. He was shocked. "It was weird," he adds. After authorities released Eric's name, Gonzales called his boss and said he had interviewed Eric the week before. He was told not to speak with anyone, but word got out and the Lakewood recruiting office was so mobbed with reporters that Gonzales had to go out the back door. That lasted about a month.

★★★

The Klebolds knew Dylan played *Doom* — lots of it. And Tom Klebold was concerned about the violent films Dylan watched — *Matrix, James Bond, Lethal Weapon* — but figured that's what kids do.

Tom Klebold also thought he and Dylan had similar personalities, and Dylan was his best friend. Although Dylan sometimes gave one-word answers, they talked a lot, and he seemed like a typical teen. Tom and Dylan would play chess and work together on Dylan's BMW, like building speakers for it. (Dylan didn't like helping repair the rental properties.) The Klebolds split season tickets to the Colorado Rockies baseball team with four families, and Tom usually attended with Byron or Dylan. About three years before Columbine Tom and Dylan had to stop playing sports together when Tom got rheumatoid arthritis.

The Klebolds were OK with Dylan's friends, who they described as quiet, intelligent, nice, polite, and "maybe shy." They were definitely not the most popular kids in school, the Klebolds thought, but they seemed happy and healthy, like laid back kids without social pressures. Some were members of a fantasy baseball league Dylan joined, which had its own Web site. Or the friends would watch movies. Dylan had a sleepover at least once a month at a friend's house, including Eric's.

The Klebolds thought Eric was "quieter" and respectful, but didn't hang out much at their house. Eric would get mad at Dylan if he "screwed something up" yet the Klebolds did not see a leader amongst the two. While Eric and Brooks had their falling out, Dylan didn't seem to hold a grudge against Brooks. When Brooks had a band in elementary school Dylan played drums, and in the year before Columbine, the two discussed writing a play.

In the months before Columbine Dylan himself would say he was still in love, and still depressed. He filled his diary with huge hearts, wrote that he had stopped masturbating, and still hinted at the shootings: "I hate this non-thinking statis. I'm stuck in humanity. Maybe going 'NBK' w. Eric is the way to break free. I hate this."

***

Dylan was also applying to college. According to information obtained through the Arizona Public Records law and never before released, the University of Arizona at Tucson received Dylan's college application on January 15, 1999.

Dylan's college essay is a classic example of his, and Eric's, mindset: Still dorks. But able to fool people into thinking they were normal while angry enough to keep fueling their plot. Dylan does not flaunt his goofy sense of humor, nor any of his creativity in the essay. He plays it safe, and comes across as a boring flat-liner but alludes to some problems.

Dylan filled out the boilerplate sections by listing his father on the line for parent, and said no other relative had ever attended the school. He intended to enroll in the fall in the College of Engineering and Mines to major in computer engineering. His 2.74 G.P.A. ranked him 229 in a class of 463 in the middle of his senior year. He had taken the SAT in June 1998, scoring 560 in verbal, and 650 in math for a total of 1210.

The application included a single, brief recommendation from his high school counselor, Brad Butts, written in December 1998: "Dylan has great potential in the computer science and technology field. He is very bright and I believe is beginning to mature in his attitude toward school and his future. His grades show an inconsistent pattern of performance, but he has continued to take challenging courses. His current grades are Video Production – A, Government – B, AP Calculus – C, Composition for College Bound – C, PE – D. Please feel free to call if you have questions."

The essay:

Dear University of Arizona:

I would like to take this time to introduce myself to you. I have been at Columbine High School (Littleton, CO) for three and one-half years (originating from Ken Caryl Middle School). During this time, I have become acquainted with most of the staff, as well as the student body. I have participated in many extra-curricular activities, and have worked in and out of classes towards preparing myself for my future. During my freshman year, I performed above average, receiving grades that reflected my perseverance. However, during my sophomore and junior years, I had trouble keeping a high G.P.A. This was partially a result of my hanging out with the wrong crowd; not caring about my future. It took me a long time to finally realize that the decisions I was making would affect me for the rest of my life. Also, I have difficulty communicating with people, and my time management was not optimal. These are things that I am diligently working to rectify, so my grades and my people skills reflect the positive change. Through the four years, my classes have shown and will show that I have chosen relatively difficult classes, in hope [sic] to better myself and my education. For example, I had gone through French 402 by the end of my junior year, and I am also in my fourth year of math. That current class is AP Calculus. By taking difficult classes, my grades might not have been as high as possible, but I feel that I benefitted more by this, than receiving perfect grades in courses less challenging. Now, during my senior year, I am endeavoring to work harder than before, and to maintain good time-management skills, so I can achieve a better G.P.A. than in the past.

At Columbine High School, as well as during my own time, I have been a computer enthusiast. My computer experience started in Junior High, mostly by my tinkering on my home machine. Since then, I have taken three computer-related classes at Columbine. These include a structured Q-Basic class, which taught beginning knowledge of the programming language Q-Basic, Computers

A-Z, which taught the hardware and its maintenance, and also an HTML/
Web Page design class, which organized students to fabricate and maintain
the Columbine Web Page. I also did various technical tasks for staff around
the school during that time. During some of my personal time, I taught myself
beginning Visual Basic and HTML. A friend and I also got interested in server
maintenance and network administration, which led us to help maintain the
Columbine network and server. As a result of these classes, as well as personal
time spent, I have grown a passion for using, operating, and learning about
computer systems. I feel that choosing Computer Sciences and Engineering as a
major will help further my education, and my future.

Some of the major extra-curricular activities that I participated in during my
time at Columbine High School were the school plays and musicals. However,
I did not act in these, but ran the sound system for the performances. Since my
sophomore year when I started participating in these plays, I have run sound
for four plays, and have also accepted requests to run sound for various private
groups and talent shows in our school. I have also participated in stage design,
and helped co-direct one play. During the spring of this year, I and a few other
students with similar theatrical interests will attempt to produce an entirely
student-run production, done outside of the school. I have a strong interest in
sound engineering and broadcasting, and might pursue that as an alternative to
a computer-related major.

I have chosen to apply at the University of Arizona for various reasons. The
first, being that U. of A. is a highly competitive school, with a highly renounced
computer program. This is what I believe will help me further my education and
my career. I also believe I would enjoy the hot, dry climate, a drastic change from
the weather here. I feel that a large student body will add to diversify my learning
experience of college.

I truly believe that I would be a positive member of and an active leader in
the U. of A. community, and I hope that you feel the same way. Thank you for
the consideration of this application, and this letter. I look forward to hearing
from you.

Sincerely,

Dylan Bennet Klebold

Dylan also applied to the University of Colorado at Boulder. Again,
those records have never been made public. Dylan's personal essay
was the same as for Arizona, although he changed the second to last

paragraph with weak, almost odd reasons for wanting to attend the more local college:

"I have chosen to apply at the University of Colorado at Boulder for various reasons. The first being that I live in a suburb of Denver and the commute to my home is feasible. I was very impressed when I went to visit the campus. The Engineering/Science program not only sounded like what I was looking for to further my career in computers, but also has been ranked very high among colleges in the country. I was also impressed with the tour guides. They were informative, and told me a great amount about the college's history, its specialties, and the life style within. The accommodations for students at C.U. were inviting, as were the wide variety of activities and courses."

After his contrite college application, Dylan wrote an essay for creative writing class in February 1999 that was so violent the teacher flagged it with comments. It is one of Dylan's most public signs of violence.

He also used words like "pussy" and "prick," either failing to recognize, or ignoring, they were inappropriate for a class essay. The essay itself tells of a man who kills "preps" and looks a lot like Dylan. He is 6'4", left-handed, and wears a trench coat. He carries a knife, duffle, and two guns. Like the Columbine shootings, the avenger also parks his car near the scene of the showdown, and uses diversionary bombs to distract police. Dylan was still depressive, but more and more aggressive. The two killers were becoming more intertwined.

The one and one-fourth page paper was written in the form of one huge paragraph:

The town, even at 1:00 AM., was still bustling with activity as the man dressed in black walked down the empty streets. The moon was barely visible, hiding under a shield of clouds, adding a chill to the atmosphere. What was most recognized about the man was the sound of his footsteps. Behind the conversations & noises of the town, not a sound was to be heard from him, except the dark, monotonous footsteps, combined with the jingling of his belt chains striking not only the two visible guns in their holsters, but the large bowie knife, slung in anticipation of use. The wide-brimmed hat cast a pitch-black shadow of his already dimly lit face. He wore black gloves, with a type of metal spiked-band across the knuckles. A black overcoat covered most of his body, small lines of metal & half-inch spikes layering upper portions of the shoulders, arms, and back. His boots were newly polished, and didn't look like they had been used much. He carried a black duffel bag in his right hand. He apparently had parked a car nearby, &

looked ready for a small war with whoever came across his way. I have never seen anyone take this mad-max approach in the city, especially since the piggies had been called to this part of town for a series of crimes lately. Yet, in the midst of the nightlife in the center of the average-sized town, this man walked, fueled by some untold purpose, what Christians would call evil. The guns slung on his belt & belly appeared to be automatic hand guns, which were draped above rows of magazines & clips. He smoked a thin cigar, and a sweet clovesque scent eminated from his aura. He stood about six feet and four inches and was strongly built. His face was entirely in shadow, yet even though I was unable to see his expressions, I could feel his anger, cutting thru the air like a razor. He seemed to know where he was walking, and he noticed my presence, but paid no attention as he kept walking toward a popular bar. The Watering Hole. He stopped about 30 feet from the door, and waited. 'For whom?' I wondered, as I saw them step out. He must have known their habits well, as they appeared less than a minute after he stopped walking. A group of college-preps, about nine of them, stopped in their tracks. A couple of them were mildly drunk, the rest sober. They stopped, and stared. The streetlights illuminating the bar & the sidewalk showed me a clear view of their stare, full of paralysis & fear. They knew who he was, & why he was there. The second-largest spoke up 'What're you doin man.. why are you here?' The man in black said nothing, but even at my distance, I could feel his anger growing. 'You still wanted a fight huh? I meant not with weapons, I just meant a fist fight cmon put the guns away, fuckin pussy!!' said the largest prep, his voice quavering as he spoke these works of attempted courage. Other preps could be heard muttering in the backround; 'Nice trench coat dude, that's pretty cool there.' 'Dude we were jus messin around the other day chill out man' 'I didn't do anything, it was all them!!' 'cmon man you wouldn't shoot us, were in the middle of a public place' Yet the comment I remember the most was uttered from the smallest of the group, obviously a cocky, power hunger prick. 'Go ahead man! Shoot me!!! I want you to shoot me!! Heheh you wont!! Goddam pussy' It was faint at first, but grew in intensity and power as I heard the man laugh. This laugh would have made Satan cringe in Hell. For almost half a minute this laugh, spawned from the most powerful place conceivable, filled the air, and thru the entire town, the entire world. The town activity came to a stop, and all attention was now drawn to this man. One of the preps began to slowly move back. Before I could see a reaction from the preps, the man had dropped his duffel bag, and pulled out one of the pistols with his left hand. Three shots were fired. Three shots hit the largest prep in the head. The shining of the streetlights caused a visible reflection off of the droplets of blood as they flew away from the skull. The blood splatters showered the preps buddies, as they were to paralyzed to run. The next four preps were not executed so systematically, but with more rage from the man's hand cannon than a controlled duty for a soldier. The man unloaded one of the pistols across the fronts of these four innocents, their instantly lifeless bodies dropping with remarkable speed. The shots from that gun were felt just as much as they were heard. He pulled out his other pistol, and without changing a glance, without moving his death-stare from the four other victims to go, aimed the weapon out to the side, and shot about 8 rounds. These bullets mowed down what, after he was dead, I made out to be an undercover cop with his gun slung. He then emptied the clip into two more of the preps. Then, instead of reloading & finishing the task, he set down the guns, and pulled out the knife. The blade loomed huge, even in his large grip. I now noticed that one of two still alive was the smallest of the band, who had now wet his pants, and was hyperventilating in fear. The other one tried to lunge at the man, hoping that his football tackling skills would save his life. The man sidestepped, and made two lunging slashes at him. I saw a small trickle of blood cascade out of his belly and splashing onto the concrete. His head wound was almost as bad, as the shadow formed by the bar's lighting showed blood dripping off his face. The last one, the smallest one, tried to run. The man quickly reloaded, and shot him thru the lower leg. He instantly fell, and cried in pain. The man then pulled out of the duffel bag what looked to be some type of electronic device. I saw him tweak the dials, and press a button. I heard a faint, yet powerful explosion, I would have to guess about 6 miles away. Then another one occurred closer. After recalling the night many times, I finally understood that these were diversions, to attract the cops. The last prep was bawling & trying to crawl away. The man walked up behind him. I remember the sound of the impact well. The man came down with his left hand, right on the prep's head. The metal piece did its work, as I saw his hand get buried about 2 inches into the guy's skull. The man pulled his arm out, and stood, unmoving, for about a minute. The town was utterly still, except for the faint wail of police sirens. The man picked up the bag and his clips, and proceeded to walk back the way he came. I was still, as he came my way again. He stopped, and gave me a look I will never forget. If I could face an emotion of god, it would have looked like the man. I not only saw in his face, but also felt eminating from him power, complacence, closure, and godliness. The man smiled, and in that instant, thru no endeavor of my own, I understood his actions."

Teacher Judith Kelly peppered the paper with her comments. "Great details," and "well done," she said of the first few lines describing the nighttime scene. "Quite an ending," she put after the final line.

But Kelly also included this note: "I'm offended by your use of profanity. In class we had discussed the approach of using *!*! Also, I'd like to talk to you about your story before I give you a grade. You are an excellent writer/storyteller but I have some problems with this one."

Dylan replied, according to Kelly, "It's just a story." In a statement provided to police on the day of Columbine, Kelly called the untitled essay, "the most vicious story I have ever read." About two weeks later, Kelly again talked to police. She said she had spoken to Dylan's parents "at length" about the essay. "Kelly stated that they did not seem worried and made a comment about trying to understand kids today," according to the summary of her interview. Kelly added she had made a copy of the essay for Dylan's counselor, Brad Butts.

Eric, in his own way, also was telegraphing via school projects. Kelly noted that he "frequently makes machine-gun gestures and writes Marine type creative stories."

Dream analysis in Tom Johnson's psychology class was optional and anonymous. In one that Eric did he and Dylan drove up a narrow, "dirty" road to the top of a hill in Eric's Honda. Lots of others, mostly from bowling class, were also trying to get up the road. There was "lots of honking, yelling, aggressive driving," Eric recalled. They got to the top, but people who Eric didn't like were taunting him and Dylan. Fights broke out, then gunfire. Eric and Dylan needed help. In a reverse image of the actual Columbine shootings, SWAT officers rescued Eric and Dylan. SWAT were then shot at, and a "sheriff guy" in a Ford Bronco drove Eric and Dylan away to a small mountain town.

★★★

Dylan was accepted into the University of Arizona and left with his parents on Thursday, March 25 for a four-day road trip to visit the school. Tom and Sue told police they did not notice anything unusual and "that Dylan would not like to dwell on decisions and he appeared to feel comfortable with his decision of going to the University of Arizona," according to a police summary of their interview.

He had picked out a dorm room by the cafeteria, and was going to study computers. "He was looking at the girls and talking about them; it was something he had never really done before. He would nudge his dad and say, 'Ooo, she was gorgeous; did you see her?'" according to Brooks Brown's book.

Robyn Anderson thought Dylan was going to Arizona because he liked the desert; Devon Adams because it was his ticket out of Colorado. "He had the best time ever," Devon says of his visit to Arizona. He invoked his trademark humor and had pictures of himself hugging a cactus. "He was getting on with his life," Devon says. "Past high school. Past all that stuff. I mean, graduation was in what? A month?"

Sue Klebold gushed to Judy Brown about Dylan attending college. She was protective of Dylan leaving for a big campus, but he was also going to prom, and coming out of his shell. He seemed happy, and on his way.

★★★

Dylan discussed his plans to attend the University of Arizona with Peter Horvath, the dean who had disciplined him. Some kids told Horvath that going away to college also meant getting away from their parents. But not Dylan. "He was looking forward to it, you know, that it's a great opportunity for him and it was probably where he would go," Horvath said. "That he'd worked hard for that opportunity and stuff. Like any normal kid would be excited about that chance."

Although on February 20, 1999 Horvath had a different type of conversation with Eric and Dylan. They approached him in the cafeteria and told him that another student was parking too close to one of their cars and was "mouthy" with them. Horvath says Eric and Dylan were "very polite, respectful and calm about the situation." It seemed to be nothing more than "verbal sparring" but Eric and Dylan feared it might escalate to their cars being vandalized. Horvath said the conflict was not Eric and Dylan versus the jocks—the other student was not a "jock." But for Horvath, the story is more evidence that Eric and Dylan did not hold a grudge against him. Even though he had earlier suspended them, they still trusted him with their problem. Their beef was with "the system."

"The rapport we [the school] had with them and the rapport I had with Dylan was never negative. He's smart enough, he understands that you're in a position doing what you're supposed to be doing but it's not you that's doing it, it's the system that having you do what it needs to do. So he never would hold that against you," Horvath says. According to Horvath's police report, "[He] passed on the information to [the other student's] counselor, who addressed the complaint."

Then one month before Columbine a teacher suspected Dylan had been smoking pot, and Horvath had to call him in. But Dylan hadn't been smoking, Horvath concluded: He didn't have any on marijuana him, he didn't smell like marijuana, and he was acting normal.

"No way was he under the influence of marijuana," says Horvath, who notes that some teachers are more "paranoid" about these sorts of things than others.

Around the same time, Dylan's one-time fan, technology teacher Richard Long, had a problem with Dylan. Students had to pay for more than ten pages of printouts in the computer lab, and lab assistant Peggy Dodd said Dylan had broken the rule. She confronted him, and he called her a bitch. Dodd told Long, who called Dylan into his office to ask what happened.

"Well, that bitch...," Dylan started.

That was all Long needed to know. He stopped Dylan mid-sentence.

"You can't talk like that," Long said. "You're never going to be allowed on the computers again."

"Well, you know, it doesn't matter," Dylan said. "It doesn't matter.

***

Seventeen-year-old junior Susan DeWitt was with her father when she approached police shortly after the shootings and told them she knew Eric Harris. She had been at his house Saturday, three days before Columbine, on a date.

Susan was a receptionist at the Great Clips hair salon in the same strip mall as Blackjack, and had known Eric for three months – since January. She often shuttled in and out of the pizza joint to pick up orders for people at Great Clips, and he seemed nice.

Eric eventually figured out Susan's name, and began asking her friends if she liked him. A couple times, he went to Great Clips to ask for her.

The Friday before Columbine, Susan was in Blackjack to pick up an order, and gave Eric her number. He said he would call after she got off work: Her shift ended at 9 p.m. Eric later called her house but got Susan's mom. She thought Eric seemed nice, until she told him that Susan wasn't there. Eric seemed somewhat angry, but mom gave Eric Susan's pager anyway.

Eric paged her with the line to his bedroom, and they talked for about a half hour. Susan said she was at a friend's house. Eric talked about computers and how he stopped hanging out with certain friends after hearing they were talking about him and making fun of him. But he didn't seem mad. They made plans for Saturday.

Turns out Susan wasn't the only Great Clips employee Eric pursued. Tanya Worlock, who also attended Columbine, told police Eric asked her out about ten times, but she always said no because she had a boyfriend. "She didn't believe Eric was a psycho about asking her out, but he was persistent," according to her interview with police. "He was very nice and courteous when he'd ask but he didn't take no for an answer." Worlock said Eric also asked out another Great Clips employee.

That Friday night, Eric slept at Dylan's. Tom and Sue told police they had not seen Eric at their house for six months, but they recalled him bringing over a stuffed, black nylon duffle bag he had to carry with both hands. Tom assumed it was a computer. Eric left the next morning without the bag. Tom said he never saw it again, nor did he look for it.

Saturday, April 17 was prom. Various friends say Eric was turned down by a few prospective dates, and that they tried to play matchmaker, but to no avail. Eric ended up spending part of prom night at home with Susan DeWitt. He was supposed to call her in the early afternoon, but finally rang around 6:30 p.m. She agreed to go over to his house and watch a movie. She lived only about five minutes away, and got to Eric's house about 7:00 p.m. His parents had just gone out to dinner for their 29th wedding anniversary. Eric's black trench coat was lying on the stairs.

They watched *Event Horizon*, the same science fiction movie that Wayne Harris had to retrieve from the sheriff's office after Eric was arrested for the van break-in. They watched the movie straight through in the basement. The movie ended about 9:30 p.m. and Eric let his dog out, and back in. They made small talk, and Eric repeated his anger at a former friend who had betrayed him. He called him a jerk, but didn't make any threats. He seemed more hurt than angry.

Eric's parents got back around 10:00 p.m. and Susan talked with them for about five minutes. They seemed nice, and Wayne Harris said he got his hair cut at the Great Clips where Susan worked. The parents went upstairs, and Eric asked if Susan wanted to listen to music. They went into his bedroom, downstairs in the basement.

It was just about Eric's last chance to get some before Columbine.

Susan recalled a poster of the blond, one-time MTV host Jenny McCarthy, and other band posters. Ticket stubs from concerts and movies were stapled around the window. Eric had CDs he had made on his computer, and soccer jerseys hanging up. They listened to soft tunes, although Eric favored more head-banging stuff. Susan didn't notice anything suspicious. Eric didn't talk about jocks, politics, or blacks. Around 10:30 p.m., Susan's sister paged her to "get home." She stuck around for about thirty more minutes and at one point, Eric put his arm around her. When she left, he kissed her on the cheek as a way of saying goodbye.

The next day, Wayne Harris came into Great Clips. He said hello, calling Susan by name, and seemed happy. Susan thought Eric got along well with his parents.

***

About two weeks before senior prom, Robyn Anderson asked Dylan to go with her. He asked her the exact date. She told him, Saturday April 17, and he seemed lost in concentration, wrapping his mind around that day. Then he said yes.

Robyn was on a church trip in Washington D.C. for the week before prom and got back in town the afternoon of the dance. When she called Dylan he was on the computer, but they made plans. She would pick him up at his house so Tom and Sue Klebold could take photos. When she got there, the parents talked about future plans for school, and videotaped her and Dylan. Dylan wore a tux, Robyn a blue dress.

Robyn then took Dylan to her friend Kelli Brown's house to catch their limo. The prom group included about a ten others, including Dylan's buddy, Nate Dykeman. They went to dinner at Bella Ristorante in Denver, where Dylan had a large salad, a seafood dinner, and dessert. When Dylan wanted to have a smoke, he went outside with Nate and they talked about the recent Arizona trip. Dinner ended around 9:30 p.m.

Throughout the night, Dylan acted normal and seemed to be in a good mood. At prom he danced with Devon Adams and made plans to see *The Matrix* on Wednesday, April 21st, which still perplexes her. "It could mean that they had planned [the shootings] and didn't have a set date or something like that, you know," she says. "It could mean anything. But it seems 'cause Dylan never ever wanted to disappoint me. That was why he came to my birthday and confirmation party, even though he didn't want to. I mean, he didn't like disappointing people. Like every time he and his parents would get in a fight, he felt so bad because he had disappointed his parents. He always felt bad because he had disappointed them in some way to make them angry at him. And I mean, that's what's like so weird about him making a date with me on a Wednesday when, if he knew that Tuesday, you know, this was going to happen."

Jessica Hughes, who was among those sharing the prom limo with Dylan, talked with him about a reunion party a couple weeks away for their elementary school gifted program. Dylan was going to bring pizza because he worked at Blackjack.

The prom dance was at the Denver Design Center, and ended around midnight. Robyn and Dylan then took the limo back to Kelli's and changed clothes. Robyn drove herself and Dylan to the after-prom at Columbine where Eric, wearing a blue flannel shirt, met them.

Monica Schuster, who was with the prom group, said Eric seemed normal at the after-prom. She spent time with him, "just goofing around going to the various sites and playing the various games." Robyn says Eric, Dylan, and their buddy Chris Morris gambled at the casino.

Robyn left the after-prom with Dylan at about 3:00 a.m. and drove them back to Kelli's house, where Dylan had left his tuxedo. She got Dylan home at 3:45 a.m. Sue Klebold was up, and asked Dylan how prom went. He flashed her a flask of schnapps, but said he only drank a little. The rest of the group was going to breakfast, he said, but he just wanted to go to bed.

The Klebolds usually reserved Sundays for family dinners. But when she spoke with police ten days after Columbine, Sue Klebold could not recall whether they followed through the Sunday before the shootings.

★★★

The diary entry is undated, but if all was going according to plan, Dylan wrote at around 9 a.m. Monday:

"One day, one is the beginning? the end. hahaha. reversed, yet true. About 26.5 hours from now, the judgment will begin. Difficult but not impossible. necessary, nervewracking & fun. <u>What fun is life without a little death</u>? It's interesting, when 'm in my human form, knowing I'm going to die. Everything has a touch of triviality to it. Like how none of this calculus shit matters the way it shouldn't. the truth. In 26.4 hours i'll be dead, & in happiness... Little zombie human fags will know their errors & be forever suffering and mournful, HAHAHA, of course i will miss things. not really."

On the next page, Dylan scrawled "WILL," and wrote, "OK, this is my will. This is a fucking human thing to do, but whatever. [name deleted] – You were a badass, never failed to get me up when i was down. Thx. You get..." The next word is unintelligible. That's it.

That same day Eric and Dylan went to 6:30 a.m. bowling class at the Belleview Bowling Lanes. Dustin Gorton, who was in the class, remembers Eric shooting a pellet gun at a wall outside the alley. At 7:15 a.m. Eric and Dylan went with Nate Dykeman and others to a nearby King Soopers supermarket. Eric and Nate then had video class together; Eric kept falling asleep, and the teacher told him to go to the nurse's office.

That Monday was the last time Robyn Anderson saw Dylan. They had second period calculus together in the morning and he was quiet, but that wasn't unusual; he would sleep until noon or 1:00 p.m. on the weekends if he could.

Various classmates have recollections of what Eric and Dylan did next that Monday. Dustin Gorton and Eric Jackson say that around 9:50 a.m. they went to a nearby Burger King drive-thru as part of a film as Gorton drove his 1972 Chevrolet Chevelle with Dylan in the front and Eric in the back. They bought food, drove back to school, ate breakfast in the parking lot, then went to the school's video production room.

Nate Dykeman had fourth period creative writing with Eric and Dylan at around 10 a.m. Dykeman says the teacher didn't arrive on time, so Eric and Dylan ditched. Then Susan DeWitt says she saw Eric, and they spoke for five minutes. He seemed anxious and irritated.

Brooks Brown says that by the time of Columbine, he had reconciled with Eric. They had a couple classes together that final semester, and Brooks figured it was time to "bury the hatchet." Brooks also felt bad for Dylan, who was caught in the middle of the feud.

"We were both immature," Brooks said to Eric. "I just want to move on. He [Eric] shrugged and said, 'Cool.'"

So the day before Columbine, Brooks says he invited Eric and Dylan to skip fourth period and go to McDonald's for lunch. They said OK, but first had to stop at Eric's house. Around 2:30 p.m., friend Nicole Markham saw Eric and Dylan in the student parking lot. She thought it was strange because it was after school, and she never knew them to stay after school for anything.

At one point in the day, Columbine student Andrew Beard told police he talked to Dylan on the phone about their fantasy baseball league. Beard was trying to trade some players with Dylan. "I'll think about it and let you know tomorrow," said Dylan, who did not seem troubled.

The night before Columbine, Dylan told his parents he was going to Outback Steakhouse with Eric and some friends. He said it was Eric's favorite restaurant, and Eric had coupons. Dylan left around 6:00 p.m. When he got back, his mom asked him if he had a good time. He said he did. He had steak.

But Nate Dykeman says he knew of no dinner at Outback on Thursday. What is clear is that Eric met with gun supplier Mark Manes that night.

Eric still wanted Manes to get him some ammunition and called him around 8:00 p.m. Manes felt bad and quickly went to Kmart. On his way back Manes called Eric and told him to come over to his house. Manes, tall and thin, wore his long brown hair in a ponytail. That night, he waited in his driveway as Eric pulled up and gave him $25 for two boxes of 9mm cartridges - 100 rounds.

Eric had been all but officially rejected, but talked to Manes about the Marines.

"It's the last option I have," Eric said.

Manes asked Eric if he was going target shooting that night.

"Maybe tomorrow," Eric replied.

Eric recorded his thoughts on a tape labeled "Nixon," which has only been excerpted by the sheriff. "It will happen in less than nine hours now," he said. "People will die because of me It will be a day that will be remembered forever." (It is unclear why the tape is labeled Nixon, but it may not be connected to the shamed president. Eric once wrote about a friend named Nixon, and he may have simply recorded over an old tape.)

Zach Heckler figured he talked on the phone every night with Dylan. They would discuss school, and the computer death match game "Quake."("Arm yourself against the cannibalistic Ogre, fiendish Vore and indestructible Schambler using lethal nails, fierce Thunderbolts and abominable Rocket and Grenade Launchers," reads the description.) But when Zach called Monday night, Dylan said he was on the phone with someone else. He told Zach to call back. Zach tried again at 10:30 p.m. Dylan said he was tired and going to sleep. That was odd, Zach thought. Dylan didn't usually go to bed until 12:30 a.m. or 1:00 a.m.

***

Eric and Dylan never articulated why they chose April 20th. On the basement tapes they say at one point, "Today is the 11th, eight more days," and indicate the shooting will come on a Monday. But they do not note that the 19th is the anniversary of the 1993 Waco siege, or the 1995 Oklahoma City bombing. If they were set on the 19th, they may have missed that deadline and had to wait an extra day simply because Manes forgot to buy the ammunition.

The 20th has its own logic as the 110th anniversary of Hitler's birthday given Eric's obsession with the Nazis, but that connection is never stated. In a December 20, 1998 diary entry Eric noted that the album "Adios" by one of his favorite bands, KMFDM, was coming out "in April," although he already seems settled on a date. Still Eric wrote, "How fuckin' appropriate, a subliminal final 'Adios' tribute to Reb and Vodka. Thanks KMFDM... I ripped the hell outa the system." The album was released on April 20, 1999.

But Eric and Dylan had April 1999 in their sights for at least a year. What makes sense is that they saw the month as the appropriate time for their own send off. This would be their graduation ceremony. And an ending they would control.   They approached it with military precision. They made figure drawings to show how guns, ammo and napalm tanks (never used) would fit on their bodies. A spreadsheet shows they produced dozens of cricket bombs on various days, and that the quality ranged from "OK" to "excellent." Tests on thirteen batches of napalm showed that one was "worthless," another was "shitty but in a fix would do OK," and one was "good burning. very slick." Budget figures ranged from $20 for gas to $200 for explosives. But Eric's list indicated he still needed to get laid.

In Dylan's car police found an undated list titled "DO SHIT FOR NBK": "fire off clip, buy suspenders, buy cargo pants, work out carrying gear plan, find out how to carry TEC-9, get pouches, get napalm containers, buy straps, figure out how to carry knife, get bullets, get shells, give Reb powder, buy adidas soccer bag(s), give Reb glass containers, fill up gas cans, find volatile combo of gas and oil, look for voltage amplifier, buy 'wrath' t-shirt, buy punk gloves."

A schedule for the day of Columbine indicated they would get up around 5 a.m. and meet at "KS" (probably King Soopers market) at 6 a.m. They would get gas, propane, and carry out other last minute preparations. They had plotted the ebb and flow of the cafeteria lunch crowd to maximize their killings:

10:30 a.m. to 10:50 a.m.: 60-80 people scattered
10:56 a.m.: lunch ladies bring out shit
11:08 a.m.: up to 220 people
11:15 a.m.: 500+

They also plotted their mindset. 11:16 a.m.: HAHAHA

***

On the 20th Eric and Dylan filmed themselves in the family room on the main level at Eric's house for the final segment of the basement tapes. It was just before 11:00 a.m.

"Say it now," Eric says.

"Hey mom, gotta go," Dylan says. "It's about half an hour before our little judgment day. I just wanted to apologize to you guys for any crap this might instigate as far as (inaudible) or something. Just know I'm going to a better place. I didn't like life too much and I know I'll be happier wherever the fuck I go. So I'm gone. Goodbye."

"I just wanted to apologize to you guys for any crap," Eric says. "To everyone I love, I'm really sorry about this. I know my Mom and Dad will be just like just fucking shocked beyond belief. I'm sorry alright. I can't help it."

"It's what we had to do," Klebold interjects.

"Morris, Nate," Harris says, apparently referring to Chris Morris and Nate Dykeman, "if you guys live I want you guys to have whatever you want from my room and the computer room."

Klebold says they can also have his possessions.

Harris wills a CD, *Bombthreat Before She Blows* (by the band Fly) to a girl. "Susan, sorry," he says, possibly referring to Susan DeWitt. "Under different circumstances it would've been a lot different."

"That's it," Harris says. "Sorry. Goodbye."

Klebold sticks his face in front of the camera: "Goodbye."

Heartbreak

2 student gunmen terrorize Columbine High in deadliest school shooting in U.S. history. 2A

George Kochaniec Jr./News Staff Photographer

Columbine students are overwhelmed by emotion during Tuesday's rampage. As many as 25 people, including the gunmen, were killed, and 21 were wounded.

GEORGE KOCHANIEC JR.

This photo and headline ran together the first day after the shootings, and they have come to symbolize Columbine. *Rocky* editor John Temple explained it this way: "Our approach to Columbine started on the first day. Our headline, 'Heartbreak,' tried to convey that we are part of this community, that we are neighbors, that we care."

Unidentified students outside Columbine High the day of the shootings. This is among the work that earned the *Rocky Mountain News* the 1999 Pulitzer Prize for breaking news photography. The *Rocky* donated its $5,000 prize to the HOPE committee, a group of families of Columbine victims raising money to build a new library at the school.

RODOLFO GONZALEZ

Students from Columbine High and other schools in prayer and song a day after the shootings.

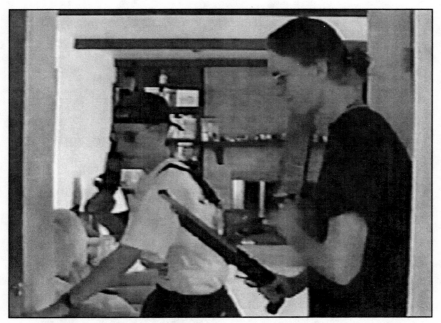

A "frame grab" of Eric Harris, left, and Dylan Klebold, right, in one of their homemade videos titled "Radioactive Clothing." The short, mostly goofy skit followed Eric and Dylan as they investigated contaminated clothing. The guns are probably fake, but this image of them is not far off from what they looked like the day of the shootings.

A rare glimpse of a killer's parents: Wayne and Katherine Harris at the federal courthouse in Denver for depositions in 2003.

Tom Klebold leaving the federal courthouse in downtown Denver in 2003 for depositions in Columbine lawsuits. "I've had better days," he told the *Rocky Mountain News*.

Sue Klebold, also leaving the federal courthouse as part of Columbine depositions in 2003. It appears to be the first time victims families were able to see the killers' parents.

President Clinton, who was in office at the time of Columbine, at the groundbreaking for the Columbine Memorial on June 16, 2006. At the groundbreaking, Clinton pledged $50,000 to help build the memorial.

Doves released at the dedication of the Columbine Memorial on September 21, 2007—thirteen at first, then some 200 more.

Randy and Judy Brown filed numerous complaints regarding Eric Harris and Dylan Klebold with the Jefferson County Sheriff's Office for more than two years before Columbine. After Columbine they were among the fiercest critics of how sheriff's deputies investigated those complaints, and the actual shootings.

MATT MCCLAIN

On the eight-year anniversary of Columbine the father of slain student Isaiah Shoels visited the campus of Virginia Tech in Blacksburg, Virginia. Four days earlier, a gunman had killed thirty-two before killing himself. The stones and flowers arrayed behind Michael Shoels represent the dead, including the gunman.

There was no script to follow as Michael Shoels steps forward and places a flower on a memorial after the noontime moment of silence for the Virginia Tech victims on April 20, 2007

TRAGEDY AT COLUMBINE

DAY OF REMEMBRANCE

CASSIE BERNALL

STEVEN CURNOW

COREY DePOOTER

KELLY FLEMING

MATTHEW KECHTER

DANIEL MAUSER

DAN ROHRBOUGH

DAVE SANDERS

RACHEL SCOTT

ISAIAH SHOELS

HOSPITALIZED
RICHARD CASTALDO
SEAN GRAVES
ANNE MARIE HOCHHALTER
PATRICK IRELAND
LANCE KIRKLIN
LISA KREUTZ
JEANNA PARK
KASEY RUEGSEGGER
VALEEN SCHNURR
MARK TAYLOR
UNNAMED BOY, 15

JOHN TOMLIN

LAUREN TOWNSEND

KYLE VELASQUEZ

STORIES OF THE 13 SLAIN. PAGE 11AA

TREATED AND RELEASED
BRIAN ANDERSON
JENNIFER DOYLE
STEPHEN AUSTIN EUBANKS
NICK FOSS
MAKAI HALL
JOYCE JANKOWSKI
MARK KINTGEN
ADAM KYLER
STEPHANIE MUNSON
PATRICIA NIELSON
NICOLE NOWLEN
DAN STEEPLETON

32-PAGE SPECIAL SECTION

The Sunday front page of the *Rocky Mountain News,* five days after the Columbine shootings.

PART TWO: RECOIL

TWELVE

Violent Profiles

Psychopaths run the gamut, according to various interpretations, from serial killer Ted Bundy to murderous psychiatrist Hannibal Lecter in the movie *Silence of the Lambs*.

Intellectually, psychopaths have an icy sense of superiority: They are arrogant, excessively opinionated, self-assured, cocky, charming, and glib.

That is coupled with a mean hot streak: They are impulsive, irritable, and aggressive. Also called antisocial personality disorder, psychopaths may repeatedly steal, destroy property, harass others, or pursue illegal occupations, according to the *Diagnostic and Statistical Manual*, the Bible of mental health diagnoses.

Psychopaths may act that way to avoid being pushed around. They may also say their victims deserved it because they're foolish, or a loser. Or because life is unfair.

Psychopaths move through life with reckless abandon. Yet they are not necessarily violent. The death they leave behind may come in pursuit of other goals. What stands out is their manipulation. The psychopath may be the confidence man in a sharp suit who extracts someone's trust and then empties their bank account. They have no care for the feelings of others. That intellectual underpinning, a lack of conscience, may be scarier than the violence they sometimes embody.

Eric Harris, say some experts, was a psychopath. He remained calm on the surface, and told people what they wanted to hear. He got through his diversion program with flying colors by seeming motivated and apologetic, writing a perfectly contrite letter to the owner of the van he broke into. In school, he wrote an "I feel sorry for myself" essay about how he learned a lesson from the break-in. He looked Judy Brown in the eye and told her he was sorry for flipping out over his backpack after the cracked windshield. It was all fakery (although Judy Brown was the one person who appears to have called him on it). He didn't care. But he did keep plotting a school shooting.

Dwayne Fuselier, a psychologist who was the FBI's lead Columbine investigator, is among those who believes Eric acted like a psychopath. He says that when psychopaths do become violent, it is extreme. "Eric Harris wanted to hurt people," he adds. "It made no difference who it was."

Psychopaths are not crazy or "psycho," as everyday usage may imply, but rational, calculating, and aware of their actions. They cannot plead insanity when faced with their crimes. When a schizophrenic says they killed someone because they were under orders from a Martian, for example, "we deem that person not responsible 'by reason of insanity,'" psychologist Robert Hare writes in his book about psychopaths, *Without Conscience*. "When a person diagnosed as a psychopath breaks the same rules, he or she is judged sane and is sent to prison."

Hare adds: "Still, a common response to reports of brutal crimes, particularly serial torture and killing, is: 'Anyone would have to be crazy to do that.' Perhaps so, but not always in the legal or the psychiatric sense of the term."

Treatment programs, such as diversion, don't work because psychopaths don't want to be cured. "Psychopaths don't feel they have psychological or emotional problems, and they see no reason to change their behavior to conform to societal standards with which they do not agree," Hare writes.

In therapy, psychopaths learn to manipulate the sessions and say the right things: "I was an abused child," or "I never learned to get in touch with my feelings," Hare writes.

Aubrey Immelman, a professor of psychology at the College of Saint Benedict/Saint John's University in Minnesota, comes from outside the ranks of law enforcement. He specializes in political psychology and criminal profiling, and has thoroughly reviewed the files on the Columbine killers. He generally agrees with the premise that Eric was a psychopath.

Immelman adds that psychopaths try to reroute the blame and Eric shows that when he tries to put the onus on Dylan for the van break-in. Or when his apology letter doesn't take full responsibility for the van break-in. "I let the stupid side of me take over," Eric writes. Immelman adds, "[Psychopaths] will blame their infirm grandmother for their vandalism if they have to."

Diversion may have even inflamed Eric and Dylan, another sign of psychopathy. "Here's a hypothesis for you," says Immelman. "Had they not been put on diversion, Columbine wouldn't have happened." That theory goes especially for Eric. "The thing he hates most is people telling him what to do," Immelman says. "He must have built up so much anger going through the anger training and having to deal with law enforcement, having to give the urinalysis."

★★★

To be sure, Eric's diagnosis of psychopathy is not 100 percent. Psychopaths do not tend to be suicidal, or seek fame. They usually come from the ranks of "low socioeconomic status and urban settings," according to the DSM. Psychopaths must also show certain patterns of behavior as juveniles that include animal abuse. Eric, in all his writings, never mentions that, nor is there any evidence of such behavior. His extreme violence is not a trademark of psychopaths. And Eric does show emotion and feeling: He laments the loss of his childhood friends, he wishes he had more friends at Columbine, and he worries what will happen to his parents after the shootings. (Although Fuselier points out that if Eric really did care about his parents, he wouldn't have undertaken the shootings.)

Their pell-mell behavior makes psychopaths poor employees, yet Eric was a model worker. Lying for the sake of lying, or duper's delight, is another sign of psychopathy, and Eric told multiple lies. Although he himself also indicates he lies for a specific purpose, or as he says in his diary, "just to keep my own ass out of water." In other words, Eric needs to lie to stay out of trouble. It doesn't appear to be for fun.

★★★

Immelman's more specific diagnosis of Eric as a "malevolent psychopath" may reconcile some of these differences. The term psychopath would not seem to need a qualifier terming it malevolent, or "especially vindictive and hostile." But that could explain Harris' uncharacteristic–for a psychopath–violence. Such psychopaths have a "cold-blooded ruthlessness, an intense desire to gain revenge for the real or imagined mistreatment to which they were subjected in childhood," according to psychologist Theodore Millon. They do not want to be seen as weak, have a "chip on the shoulder attitude," and "rigidly maintain an image of hard-boiled strength."

Immelman also believes Eric had streaks of narcissism and sadism; the sadism because he didn't just kill but teased, taunted and tormented his victims at Columbine. Before the shootings, he wrote of killing Brooks Brown but also torturing and urinating on him. Immelman contrasts that with the actions of the Washington D.C. area snipers, who stealthily killed ten during a 2002 shooting spree. "You hide, you try to get a clean kill," Immelman says of the snipers. "You don't want to make the person suffer, you're just interested in the effect that you're going to have on the public, on the community. Over here [at Columbine] they wanted their victims to suffer personally. For sadists, it's always the humiliation, and the dominance." Immelman also points to the sadism in Eric's sort of rape fantasy in his November 17, 1998 diary entry:

who can I trick into my room first? I can sweep someone off their feet, tell them what they want to hear, be all nice and sweet, and then 'fuck em like an animal, feel them from the inside' as [Nine Inch Nails lead singer Trent] Reznor said. ...I want to tear a throat out with my own teeth like a pop can. I want to gut someone with my hand, to tear a head off and rip out the heart and lungs from the neck, to stab someone in the gut, shove it up to the heart, and yank the fucking blade out of their rib cage! I want to grab some weak little freshman and just tear them apart like a fucking wolf. show them who is god. strangle them, squish their head, bite their temples into the skull, rip off their jaw. Rip off their colar bones, break their arms in half and twist them around, the lovely sounds of bones cracking and flesh ripping, ahh so much to do and so little chances.

As for the narcissism, psychopaths do not typically seek the limelight. "They want credit for their crime," Immelman says, but adds, "Psychopaths aren't interested in making it into the history books. Psychopaths want to take for themselves what they believe the world owes them."

Eric, however, does want to go down in history. He writes in his journal, "Don't blame anyone else besides me and V for this."

And Eric wants power. But grandiose schemes often bring down narcissists. "Which is often why they are self-destructive, because they bite off more than they can chew," Immelman says. "With Hitler, really to take over the whole world, to create a master race, things that really cannot be done in the real world. Sometimes it's just referred to as megalomania."

★★★

Eric also told us why he did it, but I would argue he seems to give two different reasons in two different places. In the Web writings, Eric's violence is often propelled by a sense of superiority over the dumb, the ignorant, and those who cannot play *Doom*. The Web writings, it could be expected, were also more targeted for public consumption.

But the diary entries tell another story. And because they were not necessarily meant to be public, they may be seen as more truthful. In two of the most telling views into Eric's mind, he is Dylan Klebold: A sad, lonely, depressive. If Eric truly felt superior, it came from a sense of inferiority:

In late 1998 Eric writes:

Everyone is always making fun of me because of how I look, how fucking weak I am and shit, well I will get you all back: ultimate fucking revenge here. you people could have shown more respect, treated me better, asked for knowledge or guidence more, treated me more like senior and maybe I wouldn't have been as ready to tear your fucking heads off. Then again, I have always hated how I looked, I make fun of people who look like me, sometimes without even thinking sometimes just because I want to rip on myself. Thats where a lot of my hate grows from. The fact that I have practically no selfesteem, especially concerning girls and looks and such. therefore people make fun of me .. constantly..therefore I get no respect and therefore I get fucking PISSED as of this date I have enough explosives to kill about 100 people, and then if I get a couple of bayonets, swords, (illegible), whatever I'll be able to kill at least 10 more and that just isnt enough! GUNS! I need guns! Give me some fucking firearms!

This diary entry apparently comes in April 1999 (the first Friday of the last month, Eric indicates):

Why the fuck can't I get any? I mean, I'm nice and considerate and all that shit, but nooooo. I think I try to hard, but I kinda need to considering NBK is closing in. The amount of dramatic irony and foreshadowing is fucking amazing. Everything I see and hear, I incorporate into NBK somehow. Either bombs, clocks, guns, napalm, killing people, any and everything finds some tie to it. Feels like a Goddamn movie sometimes. I wanna try to put some mines and trip bombs around this town too maybe. Get a few extra frags on the scoreboard. I hate you people for leaving me out of so many fun things. And no, don't fucking say, 'Well that's your fault' because it isn't, you people had my phone#, and I asked and all, but no no no no don't let the weird looking Eric KID come along, ooh fucking nooo.

For Fuselier, the passages still support the psychopath diagnosis because "Both seem to serve the purpose for Eric to shift the responsibility for his actions to others. E.g., Since I get no respect from you guys, I don't have any self esteem, and therefore get pissed, and so it is your fault if I want to kill you."

Immelman says the passages are consistent with Eric's narcissism and quotes the DSM: "Vulnerability in self-esteem makes individuals with

Narcissistic Personality Disorder very sensitive to 'injury' from criticism or defeat. Although they may not show it outwardly, criticism may haunt these individuals and may leave them feeling humiliated, degraded, hollow, and empty. They may react with disdain, rage, or defiant counterattack. Such experiences often lead to social withdrawal or an appearance of humility that may mask and protect the grandiosity."

★★★

In *Without Conscience* Hare reviews a number of possible causes behind psychopathy. He concludes it is "a complex – and poorly understood – interplay between biological factors and social forces." Hare adds, "This doesn't mean that psychopaths are destined to develop along a fixed track, born to play a socially deviant role in life. But it does mean that their biological endowment... provides a poor basis for socialization and conscience formation."

Eric's extreme violence makes his psychopathy appear inherent, and predestined. Yet the environmental firing pins that set him off - Columbine, maybe diversion - are easier to identify.

★★★

Eric's violence is more eye-catching. But he's the outlier. When it comes to other school shooters, they look more like Dylan Klebold. And while it is said that Eric was the deceiver-in-chief, Dylan was the one who fooled everyone. From the first minutes of Columbine, and through the many years of revelations, people express little surprise it was Eric. Dylan is the one who confounds people. Yet he is the type to watch for.

★★★

Dylan's writings sum up his diagnosis: depressed. As Fuselier puts it, he showed, "fairly dramatic emotional swings, e.g., from 'I've found my soulmate, and the love of my life, to (paraphrasing now) 'she doesn't know who I am, therefore my life is worthless, so I'll kill myself.'" Immelman sees the same depression in Dylan: sensitive to humiliation, dying a thousand deaths each day. Immelman also calls Dylan "avoidant personality disorder," or basically shy. He wants to be part of the group, but cannot.

For Immelman, a secondary characteristic of Dylan is passive-aggressive personality disorder, or what is technically termed "negativistic." Such persons show a negative attitude and "passive resistance" to work and social demands, according to the DSM. They procrastinate and forget to do things. They may be "sullen, irritable, impatient, argumentative, cynical, skeptical and contrary" and feel "cheated, unappreciated, and misunderstood and chronically complain to others." They especially hate authority figures, and anyone who the authorities favor (in Dylan's case, quite possibly the jocks). When authorities tell a negativist what to do, they become stubborn, and inefficient. They blame their failures on others, or will apologize and promise "to perform better in the future," according to the DSM.

For Immelman, Dylan shows passive-aggressiveness in the diversion program with his time-management essay that uses an oversized, odd font and is bothersome to read. This is someone trying to sabotage authority. At school, he procrastinates. Dylan is suspended for scratching the locker of someone who has angered him. "Does he go and confront the student? No," says Immelman "He goes behind the student's back and he scratches his locker. That's exactly what passive aggressive is. By its very definition."

Dylan also shows passive-aggressiveness in the greeting cards he writes to friend Devon Adams. He shows affection, but also teases her (calling her a "voodoo priestess"). "It seems like when he [Dylan] helps a person, he's hurting a person," Immelman says. "In other words, he undermines or sabotages helpful acts at one level with passive-aggressive behavior on another level."

Dylan's essay of a man in a black trench coat who not only shoots jocks but first toys with them shows sadism, as does his taunting people the day of Columbine, but Immelman and Fuselier agree Eric's sadism was more pronounced. For Dylan, it was not a guiding light.

★★★

If Dylan was a depressive who wanted to kill himself, why did he kill others? Like other school shooters, his depression manifested itself as anger. He hated himself, but also others, and blamed them for his problems.

Fuselier says Eric portrayed a mass shooting as a solution to Dylan's depression: "It's 'their' fault, they are the 'zombies,' 'we' are superior to them... so let's show how superior we are...."

If Dylan had gone on to college, Fuselier believes, it is less likely he would have carried out a shooting. "If, for some reason, Harris had pulled out, I think it much less likely that Dylan would have done this alone," Fuselier adds. "If, for some reason, Dylan had pulled out, I think it more likely that Eric would have committed this act alone, or might have done something else like it."

Depression is attributed to both biological and environmental factors. And as with Eric, Dylan's biological factors are harder to pinpoint. The environmental ones are easier to see.

★★★

Depressives are more likely to commit suicide. Psychopaths are not. But suicide made sense to Eric and Dylan for any number of reasons. It was the ultimate way to control their own destiny and the only antidote to an uncontrollable rage – despite their school rampage, which lasted maybe forty-five minutes, they were still not satisfied. They may also have seen it as the warrior's way out, nobler than being captured alive.

And for Eric and Dylan, suicide was not a leap: Life on earth was already hell because smart kids like themselves were among the least popular. They expected more, but got less. Their fall down the social ladder was steeper because they had higher expectations.

Dylan wrote in his diary: "The framework of society stands above & below me. The hardest thing to destroy, yet the weakest thing that exists." Death would set him free. Eric would destroy everything, including himself.

Eric and Dylan, in part, were right. High school is unfair, just as life is unfair. Although their own shortcomings also sent them spiraling: People picked up on Eric's odd and violent vibrations and backed off, while Dylan's shyness and underdeveloped social skills doomed him from the start.

In one sense, Eric and Dylan weren't that bright either. They were positioned to be masters of the universe in the coming computer age if they could just stick it out another month until high school ended. Success in the real world could have been their revenge. But their violent, juvenile minds couldn't see ahead. They wanted immediate retaliation against the social hierarchy they felt had wronged them.

Probably virgins upon death and maybe the biggest losers at Columbine High, Eric and Dylan still had friends, but it didn't make a difference. Their buddies were on the same lowly rung of the social ladder.

And they didn't even recognize the friends they had. Mental illness warps reality: Eric was blinded by his rage, and Dylan by his depression.

Dylan was probably the smarter of the two, and appears to be the first to specifically mention the idea of Columbine. But Eric sharpened it into reality and carried the ball down the field because his energy was more focused on violence.

They both wanted the deadliest school massacre ever, and belittled shooters who only killed and maimed a few. And they did in fact ramp up the concept of the school massacre, adding bombs to the mix and reaching, for the moment, unprecedented levels of planning and death. But they were followers even in Columbine, using the script of other school shooters who showed them the art of the possible.

★★★

On December 30, 1974 Anthony Barbaro of Olean, New York brought a 12-gauge shotgun, a .30-06 rifle with a telescopic site, and homemade bombs to his high school over Christmas break. The eighteen-year-old honors student killed three: A janitor who was at the school; Neal Pilon as he walked along the street; and Carmen Wright as she drove past the school in her car. Barbaro started a small blaze in the hallway, which set off the fire alarm, and he wounded eight firemen who responded. State troopers and city police officers stormed the school under the cover of tear gas and gunfire and captured him at 5:30 p.m. Barbaro, wearing a white sweatshirt, threw his guns out one of the shattered windows and surrendered without a struggle. Or, according to the *Chicago Sun-Times*, SWAT found him asleep, with headphones playing "Jesus Christ Superstar."

Accounts vary dramatically in the *New York Times*, but according to one story, Barbaro hung himself "with a knotted bedsheet in the county jail." "I guess I just wanted to kill the person I hate most — myself," he wrote in a note. "I just didn't have the courage. I wanted to die, but I couldn't do it, so I had to get someone to do it for me. It didn't work out."

If Barbaro, Harris, Klebold and other school shooters were to pose for a class picture, their faces and backgrounds would be strikingly similar. They are typically white, middle class boys near the bottom of the social ladder who – in a characteristically passive-aggressive manner – blame other students for making them losers. Angry at the whole world, their shooting sprees are random killings.

These terrorists may have food, money, and good shelter, but not acceptance. Even the semi-popular are not immune. In Fort Collins, Colorado three junior high boys were charged in 2001 for plotting to carry out a school shooting near the two-year anniversary of Columbine. They were not the most popular in school, but were well-known and well-liked. Yet it was not enough to quell their anger toward the most popular "preppies."

School shooters commit their crimes not for drugs or money, but a generalized revenge against the social order. Some are on psychiatric drugs, although many mental health experts do not believe the drugs cause the shootings. Similarities among school shooters were plotted in a study titled "The Classroom Avenger," which examined sixteen shootings, including Columbine, and followed the shooters from cradle to grave. Some aspects match Columbine. Some don't. Sometimes, there is not enough information.

Co-authors James McGee and Caren DeBernardo found that the family appears normal, although it is in reality "often quite dysfunctional." Relations with siblings are "fractious beyond the typical parameters of sibling rivalry" (which seems to match Dylan, but not Eric.) There may be divorce, or friction between the boys - all are boys - and their parents, especially over control. "Fathers tend to be absent or minimally involved in parenting," and discipline is "overly harsh and applied inconsistently."

School shooters differ from traditional cases of juvenile delinquency because the parents do not appear to mete out physical abuse or neglect, although shooters may feel they cannot turn to adults such as parents or teachers.

Shooters rehearse through letters, diaries, and spoken remarks but generally stay out of major trouble until the shootings. They are intolerant of others, but prior crimes are small-scale, such as vandalism. Grades may be average, but the shooters above average in intelligence.

"The Classroom Avenger" clinical diagnosis is "atypical depression" and "mixed personality disorder with paranoid, antisocial, and narcissistic features." They show their depression as sullen, irritable, secluded, and angry, but do not appear patently crazy.

★★★

There is not just a psychological profile of school shooters, but an environmental one - one which fits both Eric and Dylan. School shootings overwhelmingly occur in suburbs and small towns, which may be rich in sports, shopping malls, and BMW's, but poor in diversity and tolerance. Deviation from the white-bread norm is punished, and the high school campus is often the sole arbiter of adolescent status. A loser at school feels like a loser through and through. School shooters have no escape hatch, and nowhere else to turn for self-esteem. Options outside of school offered by a big city are not found in small towns and suburbs: There is no Hollywood Boulevard for the punk rockers.

The template for suburban school shootings may be the inner-city, youth violence epidemic from 1985 to 1995 that "seeped into pop culture" as one study put it. Columbine, along with Littleton and the other school shooting locales, are the exact opposite of crime-infested, poverty-ridden high schools in Detroit and Watts. But thousands of Columbines across the country are tough, in their own suburban and small town way. Status and cliques are as virulent as gang warfare, and the outcasts face stiff odds. After too many marginalizations, dating rejections, or bottles thrown at them white, middle-class, disaffected youth may have hijacked the violent, inner-city solution.

The homes to school shootings have different names but the same genetic makeup: Springfield, Oregon. West Paducah, Kentucky. Pearl, Mississippi. Santee, California. They form a violent crescent through the South and West. Here, the spiritual forefathers of school shooters are Western gunslingers and Southern duels. Simply put, the psychologist Richard Nisbett notes, "The U.S. South, and Western regions of the United States initially settled by Southerners, are more violent than the rest of the country."

The South radiates a "culture of honor," where any affront, disrespect or sign of violence is to be avenged. The *Encyclopedia of Southern Culture*, according to Nisbett, is "replete with accounts of feuds, duels, lynchings, and bushwhackings." The region has a philosophy of self-reliance summed up by the proverb: "Every man is a sheriff in his own hearth." It may easily be transferred to the Wild West, where law enforcement was sparse.

The South became this way, Nisbett argues, because it was settled by "swashbuckling Cavaliers of noble and landed gentry status" who coveted "knightly, medieval standards of manly honor and virtue." After them, according to Nisbett, an even more influential wave of immigrants brought more violence: Scottish and Irish herders who were "tribal, pastoral and warlike." Their livelihood depended on protecting their animals, which necessitated violence, or the threat of it. They eventually spread to the western frontier.

Southerners and Westerners will not say they favor violent solutions, but do see it as more acceptable in light of defending their family, property, and honor, according to psychologist Dov Cohen, who has also studied violence in the regions.

Nisbett contrasts that with the Northeastern United States, "settled by sober Puritans, Quakers, and Dutch farmer-artisans. In their advanced agricultural economy, the most effective stance was one of quiet, cooperative citizenship."

That close-knit living continues today in the large cities of the Northeast, just as the sprawl of the South and West continues to promote the concept of self-defense. In the suburbs, everyone is a newcomer, and to be regarded warily; they have no history to back them up. Public places are few and far between. Where there are sidewalks, they are desolate. Where people do live together, it is a kingdom of private residences, tract home next to tract home, with cars as fiefdoms on wheels. It is an area fertile for keeping to yourself and taking the law into your own hands. A boy still becomes a man with a gun. And in the suburb and small town, the gun is the great equalizer against overwhelming unpopularity.

In the South of the 1930's Nisbett indicates that it was "impossible" to obtain a murder conviction if someone killed after being insulted. "Until the 1970s, Texas law held that there was no crime if a man killed his wife's lover caught in flagrante delicto," he adds.

Southern and Western lawmakers "vote for more hawkish foreign policies, and self-defense laws that are more lenient in allowing people to use violence in defending themselves and their property," according to Cohen. In one study, Southern and Western employers were "more likely than northern employers to give warm responses to job applicants who had killed someone in a bar fight, and newspaper reporters of the South and West were more likely than their northern counterparts to treat stories of honor-related violence with sympathy and understanding for the perpetrator." In another study, "Southerners who are insulted believe their masculine reputation has been damaged," and respond more aggressively than northerners.

White Southerners are more likely to agree that spanking is a proper disciplinary tool when compared to Northerners and Midwesterners. They are also more likely to expect a fight among children who have been bullied.

In situations involving hoodlums, student disturbances, and big city riots, white Southern males were "more likely to advocate violence" to stop such violence, Nisbett reported. Those who do not respond to a violent affront by fighting, or shooting back, are "not much of a man."

Other studies show that those in the South and West watch more violent television, have more violent magazine subscriptions, more hunting licenses per capita, and the regions have higher rates of execution. The culture of honor may push more people to carry and use weapons, according to Nisbett. And there is a circle of violence: Since people in these regions are more likely to be on the lookout for violence, they are more likely to find it.

The culture of honor is more clearly transmitted in "strong, cohesive" communities, according to Cohen. Thus, the more close-knit the community, the more efficiently its values are handed down.

But suburbs and small towns hit by school shootings may have the worst of both worlds: They often experience change with an influx of new residents – the classic small town that suddenly becomes a big-city suburb, or the suburb that balloons in size. This creates an unstable populace that mixes with a lingering culture of honor.

Yet a school shooting may also catapult communities into maturity and discipline. After facing the biggest crisis of their lives, they may emerge with a gravitas that includes better relations among residents, less bullying, and fewer walls between cliques. It is as if they must have their own, municipal civil wars before they can come together.

***

Eric and Dylan were uncharacteristically successful school shooters. Not because they killed so many others, but because they killed themselves. School shooters often crave suicide: They mention it in their writings, or ask to be killed once captured.

Not surprisingly, given where school shootings dominate, suicide rates in the South and West are above average. The Centers for Disease Control has calculated the "crude rate" of suicide from 1999 to 2005 based on population for the nation's four regions.

The rates, adjusted for age, are as follows:

Northeast: 7.75
Midwest: 10.51
South: 11.64
West: 12.20

Teens, who make up the legions of school shooters, are especially susceptible to suicide. They are more unstable, fail to comprehend the finality of their actions, and are more likely to be influenced by other suicides and take part in copycat incidents.

★★★

Whether bullying caused Columbine was taken up by the governor's Columbine Review Commission. Regina Huerter, who then ran the Denver District Attorney's juvenile diversion program, wrote a report for the commission which she acknowledged was not scientific but contained "input from a broad cross-section" of twenty-eight adults and fifteen current or past students during the fall of 2000, over one year after the shootings. "What is not in doubt is that bullying occurred at Columbine, that in some instances the school administration reacted appropriately, and in other instances the school administration's reaction is unclear or altogether unknown," she concluded in "The Culture of Columbine."

Huerter tried to address whether Columbine had an overarching jock culture that smothered the rest of the students. "I'm not sure I would agree," she wrote. While the football team had a winning season, she did not find an "abundance" of "go football" type posters. "I thought maybe this was because the school was trying to downplay the 'jock' image," Huerter added. "After talking with several people, I found this was not the case. In fact posters are limited and pep rallies or assemblies are only held if the team wins. I had heard that the winning forensics team, band and theater were not put in the spotlight. While I believe there is a strong emphasis on sports, after reading three editions of 'Rebeline' the school's bulletin, all types of successes were noted."

After Huerter's presentation before the commission, eight Columbine teachers testified that bullying was not part of the school culture, and that the school did not tolerate such behavior. Sixteen more teachers showed up to support their colleagues, and 107 signed a letter backing the speakers. Principal Frank DeAngelis testified before the commission that he did not hear of or observe rampant bullying. "If it was occurring," DeAngelis said, "it was not being reported."

But people told Huerter Eric and Dylan were "loners and often the brunt of ridicule and bullying." It was reported to be shoving, pushing and name calling, especially "faggot," although more specifics were lacking.

Yet the bullied could also be bullies. Dylan and especially Eric "were often identified as rude and mean," Huerter notes.

★★★

In recent years, suburban teen shooters may have influenced a new realm of killers. Native American Jeff Weise killed nine, seven at his school and two in a home, before killing himself on a Red Lake, Minnesota Indian reservation in 2005. Red Lake was the opposite of white, somewhat wealthy Columbine. So was Weise himself. But the unpopular sixteen-year-old learned the same style of revenge from Columbine, down to wearing a trench coat and identifying with Nazis. Part of Red Lake falls in Beltrami County, the county with the highest rate of suicide for those under thirty-five in Minnesota.

In 2006, it appears two adults adopted the school shooter manifesto. In Bailey, Colorado, located in a county adjacent Columbine, fifty-three-year-old Duane Morrison sexually molested female students after sneaking into Platte Canyon High School. He eventually killed one girl and then himself. Morrison's final letter penned the day before his rampage indicates that his father physically abused by him. (Oddly, he says that as a boy, he found a safe haven at school, the same place he turned into a crime scene.) Morrison also shared Dylan's depressive state, noting, "I'm tired of living, and for the last 15 years or so I'm tired of living in pain. Constant pain."

Just days later thirty-two-year-old Charles Carl Roberts IV attacked an Amish school house in Pennsylvania and killed five girls. He then killed himself.

In 2007 another adult became a school shooter, twenty-three-year-old Cho Seung-Hui. He superseded Columbine in numbers when he killed thirty-two, then himself at Virginia Tech university. It is the deadliest mass shooting in U.S. history, and came four days before the eight-year anniversary of Columbine, on April 16.

Columbine retains a deeper national resonance because it solidified in the minds of the public as the first, modern-day mass shooting. It was directed at a more vulnerable, high school population, and carried out by two high-schoolers. It played out for hours live on television. And because Virginia Tech victims were from across the country, and across the world, the grief was not as focused on a single locale.

Yet Virginia Tech has similarities to Columbine, and other school shootings. The school is located in small-town Blacksburg, where the ghosts of the South, honor, and violence, still roam. The grassy, central quad area that became ground zero for mourning and memorials after the Virginia Tech shootings had long been named for the use of force: Drillfield, where the school's corps of cadets still marches.

★★★

If anyone might stop school shooters, it is school shooters themselves. Deconstructing them might diminish their appeal, and any aura of power. Publishing photos of the dead, bloody bodies of Eric and Dylan might be a deterrent or, as one study put it, "To the extent that there is a copycat thread connecting the recent school shootings, this presents the possibility that it could run its course, as the infamy of being just one more suicidal loser dims."

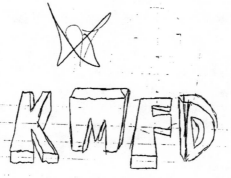

KMFD

12g.
Browning cutoff s/s crack shotgun : 300 pellet 12g. shells
Uzi 9mm, short barrel : 10 35 rd. mags.
(2) Calico Liberty III 9m semi-auto 4 100 rd. clips
Wildey .45 magnum semi-auto 30 12rd. clips

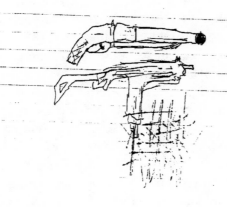

THIRTEEN

The Klebolds: Searching and Dueling

In the few days before Columbine Tom Klebold thought Dylan's attitude had been "good" and he was "very communicative." Nothing seemed amiss. If there was a problem, Tom thought, Dylan would say something.

Although Tom did think Dylan's voice was "tight'" the Friday before the shootings and made a "mental note" to talk to Dylan about it. Tom also told police he "may have even mentioned his concern to his pastor." But Tom never had that chance to talk with Dylan before the shootings. And it does not appear the Klebolds had a pastor when Columbine struck.

On the morning of Columbine, Tom and Sue didn't see Dylan leave for school but thought it was weird the way he closed the door and said "bye," like he was in a bad mood. It was 5:30 a.m.

Sue was going to ask him what was wrong when he got home from school. But around noon, Tom got a call from Nate Dykeman. Dykeman had left school for lunch just as the shootings started, at around11:20 a.m. When he tried to get back in the intersections were blocked. He asked classmate Jen Harmon what was going on. She said two kids in trench coats were shooting up the school. Dykeman didn't want to believe it, but thought it might be Eric and Dylan. He went home and called Tom, who worked out of his home and was unaware of the shootings.

"Oh my God!" he said, after Dykeman told him.

Tom checked to see if Dylan's trench coat was in the house. It was not. He turned on the television and called four people: his wife, Dylan's older brother, the woman who rented the pool house, and a family lawyer. Judy Brown, meanwhile, decided to head over. Also en route was Lakewood police officer Rollie Inskeep, one of the one thousand-plus officers and others who assisted Jefferson County with the Columbine investigation. Inskeep arrived around 1:15 p.m. and met up with three SWAT officers from the city of Sheridan police department. The Klebolds weren't really surprised and were "pretty level," Inskeep says. "They were kind of flat-liners, it was hard to read them." Maybe they were in shock, he figures.

Everyone was asked to leave the home and police swept through to check for anyone who was hiding. When they were inside the home,

Inskeep kept the Klebolds in one room that appeared to be a study. The home was a cut above average, Inskeep thought, but not extravagant. The Klebolds plugged him for more details on the shootings, but he was out of police radio range. When he tried to get information via radio, he found that the television was putting it out faster. So they watched the reality show they were part of unfold on television.

Tom agreed to speak with Inskeep, "with the knowledge of his attorney" and provided a brief record of Dylan's life, starting with his son's date of birth and car, the black, 1982 BMW. Tom noted that he himself opposed guns, and so did Dylan. The house only contained a BB gun, Tom said, originally a gift to Dylan when he was around ten years old.

Sue told Inskeep she had not noticed anything unusual about Dylan and in fact he was "extremely happy because he had just recently been accepted at the college of his first choice, which was the University of Arizona in Tucson." Although Dylan was "not a mainstream type kid," he was not unhappy, Sue said. But he did play computer games and that bothered her. When Inskeep asked about family dynamics, Sue said Dylan and his brother "were beginning to develop a good relationship."

Among the most intriguing comments Sue Klebold has ever publicly made were in Inskeep's written report: "When asked about guns or explosives, she stated that Dylan has always been fascinated by explosives and guns. She stated that Dylan wore combat-looking boots and that he liked the look that he had established."

The rest of the world now knew Dylan was fascinated with guns and explosives. Yet it was news that his mom seemed aware of that fascination before Columbine. But as in Dylan's diversion file, Sue was quick to change her mind if anything she said seemed culpable.

"She then recanted her previous statement and stated that Dylan did not really talk about explosives and guns but he just likes to have the look of the trench coat and boots," Inskeep wrote.

After speaking with Sue, Inskeep spoke with their attorney, Gary Lozow. "Gary indicated that the family would be willing to remain cooperative with us and assist us." Tom also indicated "he would be willing to respond to the high school in an attempt to talk Dylan out of the school if in fact he was involved."

Jefferson County District Attorney Dave Thomas was at Columbine, and Lozow called Thomas' assistant.

"Tom Klebold had heard his son's name on television," Lozow said. Word was relayed to Thomas. Thomas turned to a sheriff's department commander. "Would it be of any assistance if Tom Klebold came on the scene?"

Don't bother, came the reply; officers didn't even have contact with the shooters. It was close to 2:00 p.m. In fact, Eric and Dylan were about two hours dead.

Byron Klebold told Inskeep he had not been close with his brother since moving out two years earlier. Byron said Dylan was somewhat detached because he was a "pissed off" teenager. Dylan acted tough and had knives, but was also "normal" and gave no indication of carrying out a school shooting.

Guesthouse tenant Stephanie Juenemann, then twenty-seven, was a friend of the family who had been staying with the Klebolds for a year. "Dylan was always very polite to her and seemed like a 'nice guy,'" she told police.

Inskeep then spoke with Judy Brown. He noted that she became "extremely emotional" and indicated she had "gone to the Jefferson County Sheriff's Department approximately one year ago and told them that this was going to happen."

Tom and Sue repeated that there was no way Dylan could have been involved in something like this. They said police would find no guns and bombs in their home. But investigators who entered the home with a search warrant found homemade brass knuckles, shotgun wadding, shotgun shell casings, a shotgun barrel, four boxes of 9mm bullets, two BB rifles, a BB pistol, and an inert grenade. When police later asked about the pipes in the Klebold garage, no doubt because of the pipe bombs Eric and Dylan built for Columbine, Tom said they were for repairs at the rental homes. Tom had no idea why Dylan would want to participate in the killing of twelve fellow students and a teacher.

Around 8:00 p.m. a Jefferson County sheriff's deputy arrived and told the Klebolds they had to leave but could get some clothes. Tom went first, accompanied by Inskeep and the deputy. Susan was next, and left with two birds and two cats. Emotion then broke through. Byron started crying and hugged his dad. Tom, Susan and Byron then left in separate cars. Each parent was accompanied by at least one friend.

***

Tom and Susan contacted Gary Lozow after being referred to him by a civil attorney. Lozow works at the well-connected, well-respected Denver firm of Isaacson, Rosenbaum. Lozow, who has a long face and thinning gray hair he slicks back, is known for his criminal defense work. He is not a talking head, although his clients often make headlines. His law firm bio cutely thanks his mom for helping launch his career: "My brother was a criminal defense attorney and if he hadn't hired me, my mom would have screamed at him."

In 1993, Lozow delved into the savings and loan scandals, successfully defending Silverado Banking Chairman Michael Wise. (Wise later plead guilty to financial wrongdoing in another case.)

In an unusual move, Lozow and another attorney once paid $350,000 to settle claims against themselves. Lozow and Stuart A. Kritzer represented Mitchell and Candace Aronson, who claimed their neighbors tried to drive them from their pricey, Jefferson County foothills neighborhood because they were Jewish. The neighbors, William and Dorothy Quigley, filed a countersuit accusing the Anti-Defamation League, which had worked with the Aronsons, of defamation, and illegally tape-recording phone conversations.

The Quigley's won $10.5 million in 2000 from the Anti-Defamation League. Lozow and Kritzer made their payout given their representation of the Aronsons. Jefferson County District Attorney Dave Thomas also apologized to the Quigleys in 1995, one year after his office filed criminal hate-crime charges against them. In addition, the county's insurers paid the Quigleys $75,000.

Another Klebold criminal defense attorney, early on, was Rick Kornfeld, a former assistant U.S. attorney in Chicago who was working at Isaacson, Rosenbaum when Columbine struck. Kornfeld, who went on to successfully defend the Denver-based independent bookseller Tattered Cover for refusing to give police a customer's list of purchases, considered Lozow a mentor.

The days surrounding Columbine already had some weird overtones for Kornfeld. "April 20th is my wife's birthday," he says. "It was also Hitler's birthday. My father-in-law's birthday is April 19th, which is the Oklahoma City [bombing], so we sort of have the psycho trifecta of birthdays."

The day of Columbine Kornfeld got back to the office at 1 p.m. after a birthday lunch of Mexican food with his wife, and learned he too was now on the Klebold case. Sometimes, Kornfeld explains, the circumstances of a case may be clear cut: "You know, sometimes a guy will call and say, 'The police are at my door with a search warrant, what should I do?' Well, I'll say, 'Read the warrant. If the warrant's legit, like the Grateful Dead say, step aside, they're coming in.' Don't create more problems for yourself. It's not that fancy."

Columbine was the opposite. In those first hours, the case was unfolding as fast as the television images.

"We were watching the news like everybody else," Kornfeld says. "The police were not busy informing us what was going on, nor would I expect them to. The media strategy was to sort of try to hold things at bay and not comment until we had something to say."

"It wasn't the typical, I've been charged with 'X' I'm in trouble. Help me deal with this case," Kornfeld adds. "This was just a bad, bad, bad situation, and they [the Klebolds] knew that they needed a lot of advice, and I think they wisely perceived that among the types of advice they would need, someday, in some context, was quote unquote legal advice."

Another attorney at Isaacson, Rosenbaum, Stephanie O'Malley, was a former Jefferson County deputy District Attorney (and the daughter of then Denver mayor Wellington Webb). She checked with the DA's office to see what she could find out.

Still, the clients only became clear at the end of the day. "The [legal] representation clearly became the family because Dylan was, was gone," Kornfeld says.

The Klebold attorneys not only concerned themselves with the legal, but the workaday. "There were significant issues about the family's privacy. Logistics surrounding that. Where would they go? How would they get clothes, etc.?" Kornfeld says. "And then the next, the real obvious legal issues, whether it was the second day, I don't really remember: Are these parents in any type of criminal, legal peril? And if so, determining that, because that of course tempers your advice about how and to what extent, and under what terms and conditions, to cooperate with authorities."

If the Klebolds were not suspects, they might still be witnesses. And a promise or letter from prosecutors absolving the Klebolds would not be ironclad. "You can walk into a meeting as a non-target, and depending on what you say, you can end up as a target," Kornfeld says. Parents are generally liable for the criminal behavior of their children if they willfully assist them. But for Kornfeld, the flipside was trouble too.

"Maybe you stick your head in the sand and you know your kid is experimenting with pipe bombs and then subsequently the kid plants a pipe bomb somewhere," he says, "I think you've got problems, even though basically, you facilitate it by doing nothing as a parent. I think a prosecutor could make a case and certainly a civil lawyer can make a very good case that you were acting negligently."

Maybe it's no surprise that the Klebold attorneys had reached their own conclusion: They didn't believe the parents had "direct criminal liability." "The parents also wanted to cooperate with the authorities and were willing to do so, and so over the course of several days, that was arranged; the logistics of that, you know, the conditions, the place, who was going to be present," Kornfeld says. "Were the feds involved? Were the locals involved? Who was running the show? Who was in charge? Who had the authority to make charging decisions, etc.?"

There was "gamesmanship" in choosing a location. "If it's at our office, it's our show. If it's at their [the police] office, it's their show," Kornfeld says. Ten days after Columbine, the meeting with police was held at Kornfeld and Lozow's downtown Denver office.

The Klebolds have never been charged with a crime, although victims' families did sue in the civil courts. But that was not Kornfeld's main concern early on. "I mean, this is America, people are going to get sued, there's no question about that," he says.

Those early days were, for the Klebolds, "I think just absolute shock, disbelief, out of body experience," Kornfeld says. "A bad dream."

Since then, a long-standing representation has emerged between Lozow and the Klebolds. But Kornfeld does not believe the Jewish identity shared by Sue Klebold and Lozow was a factor. "He [Lozow] is a great lawyer. Very deep-feeling guy, I think he related to them on a human level, but it was happenstance, I mean they called him," says Kornfeld, who is also Jewish. "I wasn't there. I was at lunch with my wife. We're in court a lot. What would have happened? Would they have called someone else if Gary were not there? If Gary weren't there and I was there I would have got the call? I mean, you know, who knows? It was somewhat unusual, over the lunch hour on a Tuesday or whatever it was, that Gary would even be around."

***

The Klebolds, at first, seemed to hold more emotion, and more willingness to unlock the secrets of Columbine. They quickly spoke with police. They said they wanted to help find answers to school shootings. They were open to meeting with victims' families, but the attorneys squashed the plan, according to their pastor. Because many perceived Dylan as the follower, Tom and Susan even seemed to carry less blame: Better to raise a foot soldier than an evil mastermind. "I think [the Klebolds' image] is partially a reflection of the Klebolds; you are who you are, even in a crisis, and they wanted to try and figure out what had happened and why it had happened," Kornfeld, says, although he also allows that, "I don't know if it's because of the advice they received, whether it was legal, or from friends."

But if the Klebolds truly wanted to help the world learn about their son and help figure out what happened at Columbine, they indeed had an odd way of doing it. In fact, aside from their police interviews, condensed and relayed to the public second-hand by police, the sum total of their media interviews over an eight-year span is one, with *New York Times* columnist David Brooks, who mostly covers national politics and trends with a conservative slant. Brooks concluded in a single, 777-word column that the Klebolds had faced down Columbine "bravely and honorably."

The Klebolds otherwise spent their time engaging in hand to hand legal combat to stop the release of information on Dylan, and the shooting. Should the basement tapes be made public? Or Dylan's autopsy, which is by default considered a public document? No and no, the Klebolds and their attorneys said to those, and other questions, of public access. The Klebolds even considered suing the sheriff's department for not warning *them* about Columbine.

Those who know the Klebolds, and who knew Dylan, say it was as if Dylan lived a secret life. The Dylan who committed Columbine was not the Dylan they knew, nor the Dylan who Tom and Sue raised. But if Dylan worked to keep his plans a secret from his parents up until Columbine, his parents fought to keep his life a secret after Columbine.

As to how the Klebolds cope with Dylan's legacy, the one word answer may be this: Suicide. Sue Klebold, shortly after the shootings, relayed to this author through an intermediary that she believed a study of suicide would reveal why Dylan went on his rampage. And in their interview with the *Times,* Tom and Sue emphasized that point. (A donor named Sue

Klebold is also listed in the Suicide Prevention Action Network Winter 2006 newsletter.) In one way, Tom and Sue are not far off. But they cannot make the other leap that Columbine was also mass murder.

***

The day after Columbine Susan Klebold had her hair done. As thousands of people — cops, reporters, students, families, politicians, well-wishers, hangers-on, looky-loos, loons, locals and publicity seekers– massed about the school, Susan was one mile away in a strip mall at Dee's Four Star Images, sliding into a salon chair. It is the same strip mall where Eric and Dylan worked at Blackjack Pizza, although Susan had never mentioned to her hairdresser that her son worked a few doors down. In fact, Susan had never talked about her children in the one year she had been seeing Dee Grant, and coming in about once a month.

Dee doesn't know how Susan first came to visit her. She remembers that Susan was always on time and always tired. Renting out their converted Victorian in Denver was a lot of work. But Dee wasn't surprised when Susan called on the worst day of her life–the day of Columbine, Dee recalls–to reschedule her hair appointment for the next day. "I always had the feeling that she was a reasonable person, you know and I thought she was a good person," says Dee, who is in her 60s. "And see, for her to call me and change an appointment because something happened, to me just says she's a creature of habit of responsibility. You don't break appointments. You don't have to tell anybody why you're changing it, but you don't leave somebody in the lurch. She's being responsible at all times. Because that's her mode. She doesn't know how else to do it."

Dee's small store smells of nail polish and on a hot spring day, she has on a thin black dress with white and green leaf prints. She has brown hair, and black pumps. Another woman's hair is setting while Dee does the woman's nails. In the waiting area are the magazines *Midwest Living* and *Essence*, an odd choice given the paltry number of blacks in the Columbine area.

The day after Columbine, Dee's grandchildren were in the shop. Susan commented how nice and innocent they were, and reminisced about her own children. Dee had already made the connection between Susan and Dylan. That's why she called police before Susan came in.

"I thought, with everything that has gone on, which is so horrendous, that I needed to let them [the police] know she was here for either her protection, my protection, or just their knowledge," Dee says. "Because maybe they're looking for her and I didn't want to be a part of anything that isn't supposed to be going on. I didn't want anything to fall on me down the road. So it was just kind of, but it was really in everyone's best interest. Because who knows who's following her? Who knows if violence was going to follow her as well?"

Dee told the police she didn't want them coming into the shop but, "I just want them to be aware of it, and if they feel like they want to patrol the shop while she's here, that's fine, but not to come in. They said it wouldn't be necessary."

Dee also went to confession to talk to a priest about Susan coming in the next day. "Maybe because I'm Catholic and you think you have to tell everything to the priest," Dee explains. "But I guess I wanted to feel like I was doing the right thing by having her come over. I was kind of, you know, because I wanted to treat her like I always treated her because she's always been right with me and I know her family has a crisis now, and I didn't want; I knew the whole world was against her and I just kind of identified with her situation. Kind of put yourself in someone else's shoes, you know? And I had no reason to believe she was in any way, shape or form the cause, or evil herself, through my relationship with her. So I wasn't judging her. I was just trying to treat her as a mom who was in crisis now."

Susan came in for a color and a cut. That's about $55. Dee says plenty of women end up sitting in her stylist's chair after a tragic incident. Now Susan Klebold examined her own life: What happened here? We thought we were doing everything right. Did we do anything wrong?

Susan thought Dylan had all the right boxes checked off: He was "going forward" after his run-in with the law. He went to prom. He was going to graduate. He had picked out a college. "You know how you kinda see the light at the end of the tunnel, and she kinda saw that as, you know, I think we're going to have a chance now," Dee recounts. "Dylan's a smart boy, you know, we're going to put him in with some others, once he goes off to school. You know how parents always hope. How they always hope. Especially if they have a problem child."

Susan wasn't a big fan of Eric Harris. "I think there was just probably; you know how you have a little gut feeling like, 'Well, I wish he [Dylan] would kinda pick another friend, you know, this one is a little complicated,'" Dee says. Yet while Susan felt she couldn't keep two kids apart at that age, she figured Dylan's going off to college would break that bond.

After the killings Dee said Susan flagged Dylan's computer marathons as a warning sign. But she had hesitated to cut him off. "Computers is where it's at, you know, he's learning a lot about it, and that's a good thing, it'll give him an edge,'" Susan thought, according to Dee.

Susan was flummoxed by testimony that Eric and Dylan were prejudiced. "Dee, we're not prejudiced," Susan said. "I'm Jewish. You know? We don't teach prejudice.'"

Of reports that the two brandished Nazi slogans, Susan said, "Dee, that's ridiculous."

Susan seemed "sad and numb" when they spoke the day after Columbine, tears sometimes welling up in her eyes. "She really didn't know what to make of it. Then of course she says, 'Well, Dee, I really don't know if I'll see you anymore because I don't know where our lives are going to lead now. I don't know if we'll have to change our names, move, I don't know.' So you know, she thanked me, and I wished her good luck and like that."

Dee has not spoken to Susan since then, although her daughter sent Susan a card for Mother's Day.

The same day Susan got her hair done, she and Tom issued a statement on Columbine. "We cannot begin to convey our overwhelming sense of sorrow for everyone affected by this tragedy. Our thoughts, prayer and heartfelt apologies go out to the victims, their families, friends, and the entire community. Like the rest of the country, we are struggling to understand why this happened, and ask that you please respect our privacy during this painful grieving process."

The Klebolds also called Dylan's friend, Devon Adams, the day after the shootings to invite her to Dylan's funeral. "I wasn't there to talk to them, but they called us and I had told my parents if they called to tell them that I was there for them if they needed me," Devon says. She ended up attending the funeral for slain student Rachel Scott instead, which was the same day. "Possibly my biggest regret of my life is attending Rachel's funeral and not Dylan's," Devon now says.

★★★

The day of Columbine Rev. Don Marxhausen was thinking to himself, "Who the hell are the dumb parents?" Then a parishioner and neighbor of the Klebolds came up to Marxhausen while he was handing out the Eucharist.

"It's the Klebolds," the man said.

"What?" Marxhausen said.

"Police cars are all over the Klebold property," he replied. "It's the Klebold family. It's their son."

"Oh, really," Marxhausen said to the neighbor.

"Body of Christ," Marxhausen said to parishioners, continuing to hand out bread wafers.

"Keep it going," Marxhausen said to himself, trying to maintain appearances.

Then he took action. "So I said through the grapevine, let them [the Klebolds] know if they need me, I'll be available. Well, it turns out the grapevine never got to them, Tom just called me on his own. 'Would you help?' Of course. A Christian needs to go where it's the darkest. And that might be Jewish as well. Not for voyeurism, but because if you have some candle, you got to light that darkness. So I didn't have to think about this. Of course I'll be there."

Marxhausen is a burly, bearded, liberal of a man with a sharp wit. He loves to laugh, but is no stranger to difficult situations, having been a social worker for six years in inner-city Chicago. Dylan's funeral was held on Saturday, April 24 at a local funeral home and about fifteen people attended, including a Klebold aunt and uncle; Randy and Judy Brown; and Nate Dykeman's mother and stepfather. Dykeman himself did not attend, he contends, because he was not told.

Gary Lozow did not attend. Another attorney from his office did, but not for legal reasons. "This was a very sort of intense relationship, and I think that the people that were there for them, we were among those people, I hope," says attorney Kornfeld, although he did not attend the funeral either. "This relationship, especially at the beginning, was an unusual kind of attorney-client relationship. We were there to help, and we weren't there to judge them. I think that's what a lawyer should do anyway. Certainly in this case, that's what we tried to do, and, we didn't think they did anything wrong."

Marxhausen's wife was also there, for a reality check, along with another Lutheran pastor, and a police officer. Robyn Anderson recalls being invited through another friend of Dylan's, but says she didn't get the message until after the fact. Tom Klebold wore a charcoal suit; Susan had on a dress. Before the service got underway, Marxhausen picked up on the tension among the small group and came up with an idea. "I said we just needed to talk first. We talked about forty-five minutes and out came all this love [for Dylan]."

There was a sort of funerary loophole Marxhausen was on the lookout for. "I've heard people, they don't speak ill of the dead, then nothing got said," he says. But people did talk, and it wasn't about Dylan the mass murderer. It was about Dylan the Boy Scout, Little Leaguer, and ten-year-old who enjoyed grossing out his mother with a handful of leeches from a creek. He wasn't a bloody mess, but the same old Dylan in an open casket.

The positivity left Marxhausen confused. "People told how much they loved Dylan, how really they thought he was a good guy, and I had several families there and afterwards come and tell me that the Klebolds did a marvelous job in raising him," he says. "So, if you were at the funeral...you'd have a difficult time figuring out what was reality."

Marxhausen asked the attorney whether he should "shut up or talk to the press."

"Why don't you tell people what you saw here today?'" he replied.

Tom Klebold knew that Marxhausen had put himself on the line by performing the service. "You made yourself vulnerable," he said.

The Klebolds released a statement after the funeral: "Today we had a private service for our son, Dylan Klebold, whom we loved as much as we knew how to love a child. Our sadness and grief over his death and this tragedy are indescribable. We again apologize to all those who have also suffered a loss of their loved one and we continue to pray for the recovery of those who are injured. We would also like to extend our gratitude to those who have offered their support and sympathy during this grieving period."

On Friday April 30, ten days after Columbine, the Klebolds had their sit-down with Jefferson County sheriff officials: Lead Columbine investigator Kate Battan, Sgt. Randy West, and Investigator Cheryl Zimmerman. Also present was Jefferson County Deputy District Attorney Charles Tingle.

The Klebolds were represented by Lozow and Stephanie O'Malley. Jefferson County District Attorney Dave Thomas can't recall why he didn't sit in on the interview with the Klebolds. But Thomas says the meeting lasted from 4:15 p.m. to 6 p.m. He told the *Rocky Mountain News* that the Klebolds were "very cooperative" and "They were obviously concerned about everything that's transpired." The Klebolds also asked for any writings, diaries and information on Dylan's computer that could help them understand April 20th.

Kornfeld did not attend the meeting but said, "I don't think the Klebolds refused to answer anything. I don't think the Klebolds walked out the door."

The Klebolds told police they thought Dylan was gentle. There was nothing unusual about his room, although Tom didn't go in there often and had not been in there for about two weeks before the shooting. But near the end of his life, "Dylan seemed to like the way he looked and seemed comfortable in talking to anyone," according to the police report of the Klebold interview. Tom thought Dylan managed himself and his life well. Tom was "very upset" with how the media portrayed Dylan after Columbine.

★★★

Kornfeld said he worked on the Klebold case about a year, but his hours significantly dropped off after the summer of 1999, once it became clear the District Attorney would not pursue a criminal case against them. Kornfeld acknowledges that the Klebolds "clearly" missed something, but not in a criminal manner.

Edgar Berg, Tom's former colleague, spoke with the Klebolds in the days after Columbine. Like Devon, the only way Berg could figure Columbine was to point to a secret life Dylan led. "Tom acknowledged that's what his son did," Berg says. "Tom says that he just spent endless, sleepless hours thinking, 'What did I miss?' Dylan was his best friend."

The Klebolds were prepped for a television appearance that never occurred. And they went silent until June of 1999, when families of those who were killed and injured started receiving letters of apology that were mostly boilerplate, but slightly personalized to each victim. "Our hearts are breaking for you over the loss you've experienced," the Klebolds wrote to Brian Rohrbough, whose son Dan was killed. "Dan was so young, yet so full of selfless courage. He'll never have the chance to do any of the things he wanted to do because he was taken from you in a moment of madness. We'll never understand why this tragedy happened, or what we might have done to prevent it. We apologize for the role our son had in your son's death. We did not see anger or hatred in Dylan until the last moments of his life when we watched in helpless horror with the rest of the world."

"A moment of madness," however, may not have fully captured Dylan's situation: His writings, his arrest, his school suspension, his buying of guns and making of bombs, and Susan's own words–that Dylan had "always been fascinated by explosives and guns"– all pointed to a pattern. Lawsuits against the Klebolds would say as much.

If Dylan led a secret life, that did not mean much of the public felt Tom and Susan Klebold should be secret. How could they not catch one iota of planning for the deadliest school shooting in U.S. history while one of the plotters lived under their roof? How could they miss the depression that Dylan dragged with him?

★★★

After the shootings, Robyn Anderson and her mom sent a sympathy card to the Klebolds. They then called, and set a date to visit the Klebolds at their home.

That story comes from Anderson's deposition after victims' families filed lawsuits against her. The scene itself at that deposition is notable: Nine attorneys representing eight slain students and six injured students (some attorneys represented more than one client) were present. Anderson was accompanied by her own attorney, Denver-based Richard Everstine.

The parents of five slain students–Kelly Fleming, Matt Kechter, Dan Rohrbough, Lauren Townsend, and Kyle Velasquez–were also there to face down Anderson. They were all represented by attorney James P. Rouse and he reminded Anderson who they were. "Next to me is Brian Rohrbough. His son Daniel was killed there. Next to him is Dawn Anna. Her daughter Lauren Townsend was killed there."

Among the most intriguing scenarios in the deposition is what Anderson describes as a one-hour visit with the Klebolds after Columbine. But the deposition provides little insight. "We just talked about everything that had happened," Anderson said, "and how we were all in shock about Dylan and Eric."

"What exactly was said, to the best of your recollection?" she is asked.

"Basically, just how they [the Klebolds] tried to think about everything they could possibly think about as far as signs that something was wrong, that something was going to happen, as did I," Anderson says.

Did the Klebolds flag any warning signs?

"Nothing really conclusive," Anderson says, except for Dylan's odd, maybe bothered tone of voice when he said "bye" to his parents the morning before he left to kill 12 classmates and a teacher. Anderson "briefly" discussed with the Klebolds her buying the guns. "Just that we had gone several months before, and that I had shown my ID to help them get the guns." Did Anderson tell the Klebolds she regretted the gun purchases? Were the Klebolds remorseful for Dylan's actions? How did the rest of the conversation go? Anderson cannot remember, but she adds that the Klebolds were hospitable.

Anderson is about equally blank when it comes to any warning signs she herself picked up on; except recalling that Dylan seemed a little odd when confronted with the exact date of the prom.

***

Nearly six months after Columbine, Devon Adams called the Klebolds on what would have been Dylan's 18th birthday, September 11, 1999. They still had the same phone number and she left a message. She called to "Let them know I was thinking of them. I was keeping them in my thoughts. Let them know I hadn't forgotten about them. I hadn't forgotten about Dylan, and I was still around."

Devon also had a gift for the Klebolds, and went to their house, where she spent a couple hours talking "about memories and stuff." She recounted how he helped her after her car accident.

"I think they thought it was pretty cool," she said of the car story. "We were T-boned while crossing an intersection, and Dylan stopped his car and ran up to my window and was just like, 'Are you OK? Are you OK?' and he was freaking out, and I just told him to go get my parents and tell them to come up here and get me."

Then Devon and the Klebolds got to what had brought them together: The killings. And why Dylan did it. The Klebolds were still considering, as Devon puts it, "The multiple personality possibility" but adds, "Just, I mean, any theory you've heard of... literally. I mean, we've talked about all of them."

The Klebolds cried at some points while Devon was there. "But it was probably because I was crying first; because I cried a lot," she says.

When Devon talked with the Klebolds a year later on September 11, 2000, Sue gave her an open invitation to hang out with her and Tom to watch a movie, or use their pool or tennis court, but Devon was too busy to take them up on the offer. The Klebolds also said they were putting together a photo scrapbook of Dylan.

People sometimes have a hard time describing how the Klebolds look. Devon remembers Susan wearing Dylan's jeans after his death, which is tough because Susan is not especially tall, while Dylan was around 6-feet 4-inches. But its also tough recalling much more. Devon believes it may be Susan's sadness and her eyes that always seem to be filled with tears. "It's sort of the thing where you don't want to remember; you don't want to remember pain, and Susan really embodies pain and she's pretty much been through the worst that you can go through and so you don't really; you try to block that out," Devon says. "It's obvious in everything she says; in her voice, yeah. In her eyes, and just her mannerisms."

★★★

October 1999 marked 180 days since the shootings, and the deadline for those who might sue government agencies connected to Columbine to file "intent to sue" notices. Such papers do not ensure anyone will actually sue, but are a placeholder to reserve that right should they decide to do so later. At one point nineteen victim families filed intent to sue notices against the sheriff's department and/or school district. But the name that stuck out was Klebold. Tom and Susan argued in their filing that the sheriff's department was "reckless, willful and wanton," in how it handled the Browns' 1998 report, just as Eric and Dylan entered diversion. It was maybe the one thing the Klebolds and the victims families could agree on.

While the Browns report mentioned Eric and Dylan, the Klebolds heaped blame on Eric. If the sheriff had followed up on the report and informed the Klebolds, Tom and Sue said, they probably would have demanded that Dylan stop hanging out with Eric. The Klebolds never did file suit. But in February 2000 then Sheriff John Stone appeared before the Colorado state legislature to support a pair of gun control bills when State Sen. John Evans, a Republican from the Denver suburb of Parker, asked Stone questions that remained on a lot of minds: How were the Klebolds and Harrises unaware of what their children were up to, and why hadn't charges been filed against them? One set of parents may have known about an explosive, but it couldn't be corroborated, Stone said. "There was deception in the way they stored the firearms and bombs in the house," he added.

On Columbine's one-year anniversary the Klebolds were still sad, and still sad for those whose lives their son had ruined, they said in a public statement. But part of the statement now emphasized they were ready for answers: "There are no words to convey how sorry we are for the pain that has been brought upon the community as a result of our son's actions. The pain of others compounds our own as we struggle to live a life without the son we cherished. In the reality of the Columbine tragedy and its aftermath, we look with the rest of the world to understand how such a thing could happen.

"We are convinced that the only way to truly honor all of the victims of this and other related tragedies is to move clearly and methodically toward an understanding of why they occur, so that we may try to prevent this kind of madness from ever happening again. It is our intention to work for this end, believing that answers are probably within reach, but that they will not be simple. We envision a time when circumstances will allow us to join with those who share our desire to understand. In the meantime, we again express our profound condolences to those whose lives have been so tragically altered. We look forward to a day when all of our pain is replaced by peace and acceptance."

Marxhausen says that over a year after Columbine, the Klebolds themselves still had no answer. It wouldn't do any good to talk to them, even if they would talk to a reporter. "It's too soon," he says. "I think that they're just starting to process and come up with some ideas. Then if you were to talk to them right now, it would not be the same thing were you to talk to them six months from now. 'Cause there's a whole piece of shock that was part of it; it's part of grief too." He later adds: "They're going to have to own up to, in the end, not only did they love their son, and a hell of a lot of people did, or a lot of people did, their son did a very, very, very, very bad thing. Now the mother was already there. He [Tom] doesn't want to say that yet. But in the end, they're both going to have to balance each other out. We had this kid that we loved, who was going to be our star, because the older one Byron is not an academic."

At one point, the Klebolds wouldn't even talk to their friends: Paranoia that they would talk to the media, or break confidences, became too great, Marxhausen says. A set of neighbors who had shepherded the Klebolds through the crisis, making sure they kept eating and taking walks, were among those shut out. But the neighbors then told the Klebolds one week later, "You can't throw us out." The Klebolds relented.

In the first year and a half after the shootings Marxhausen visited with the Klebolds every other month. "Probably 60 percent friend and 40 percent minister," is how he terms their relationship. Although Marxhausen will also say: "I'm not their pastor really. She's Jewish. He's still struggling with issues of faith. But I can be the God person and the Christian by simply being there."

When visiting the Klebolds at their home, Marxhausen sometimes brought flowers. He can't remember the type; his wife picked them out. Once he brought a small Christmas tree. The Klebolds might serve coffee and cookies. Sometimes they have dinner, but Marxhausen usually visits in the daytime—it's easier to see people at the locked gate at the bottom of the driveway where visitors call up to be let in.

"The Klebolds aren't going to go out every night; there's too much shame," Marxhausen says. He adds, "When you put down a credit card with the name Klebold on it, you always look for a response. It's not exactly Smith."

Marxhausen refers to the Klebolds as victims. He says Susan is "gracious" and Tom, "reads books you may not understand the title of." Tom questions how Dylan got a hold of the guns, and Marxhausen recounts a meeting with Tom Mauser, who took up gun control after his son Daniel was killed at Columbine. "Wouldn't it be interesting if Tom Klebold would join your crusade?" Marxhausen offered. But they couldn't figure out if it would hurt or help.

"I really do love them," Marxhausen says of the Klebolds. "These are good people. A meteor fell on their house. Why did the meteor fall on their house? I don't know."

The Klebolds sometimes read the newspapers, but not always. That would be too painful. Moving out of the community was not a strong alternative, Marxhausen says. "You're still going to have a history."

The support of friends, their lawyer, and "the confidence they didn't know what the hell happened" also helped keep them in Littleton. And despite the vilification, there was also sympathy. "They got over 4,000 letters of support. I mean they got gifts; you know, teddy bears, all kinds of stuff from people who had the chaos in their lives," Marxhausen says. "You know, one letter I remember: 'My son killed his beloved sister and grandfather when he was twelve or fourteen, or whatever it was, and we don't know why, so we understand. My son fell against the fireplace, the police arrested us for letting him. We do no harm to our son, and yet, this kind of thing happens.'

"There were people who brought gifts to the church that we would, I mean, just take out there. We'd screen them initially, and Lozow's office screened a hell of a lot more than we did at the church. Most of the stuff that came from the church, and I say the large percentage of it, was support and warmth, as opposed to 'You're crazy.'"

Some letters and other items would simply be addressed to "Klebolds, Littleton," or "Klebolds, St. Philip's Lutheran Church, Littleton." A small number of letters were antagonistic. "I took about three or four letters: Those of you who work with scum are scum, and blah blah blah, around the country. We pitched them. I'd say it was less than five percent," Marxhausen says.

Some months after the shootings, Marxhausen says his congregation indicated they would welcome the Klebolds. "The majority of the congregation stood up and applauded that they'd be willing to do that." But in August 2000, almost one and a half years after Columbine and ten years after becoming pastor at St. Philip Lutheran, Marxhausen delivered his last sermon there. He and his congregants differ about his departure, but it appears he was forced out, at least in part, because of his work with the Klebolds.

"He [Tom Klebold] just feels a certain responsibility that what has happened to me was part of this whole Columbine thing," Marxhausen says. "And so he feels bad about that." But Marxhausen says it was the best time of his life going "into the darkness." "It's been a good thing," he adds. "It's just chaos is scary as hell."

Marxhausen deadpans that the favorite topic with Tom and Susan is pain. "We talk about, 'it.' Anybody who is in grief, that's what you talk about is 'it,'" he says. "The whole subject. You may start off talking about, 'The Yankees are going to pull it off again.' But then it's 'it.'"

He recounts a visit with the Klebolds in October 2000. "It was a relief yesterday just to see the tears start to run. She [Susan] cried initially. And all I had to do was repeat the line, 'You loved your son very much,' which is what I said on NBC television and now that's just pourin' out, pourin' out, pourin' out, which is good, because then the grief can start to work. But they're just hurtin' just so damn horrible."

Another perennial for the Klebolds, and the topic for the public and the victims families is how could the parents not have known. Or, to borrow from Marxhausen, why did a meteor fall upon the home of the Klebolds? Didn't they see it coming?

They didn't, Marxhausen says, and cites the mental Rolodex they go through. "Well, they just try different theories. What are they? What were the clues? Did we miss anything?"

The upshot is empty. "The parents have no idea," Marxhausen says. "I gotta tell you that. They have no idea. They try to go down theory lane, and it only goes so far."

★★★

The truth is that the truth according to the Klebolds was emerging. And the Klebolds figured they were not the culprits. Glimpses of that theory began to emerge more than a year after the shootings: The Klebolds told Marxhausen that Dylan was infused with idealism and righteousness that led him to rebel against the injustices and imperfections of the world such as the social tiers he experienced at school. "This did not happen in a vacuum," Marxhausen recounts. "There were some external causes that [Tom Klebold] would like the community to address. For lack of a better word, bullying, or segregating, or whatever."

The Klebolds wanted to write a book, according to Marxhausen, and sought anecdotes about bullying at the school from his daughter, who herself attended Columbine. "I think it's up here yet," Marxhausen said of any publication, pointing to his head. "And I think they want to tell their story, honest, they want to tell their story. They would love to go out and talk to somebody, or go on television, or whatever. Their lawyers just won't let them."

By April 2001 the Klebolds were on their way to keeping silent if that was what they wanted. They and the Harrises announced a $1.6 million payout of insurance money to settle all but six out of sixteen lawsuits brought by victims families. "Mr. and Mrs. Klebold continue to hope and pray that we can continue negotiations that are ongoing with the remaining claimants, put an end to the lawsuits that exist, and at some point they can tell their story," said one of their attorneys, Frank Patterson.

In fact, the Klebolds had already talked to James Garbarino, a professor of human development at Cornell University who publishes pop psychology books and had doubled as a consultant to the Klebold attorneys. He published a book in September 2001, *Parents Under Siege*, and was prohibited from quoting the Klebolds because of his legal obligations. But their sort of cooperation fed a wave of publicity for the book, which excused the parents for any role in the shootings.

The book was dedicated to Tom, Sue, and Byron. The message was, "bad things happen to good parents," as Garbarino wrote in the preface.

The Klebolds, according to Garbarino, were "attentive, involved and loving," and "good parents." The family was "battered by the slings and arrows of outrageous fortune." Dylan, in one of the mentions Garbarino is apparently allowed to make, "successfully hid his inner turmoil from his loving parents. He put up a false front of normality..."

Just as the Klebolds put the onus on Eric in their intent to sue notice, Garbarino did the same in his book. "From what we know, it appears that Dylan Klebold was not a killer on his own," Garbarino concludes. "It took his relationship with Eric Harris to make it happen."

He might in fact be right. He just doesn't prove it.

Klebold PR supported the book. "Dr. Garbarino is a well-recognized expert on parenting skills, and the book is a serious work that supports the fact that caring, responsible and well-intentioned parents may have children who commit unexplainable acts," Klebold spokeswoman Lisa Simon told *The Denver Post*. "The experiences of the parents represented in this book are instructive, and if the book helps one parent better understand their child, then it will have achieved their goal."

Garbarino was scheduled to speak in Denver one day after Dylan's 20th birthday: September 12, 2001. He was suddenly overshadowed by September 11, but it didn't matter. The book was a superficial absolution. Not an investigation.

Tom and Sue would not repeat their speaking feat until 2004 but it was again noteworthy - not for the few morsels of information, but for how the interviewer again cleared them of any wrongdoing in just a few words. The writer was *New York Times* columnist David Brooks, who made a splash in 2000 with his book *Bobos in Paradise* (bobos meaning "bourgeois bohemians"), about America's rising, monied class of decision-makers and influence peddlers who cultivated scented candles, espresso and a bohemian ethos while maintaining establishment jobs. The style was called "comic sociology" (the Klebolds seem to favor pseudo-scientific authors wrapped in an aura of seriousness and academia). Brooks' 2004 book *On Paradise Drive* explores suburban life, although the fact that most school shootings occur in the suburbs seems to have escaped Brooks in his columns on the Klebolds.

Brooks first wrote an April 24, 2004 column about Columbine taking issue with the idea that Harris and Klebold were victims of society, and on the receiving end of bullying. He supported the idea that Harris undertook Columbine because he saw himself as superior to others. The column was more about Eric and tougher on Eric, calling him an "icy killer." Klebold, in contrast, was "a depressed and troubled kid who could have been saved," Brooks wrote.

Brooks let Dylan off easy. For participating in what was then America's deadliest school shooting, it wasn't a bad obit. Yet Tom Klebold sent an e-mail to Brooks and "objected" to the column, according to Brooks. Brooks does not make clear what Tom objected to, but a conversation ensued, and Brooks wrote a follow-up column about it on May 15. Brooks noted that the Klebolds spoke with him because "the lawsuits against them are being settled, and they trust the *New York Times*, which is the paper they read every day."

But one might argue that a columnist, especially one who has had little if any involvement in a massive and complicated story like Columbine, was the perfect mark for the Klebolds to propagate their story. And again, the blame was put on Eric, as Brooks quickly pointed out in his column: "Their son, by the way, is widely seen as the follower, who was led by Eric Harris into this nightmare."

A la Garbarino, Brooks then cleared the Klebolds as "a well-educated, reflective, highly intelligent couple." Susan still thinks about leaving the area, Brooks added, but Tom says, "I won't let them win. You can't run from something like this." There is a "moment of discomfort" when handing over their credit card at a store but Tom says, "most people have been good-hearted."

Brooks does get to the reason we have all gathered: Why did Columbine happen? And was there anything in the family that triggered it?

Brooks says the Klebolds "long for some authoritative study that will provide an answer."

Tom says, "People need to understand, this could have happened to them."

The Klebolds tell Brooks they think about the signs they missed – although Brooks does not name them. The Klebolds also say they pretty much don't know the causes of Columbine, but it wasn't the family. They maintain that "the 'toxic culture' of the school, the worship of jocks and the tolerance of bullying, is the primary force that set Dylan off."

Susan tells Brooks, "Dylan did not do this because of the way he was raised. He did it in contradiction to the way he was raised."

The most "infuriating incident," was when someone told Susan, "I forgive you for what you've done." Susan's thought was, "I haven't done anything for which I need forgiveness."

Looking at the thirteen murdered and twenty-four injured, Tom and Susan emphasize that Dylan committed suicide. "I think he suffered horribly before he died," Susan says. "For not seeing that, I will never forget myself."

"He was hopeless," Tom says. "We didn't realize it until after the end."

Brooks also notes that, "While acknowledging the horrible crime his son had committed, Tom was still fiercely loyal toward him."

Brooks does not write about some of the most compelling passages attributed to the Klebolds: That Dylan was fascinated with guns and explosives. Or that he was sullen, angry, disrespectful, intolerant, and isolated.

★★★

The Klebolds themselves had a funny way of longing for an authoritative study: They were aggressively silent.

In September 2000 I filed a public records request with the University of Arizona for Dylan's college application. Thomas Thompson, an attorney for the university, said he believed the records were open, but felt a "moral and legal obligation" to inform the Klebolds. Klebold attorney Gary Lozow then asked for a month and a half "to review the Klebolds' legal options under Arizona law." Thompson granted the request.

At 4:18 p.m. on the day of deadline, Lozow faxed a letter to Thompson. He wanted two more weeks "to see if we can obtain someone who will do what we are asking to get done...." Thompson and his boss gave the Klebolds nine more days. As the end of that day approached, Thompson had not heard back from the Klebolds and the material was released.

In June 2001, I wrote a story in the *Rocky Mountain News* using confidential settlement documents disclosing details of gun supplier Robyn Anderson's lawsuit settlement with victim families. Despite the bad blood, I called Lozow later that month.

"Jeff 'Chutzpah' Kass," is how he answered the phone.

I told him I would take "chutzpah" as a sort of compliment.

I asked once again if the Klebolds would be talking to anyone about Columbine.

"The answer is no," Lozow said, "particularly not to you."

He added that my story mentioning a copy of Anderson's $285,000 settlement check (probably from her mother's homeowners insurance) was "absolutely abhorrent." He added, "And it may have set back very delicate settlement discussions in the case."

"I appreciate you talking to me about it," I said. "I appreciate you sharing it with me."

Then he said of the canceled check: "And whoever you got it from should have his hands cut off. So that's what I think, and we're not talking to you, ever. So thank you Mr. Kass. Bye bye."

Lozow then hung up. But he and the other Klebold attorneys did not stop.

★★★

In July 2001 I made state Open Records Act requests for information on Susan Klebold given her employment with two public institutions: The Community Colleges of Colorado and Arapahoe Community College. The Colorado attorney general's office, representing the colleges, approved the request and set a date of August 15 to inspect hundreds of pages. The Klebold attorneys did not oppose releasing Susan's applications and resume, but argued that the names and locations of prior employers, and the schools she attended, were confidential. The Attorney General disagreed, but gave the Klebolds one week, until the end of the day on August 22, to file suit and block release of those specific items.

At 3:15 p.m. on the twenty-second Klebold attorneys Gregg Kay and Frank Patterson called this author. They requested five more days. "They [the Klebolds] are just really bugged by old people; old friends being contacted. So I think any of us, when we find out that some stranger is digging into our background, it just feels uncomfortable," Patterson said.

Patterson said he was puzzled over what "social issue" the Klebolds could help unlock.

"School shootings?" I hinted.

"I think shootings; but that's not the parents," Patterson said.

"According to their attorneys; according to you," I said.

"There's nobody that thinks the parents actually knew anything," Patterson replied.

"Well, there's still about a half-dozen lawsuits saying that," I said. "That's somebody."

"I don't think anybody thinks that the Klebolds actually knew a damn thing," Patterson said. "That's just people who have had a horrible thing happen to them that are looking to; for answers where there might not be any."

I said the Klebolds might discuss any warning signs or psychological problems that may have caused Columbine.

"I understand that," said Patterson. "Maybe someday we'll get to talk about that."

The talk concluded with a compromise deadline: I gave them two more days– not five–until Friday at 5:00 p.m. to decide what they wanted to do.

Friday afternoon rolled around. "Let me make a proposal to you," Patterson began on the phone. "What do you say, instead of us filing something with the court, that the two of us agree to present it to a retired judge, or mediator?"

He added: "We don't want to turn it into a big, blown out litigation fight."

If we agreed to arbitration, there would be no recourse in the courts; the decision would be final. I said I would think about it. I called back around 4:15 p.m. and spoke with Kay.

"Have you decided on this deal, or what are we doing?" Kay asked.

"I'm not going to be able to do arbitration," I said.

"Well, that's alright," Kay said. "I'll pass that on to everybody and see what we're going to do." They did nothing.

* * *

In a September 6, 2001 letter Lozow admonished me for my open records requests, most of which were granted and approved by various attorneys representing governmental institutions in different states.

"I am unalterably committed to the protection of First Amendment rights, as are my clients. Likewise, my clients and I also cherish the right to privacy," he wrote.

"You, unlike any other member of the print media have repeatedly attempted to impinge upon my clients' right to privacy," Lozow maintained in the one and one-quarter page correspondence cc'd to Tom and Susan Klebold. "By exploiting open records laws, in Colorado,

Arizona, and Wisconsin, you have accessed personal information concerning Tom and Susan Klebold."

Lozow wrote that the use of such information was "egregious." He added, without providing any examples: "Your efforts have served to disrupt Ms. Klebold's employment setting and the family's emotional well being."

"For the time being, my clients' legal energy is substantially directed at trying to settle the remaining Columbine lawsuits," Lozow continued, then added the somewhat vague admonition: "My information is that your 'journalistic efforts' have succeeded in making that effort even more difficult than it should be."

The letter proceeded, without naming names, "Likewise, we have reports from people in Susan Klebold's past that you have contacted. My clients have been told that you have been intrusive and abrasive. You should know that my clients will utilize their legal options to remedy excesses perpetuated against them on the heels of the Columbine tragedy."

The next paragraph was the last: "The Klebolds are committed to maintaining some semblance of privacy and dignity in the aftermath of Columbine. Notwithstanding your efforts, we will continue to maintain that purpose throughout."

I wrote back to Lozow on September 18, and cc'd the Klebolds. "The Klebolds can play an important role in furthering the world's understanding of what has happened at Columbine, and across the country," I noted. I said I would be happy to clear up any misunderstandings with people I had tried to speak with. Neither Lozow nor the Klebolds wrote back.

In October 2002 I worked with two other reporters to break the story on the sealed diversion files of Eric Harris and Dylan Klebold for the *News*. The Klebold attorneys responded by sending a subpoena to me and my colleague, Kevin Vaughan. We went to court, where the judge indicated that the Klebolds had issued the subpoena under the wrong Columbine case, and would have to re-file. It does not appear they ever did.

MAY

S	M	T	W	T	F	S
						1
2	3	4	5	6	7	8
9	10	11	12	13	14	15
16	17	18	19	20	21	22
23	24	25	26	27	28	29
30	31					

weekly **ACTION**PLAN

M	T	W	T	F	S	S
M	T	W	T	F	S	S
M	T	W	T	F	S	S
M	T	W	T	F	S	S
M	T	W	T	F	S	S

make TODAY count

PRIORITIES

ASSIGNMENTS

AFTER SCHOOL PLANNING

MONDAY	TUESDAY	WEDNESDAY

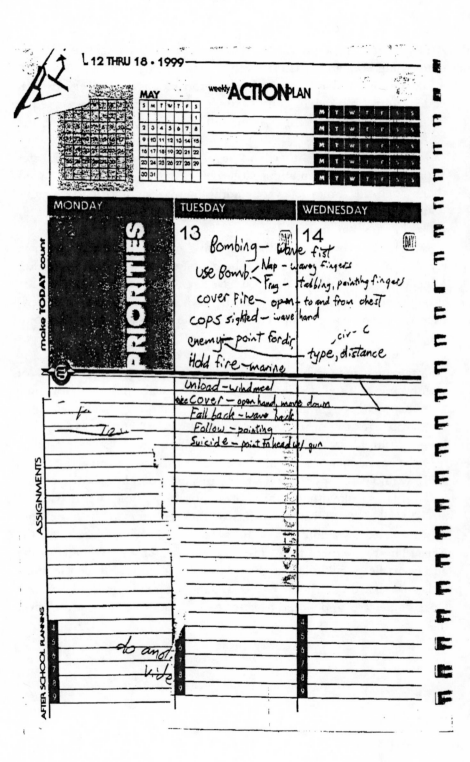

13

Bombing — wave fist

Use Bomb. — Nap — wavey fingers

Frag — stabbing, pointing fingers

cover fire — open — to and from chest

cops sighted — wave hand

enemy — point for dir

Hold fire — marine

14

civ - c

type, distance

Unload — wind meal

take Cover — open hand, move down

Fall back — wave back

Follow — pointing

Suicide — point fh head w/ gun

do and
hide

FOURTEEN

The Harrises: Immunity

Before police came to his home the day of Columbine, Wayne Harris called 911:

"This is Wayne Harris, my son is Eric Harris, and I'm afraid that he might be involved in the shooting at Columbine High School," the call begins.

"Involved how?" the police dispatcher asks.

Harris: "He's a member of what they're calling the Trench Coat Mafia."

Dispatch: "Have you spoke with your son today, Mr. Harris?"

Harris: "No, I haven't. . . . Have they picked up anybody yet?"

Dispatch: "They're still looking for suspects." And later: "Your son is with who; what gang?"

Harris: "They're calling them the Trench Coat Mafia... I just heard that term on television."

★★★

Lakewood Police detective Stan Connally is a tall, thin Texan whose accent still comes through. A former attorney who was fifty-four when Columbine struck, he has short, tussled gray hair and matching mustache. A homicide investigator since 1994, he was dispatched to the Harris home the day of Columbine.

Sitting in a small interrogation room at Lakewood police headquarters a year after the shootings, Connally is dressed in a tweed sport coat with a Western-style yoke across the chest. He is wearing a white button down shirt, and the chest pockets have the same distinctive 'V.' Connally has on khakis, and a dark paisley tie. He shrugs when asked what he was wearing the day of Columbine, and sweeps his hands over his body: "This is what I wear everyday," is the message. Connally is sure he wasn't wearing a blue blazer. He doesn't own one.

Connally doesn't recall who alerted him to the shootings that Tuesday. But he turned on the television and the gravity of what was happening hit him. His words are matter of fact, but still convey the seriousness. "I thought, 'If there's somebody in school shooting, somebody's going to get hurt.'"

Once at the Harris home Connally met up with a group of police officers from the Sheridan police department, another Denver suburb.

Connally had to consider that Eric Harris had rampaged through Columbine, escaped, and was now at home. He gladly accepted a heavy, bulletproof vest—not the thinner type some officers wear under their shirts—from a Sheridan officer. He put it on over his shirt and tie, but under his sport coat. A shutter inside the home flickered. Officers now knew someone was inside, and police took up positions around the house.

Lt. John Iantorno and Detective Grierson Wheeldon, both of Sheridan police, had been at the back of the house and now joined Connally in front. The next step, simple yet intense, was for Connally to walk up and knock on the front door. "We introduced ourselves from behind a rifle," he says.

He talked himself into the house. "I did seek to impress on them the gravity of the moment and the fact that we were there for an ongoing, violent situation and we really did not want to be trifled with."

He spoke with Wayne and Kathy Harris, and Kathy's twin sister, Karen Shepard. Connally recalls the dress of the three as "tasteful." Nothing stood out. Ditto for the house. But, "My feeling is our arrival was not unanticipated." The Harrises appeared as the Klebolds. "Maybe shockey is a good word; disbelieving but maintaining a facade," Connally says.

The Harrises in other ways mirrored the Klebolds. Wayne Harris said "the press" had already been at their door, and the family was now waiting for their lawyer. The Harrises were "reserved," and "volunteered to intercede with their son if he were in fact involved with the ongoing situation," according to Connally's written report.

Wayne, meantime, gave Connally a quick bio of Eric. Eric was looking forward to graduation and wore a black duster every day but had no interest in celebrating Hitler's birthday, as far as Wayne knew. "[Eric's] interest in 'explosives' and firearms was no more than you would expect from a person looking forward to joining the Marine Corps," Connally wrote after talking with Wayne, although Eric's rejection from the marines was all but final. Wayne said he had no reason to believe Eric would be involved in Columbine.

Officer Wheeldon's report paints a slightly different picture. He indicates the Harrises were "uncooperative," and initially forbid police to enter. Connally walks the line when asked whether he agrees. "I'm not sure it's one-hundred percent," he says, "and I'm not sure it's too far off either." The Harrises answered questions but with the most basic information and little elaboration, Connally says. He would have liked more. But he doesn't begrudge them. He himself says of the police, "Here's a group of armed strangers and I'm not sure I would have been completely embracing of their entry."

The Harris home has three levels: a basement, ground floor, and top floor. After officers were inside Kathy Harris took Wheeldon through the top floor. Then he asked about the basement. That included Eric's room, Kathy Harris replied. Wheeldon and another Sheridan police officer, Greg Miller, began walking toward it. "I don't want you going down there," Kathy said. Officers again explained that as an issue of public safety, they had to investigate. Kathy Harris relented. Wheeldon continued downstairs and, with gun drawn, entered Eric's bedroom. On the bed, he saw a clear plastic bag with shotgun shells. The other items police eventually took from Eric's room included fireworks and/or suspected bomb material, a sawed-off shotgun barrel, an air rifle with a sawed-off barrel, a page from the *Anarchist's Cookbook* titled "household substitutes," and objects with apparent bullet holes through them. There were books on the Nazis, and the movie *Apocalypse Now* was in the VCR.

From the kitchen, officers took Eric's class schedule, which was attached to the refrigerator with a magnet. From the dining room table they took high school photos of Eric, his graduation announcements, and addresses on where to send them. A drawer on the living room table with more of Eric's high school data also became part of the investigation. A computer from the second story was dismantled and carted away. From the backyard shed agents took two white, PVC pipes as possible pipe bomb material. The house was not "cleared" until 12:10 a.m. on April 21, 1999.

Police and the fire department also had to contend with a suspected bomb and gas vapors that may have reached explosive levels. Maybe Eric meant to kill his own parents. Maybe he meant to blow up the officers he suspected would arrive at his home. Regardless, the home and entire block at one point was evacuated and the bomb squad was called in.

As the Harrises and their police escorts waited outside, Kathy Harris' sister approached officer Wheeldon. She said the family feared retaliation from the parents of the murdered children. But Wheeldon wrote in his report that "neither Mr. nor Mrs. Harris appeared upset or surprised of [sic] what was happening."

***

Photos of the Harrises, like the Klebolds, emerged when they attended federal district court in Denver for lawsuit depositions in 2003. Wayne Harris, wearing dark pants, a blue dress shirt, and tie, had clearly aged compared to his military photo. At fifty-four, his nose was sharp; his hair snow white, and mostly bald on top. Katherine Harris wore dark slacks and a black, scoop neck T-shirt under a short-sleeve button down with flowers. She was also fifty-four, and has the softest look to her face of all the parents.

Before we got to fully see what the Harrises looked like, we got a feel for them: They were less cooperative than the Klebolds, allegedly pushing for immunity before agreeing to talk with authorities. They were also more of an unknown. Their public statements were thinner, and briefer than the Klebolds. Their attorneys were even less open, rarely speaking with the media. And no one, it seems, spoke out on behalf of them, at least since they had moved back to Colorado. Who were their friends? The same was true of their son. Hardly anyone who knew Eric admitted to liking him, or being friends with him.

Yet the Harrises also fought a little less over Eric's legacy. They allowed his autopsy to be released without a court fight, and did not sling subpoenas at reporters. If the Klebolds made more noise about wanting to figure out what went wrong, and offered some words here and there, the Harrises were more stoic. Although some wondered if they just had more to hide. Like the Klebolds, the first words from the Harrises came the day after Columbine, when they released a statement: "We want to express our heartfelt sympathy to the families of all the victims and to all the community for this senseless tragedy. Please say prayers for everyone touched by these terrible events."

After the shootings, the Harrises went to a nearby Marriott and would not return to their home until Memorial Day, about a month later. On Friday April 30, 1999, the same day the Klebolds had their sit-down with law enforcement, Jefferson County Chief Deputy District Attorney Mark Pautler announced the Harrises had backed away from talking unless they were given immunity. "We're not giving anybody immunity." Pautler said. A face off was now forming.

The immunity issue, at one point, became wrapped up in an odd letter writing problem. While victims families started receiving letters from the Klebolds about a month after the shootings, the Harrises soon learned that similar letters they had sent out were stalled. The Harrises had sent their letters through the school district, which handled Columbine mail. The letters were then forwarded to the sheriff's office, which said it was uneasy delivering them but unable to connect with the Harris attorney to return the letters. Attorney Benjamin Colkitt said he knew of no attempt by the sheriff to reach him.

Kathy Harris was "livid" according to a family friend. She would deliver the letters to victims families herself if she had to, and the letter incident made her chances of cooperating with police less likely. "This is not right," she said. "We're extremely upset."

The injured were eventually able to pick up the Harris letters at the sheriff's department (although six months after Columbine, *The Denver Post* reported that families of those who were killed had not received letters). One letter, to injured victim Mark Taylor, read, "Please accept our heartfelt wishes for a full and speedy recovery from your injuries. There are no words to express the tragic events of that day. We would have given our lives to prevent them.

"May you have the strength and the support to continue your healing process."

It was signed, "Sincerely, Wayne, Kathy and Kevin Harris ."

By August after the shootings, there was a turnaround. The sheriff and Jefferson County District Attorney now said the Harrises had never sought immunity and a meeting was close at hand. John Kiekbusch, by then a sheriff's division chief whose reputation was later questioned given the false information the department released, said a conversation with the Harris attorneys early on may have been "misinterpreted as a request for immunity."

"The bottom line was the Harrises' attorneys were concerned about any kind of legal exposure for their clients," Kiekbusch added.

And the proposed interview with the Harrises was always more about Eric, not any potential criminal behavior on behalf of his parents, Kiekbusch explained to the media. "Generally we want to explore Eric's personality," he added. "We would want to know about his activities, his friends, what he had to say about various aspects of his life."

Kiekbusch also said, "We've told them [the Harrises] that we want to get as much information as we can on the Columbine case itself. But we've also appealed to them on the basis that the information may help prevent this kind of thing from happening again."

District Attorney spokeswoman Pam Russell said, "In the midst of all that confusion [after the shootings] it's possible there was a misunderstanding."

District Attorney Dave Thomas, Russell added, had talked with Harris attorney Ben Colkitt several times about setting up a meeting. "Immunity is no longer an issue," Russell said. "They are not seeking immunity... somewhere along the way, that has no longer been an issue."

★★★

Before the Harrises talked with police, they mingled with neighbors. In September, they attended a neighborhood bonfire around a portable barbecue pit in the cul-de-sac meant to build community in the wake of Columbine. In the hectic months following the shootings, neighbors had little time to speak to each other. Now the Harrises were among those gathering around cookies and drinks in the middle of the street.

Neighbor Michael Good had wondered how he could ever look at the Harrises again after the shootings, and was bothered that they had not spoken with authorities. But he also thought there might not be an explanation for what happened. Or at least the Harrises didn't have one. He had read, and heard, they were "typical parents trying to do the right thing for their kids."

Good, then a forty-two-year-old firefighter and father of four, also thought Columbine could happen to him. He didn't know what his kids were doing every moment of every day. As for the gathering, he said about a dozen people were there, and he only talked to the Harrises after the barbecue. "They're not the ones that pulled the trigger," he said, and added, "We all feel very badly for them too."

For a newspaper story on the barbecue, the Harris attorneys issued a statement: "Wayne and Kathy Harris have been devastated by what their son, Eric, did. They continue to grieve for all of the victims and their families. Hopefully, there will come a time when they feel they are ready to speak publicly about their son and the horrible acts that he committed, but now is just not that time."

The stars finally aligned for a formal sit down with police on October 25, six months after Columbine. The Harrises, their attorneys, and a private investigator met with Kiekbusch, Sheriff John Stone, undersheriff John Dunaway, lead Columbine investigator Kate Battan, and District Attorney Dave Thomas. Thomas also recalls sheriff's Sgt. Randy West attending.

But we wouldn't learn much more. "The Harrises answered detective's questions, and all parties anticipate that future meetings will take place," according to a sheriff's press release. "No further details about any of the meetings will be made available, including time, date, place and content. No further information is available."

As time went on the sheriff's department would only seem more secretive. In November 2000, Jefferson County District Judge Brooke Jackson forced the sheriff to release eleven thousand-pages of police reports. The documents sometimes provided great detail, down to the type of clothing various students wore the day of Columbine. The meeting itself with the Harrises had already been made public, but not one official police document mentioned it. Jefferson County spokesman John Masson offered an answer for that: In fact, the Harrises had questioned police during the meeting. "There was nothing of substance that occurred during the meeting; not enough to generate a report," Masson said, and added that the sheriff's department had offered to meet with the Harrises again, "but that offer was never taken up."

Yet there was more to be gleaned from the meeting, as the Harrises gave a history of Eric's life up until Columbine, Dave Thomas says. His account begins to fill in some of the details the sheriff's office will not discuss.

The approximately two-hour meeting took place at the law offices of Harris attorneys Ben Colkitt and Abe Hutt; Thomas sat next to Wayne Harris at the conference table.

"I could have asked questions, and I may have asked one or two, but by and large the questioning was done by the sheriff's department, and most of it with the Harrises wasn't question and answer anyway," Thomas says. "They [the Harrises] basically narrated for a couple of hours."

Wayne and Katherine Harris (brother Kevin Harris was not there) came across as "a pretty normal, suburban family who obviously cared about their son, cared about their family, thought they did things the right way," said Thomas. He thought they were more cautious than the Klebolds. Wayne looked to be controlling his emotions, possibly owing to his military background. Nothing struck Thomas as inappropriate in the way the Harrises acted.

The Harris attorneys did not make any remarks. But Thomas looked to see if they coached, or impeded, their clients. He says they did not. "There was no humor," he says of the mood in the room. "There was no lightness at all. It was just a very somber occasion. We were introduced and basically the Harrises did virtually all of the talking."

The Harrises, apparently, had thought through the presentation of Eric's life they would give, but it did not seem canned, according to Thomas. Katherine Harris talked more than her husband.

"They had a lot of photos with them," Thomas said. "They passed them around and let us look at them and I think at least the sense that I got is that they were very passionate about wanting us to understand that this was a young man not unlike most young men. That he wasn't some diabolical monster, or that he had been causing trouble throughout his life and was somehow; was a bad seed, so to speak. That's the impression I got. Lots of family photos, and birthday parties, and soccer pictures, and places they'd lived; photographs of places they'd lived.

"And I think we were; I think all of our position was we were very respectful of just wanting to listen and let them say whatever they wanted to say. I remember very few questions being asked. They just narrated mostly, cause I think all of us viewed it as a starting point. We were just getting started with what ultimately might be a series of interviews. It just hasn't happened that way, but nobody seemed to be in a big rush or in a big hurry: 'Well, let's get on to what happened when he got to high school, and what happened the weekend before [Columbine].' Nobody did that. Everybody was very patient."

Investigators asked small-time questions, such as clarifying when the Harrises moved from one place to another. Wayne Harris talked about being a military family, and that Eric was often the new kid in school.

"Did that seem to cause any problems for him" someone asked.

"No, not that we were aware of," Wayne said. "I mean, he seemed to adjust very well."

But the story stopped at Columbine High.

"And I think primarily it stopped because we were getting into current events and they were; they and their lawyers were a little bit unsure of whether; how and whether they wanted to proceed so, plus we'd been going for a couple of hours," Thomas said. "It was, I think during parts of it, very emotional. I mean they were very distraught. I think both the Harrises expressed dismay at how this; how their son could have been involved in this. I would describe them as agonized. Physically, they appeared to really to be in agony over all this."

Wayne Harris groaned whenever events at Columbine were mentioned. "It was just like complete disbelief," Thomas said.

Katherine Harris, Thomas believes, cried at one point. "Obviously, in conflict about, I think, some mixed feelings," he said. "I mean, she obviously loved her son a great deal but obviously was pretty much aware of what he'd done but very conflicted over, 'How could this be?' I mean, 'How could he have done these things?'"

★★★

In September, 2000 I called Wayne Harris at Flight Safety Services in the suburb of Englewood and asked some questions. He recalled receiving an introductory letter from me, but was not ready to talk. "I'll tell you, we're not really in a position to do anything with that right now," he said. "We think there's a lot of stuff to go on before we can even think about anything like that. So, we're just not going to be able to do anything at all right now with that, I don't think."

I asked him if legal issues were getting in the way of him speaking. "Yeah, there's probably a lot of things involved, and I think that's probably a real big part of it," he replied.

I asked Wayne if he could at least talk about Eric's life without directly commenting on Columbine. "Well, I tell you, we really haven't, uh, considered anybody writing a book on this yet," he said. "You know, it's probably going to be done, but we're just not able to really think about that right now."

Was there anything else he might want to speak about right now? "No, not right now. I really don't think so," he replied.

I hoped something would change that would allow him to talk. "Well, I hope so," he said.

★★★

The public still wanted to hear from the Harrises. And the police wanted to hear more. But the Harrises didn't want to be prosecuted, or make civil litigation against them any easier. Thomas came up with a compromise.

If the Harris attorneys talked about the family, Thomas could garner details but could not use that information against the Harrises themselves because it was hearsay. "He [the lawyer] can say what if, Mr. Harris said this, this, this and this and this. Well then I can at least analyze it and say,

'If that's what he was going to tell me, then I would not; that would not be the subject of a criminal prosecution,'" Thomas explained.

Thomas memorialized his proposal in an undated letter to Harris attorneys Ben Colkitt and Abe Hutt in an attempt to broker another meeting. Immunity is not mentioned, but alluded to.

"We are at a stage now that you have requested some assurances from me with respect to my use of statements made by your clients," Thomas wrote in a letter cc'd to Sheriff Stone and Division Chief Kiekbusch. "I have discussed this issue internally and with the Sheriff's Office. It is our position that I am not in a position to make any promises or concessions with respect to statements made by your clients. I only know general details of what might come out of further discussions. One possible alternative is to have the attorneys provide information rather than having actual statements by the clients. If you have any other suggestions I would consider them."

On January 30, 2001 Thomas met with Hutt and Colkitt, and about a month later penned a letter to them regarding "complete interviews with the Harrises."

"I have struggled over this issue and arranging such a situation for a good portion of the last year and a half," Thomas wrote on February 21, 2001. "Obviously, I, the Sheriff's Department and the community are interested in everything that the Harrises have to say and to contribute to our understanding of the events of April 20, 1999. But, I continue to be concerned about what it is they want from this office and the situation it creates."

Thomas repeated the key quandary: "What benefit do I and this office derive from an agreement that no statements by Wayne or Kathy Harris would ever be used against them in a criminal case? I do not know the surrounding circumstances concerning the possible discovery and subsequent destruction of a pipe bomb in 1998 by Wayne Harris."

There of course were - and are - other questions. Did the Harrises know about Eric's writings? His weapons?

Thomas also repeated the idea that the Harris attorneys could relay the sensitive information: "How did Eric and Dylan manage to build the bombs, apparently at the Harris home without the knowledge of the Harrises?" he added, but also noted, "As you know, I have never threatened any of the parents with criminal prosecution nor do I possess sufficient information or evidence to suggest that any criminal prosecution would be considered or would be appropriate."

As of August 2001, Thomas told me, he had spoken with the Harris attorneys "no less than ten times." He often spoke with Colkitt and Hutt, with both of them on speakerphone. He called them "very good lawyers" and added, "I think they've given up on me saying I won't ever prosecute. I really think the Harrises want to tell their story and I think they will through civil lawsuits [filed by victims families]."

Yet Thomas also pegged the civil lawsuits as holding up his attempts to talk to the Harrises. "The civil case has interfered to a large extent with us carrying on those conversations, so I don't know if it will ever happen or not to be honest," he said.

I asked Thomas if immunity was the holdup. "It's still there. It's still an issue," he said, but added, "And I won't describe it as immunity because that's a problem. We have a little semantic difference here."

He returned to the alleged father-son pipe bomb incident to illustrate the potential parental liability. "The one extreme is that he [Wayne Harris] finds this thing and he says, 'Eric, what the hell's going on? What is this?' And he says, 'Ah, I was just playing around, it's a science project. I was reading in a book about how the ancient Chinese were making rockets and that's really what I had in mind, but I got kind of carried away and I made this thing to see if it would explode. And I though it'd be pretty fun.' And dad says, 'You idiot. You know, what kind of idiot are you, I mean, you know, you're not supposed to be doing stuff like this. We're going to go destroy this. And I don't want you ever doing anything like that again! That's one extreme," Thomas says. "The other extreme which I will tell you I don't think happened is, 'What are you doing? Oh, I'm building this pipe bomb because I'm going to take it to school and I'm going to blow up a bunch of people because I hate 'em. I hate 'em! And dad says, 'Fine, you know go ahead, go do what you want to do.' That didn't happen... But I don't know. I don't know when it happened exactly. I don't know the circumstances. I don't know what kind of pipe bomb it was, I don't know how it ties in with other things that we know in this case. So for me to say, 'Mr. Harris you can come forward and you can tell me all of these things, and I don't know what you're going to tell me, but I'll tell you in advance that I will never use this in a criminal prosecution, I can't do it.' And I told him I can't do it."

"As impossible as it might sound," Thomas adds, "what position would I be in if Mr. Harris said, 'I spent the weekend building pipe bombs with my son?'"

The Harrises, from what we know, never talked to police again.

★★★

When the Harrises made news in December 2001 the situation again seemed to reveal as much about them as the sheriff's department. The occasion was the *Rocky Mountain News* and the local, alternative weekly *Westword* reporting on previously undisclosed writings of Eric that showcased more of his plans for killing. An unnamed source or sources quietly gave the media the documents, which appeared to have come from the sheriff's department. Yet the sheriff hinted that it may have been the Harrises themselves who surreptitiously released the information, although it contrasted with their quiet nature and fights against public records. There was also no clear reason the Harrises would want the material public. The Harrises sent out a statement saying they "were horrified by the unexpected publication of their son's journal entries and drawings," and that it might cause copycat incidents.

They also said, "On April 20, 1999, the Jefferson County Sheriff's Department seized numerous papers and other items from the Harrises' home. In June, 2001 the sheriff's department furnished Mr. and Mrs. Harris with a copy of some of the papers that had been taken from their home. The copies which Mr. and Mrs. Harris received from the sheriff's department in June differ in appearance in many respects from the copies published by the Denver media."

Perhaps the most interesting aspect of the Harris' remarks was their stated fear that Eric's writings could spawn copycats. That was a bit duplicitous given that they were so tight-lipped about information on their son that could explain what made him tick and realistically prevent other school shootings.

★★★

After Columbine Katherine Harris' parents, Richard and Elaine Pool, still lived in the unassuming house in quiet south Denver where their girls grew up. A man in a plaid, wool shirt, dark pants and gray hair straight and neatly combed answers the door. "No, I'm not interested," he says when asked if he would like to speak about his family.

Eric's birthday falls eleven days before Columbine and Pool neighbor Steve Ferguson recalls Dick attending a party for Eric sometime in the two weeks before the shootings. On the day of Columbine Ferguson got home around 6:00 p.m. and saw a small platoon of cars he recognized as belonging to relatives. He had a feeling it was due to the shootings - why else would so many people gather on a Tuesday night? But he didn't know the exact connection.

Ferguson, who was then in his forties, says he didn't go over to the Pool's home that day but waited, he thinks, two days before contacting them. He called from work.

"I said, 'Elaine, so what's going on? I noticed the cars over there the night of Columbine,'" Ferguson says as he sits in his house across the street from the Pools. "I said, 'Did something tragic happen to a grandson or granddaughter?'

"And at that time, Elaine said, 'Yes, I had a grandson that was killed, that was killed in the Columbine shootings.' And I expressed my condolences, and extended my sympathy and that kind of stuff."

"Which one was he?" Ferguson asked.

Elaine broke down and said: "My gosh, he was the killer."

Ferguson asked the name of the grandson. "Harris," his grandmother said. "His name is Harris."

The weekend after Columbine Ferguson was doing chores outside his house. Dick came over with tears streaming down his cheeks.

"He was emotionally shot, and uh, he tried to explain a little bit what was going on, and that kind of stuff," Ferguson recalls. "'Dick,' I said, 'You don't have to explain.'"

"Again, I extended my condolences and my feelings," Ferguson added. "I said Dick, this has got to be tearing you apart type of thing. And he acknowledged that, and he just; said it's tough. I really cannot remember verbatim what he said, but he said it's eatin him alive. He said he can't sleep."

Dick told Mary Ferguson, "It will never be the same for us, ever."

After Columbine the waving, the smiling, and the visits to the Ferguson house stopped. "They were just different people," Steve said.

Steve does not believe the Pools mentioned their grandson ever again, and it was about three years before they looked like they were back to normal, at least on the outside. Mary Ferguson says the Pools seemed to have fewer family gatherings at their home after Columbine. And every year for the anniversary, Dick and Elaine travel out of state to get away from reporters. Mary does not want to say where. "It's kind of like unspoken word," she says. "When April comes around every year, he

[Dick] says, 'You know we're leaving, for this week.'"

★★★

Just before 9:00 a.m. on August 9, 2002 Wayne Harris shows up at federal district court in Denver for his deposition in the Luvox case. I do, but don't recognize him at first. His face is longer and thinner than the official military photo used as a default "mug shot" of him after the shootings. His build also seems thinner than his military photo would let on. He is an iteration of his former self.

His hair and mustache are white. He is dressed in a dark slacks with a cell phone attached to his belt. A dark and light striped polo shirt hangs on him loosely and he looks more like a pro golfer than a man about to enter a deposition. This also throws me off.

Once inside the courthouse, I find myself sharing the row of urinals with him in the men's bathroom.

"Are you Wayne Harris?" I ask.

"What makes you think that?" he says, and chuckles.

I say he looks like Wayne Harris. There is a pause, and I ask if he is here for depositions. He says he is there for a lot of things. A very lawyerly response. I suppose he should know by now.

Yet his demeanor is almost cheery, as if he enjoys the verbal jousting. I ask if he thinks Luvox caused the Columbine shooting. "I think it will all come out," he says.

I ask if there's anything else he wants to say. No, he says. I ask if he thinks he'll ever talk. "Oh no," he adds, although the possibility still seems open.

The Solvay depositions are closed to the public, but I and a photographer wait outside the courthouse. When the depositions are done, Wayne Harris and one of his attorneys come barreling out of the courthouse a little after 1:30 p.m. as if to avoid us. The photographer snaps some pictures. The attorney and Harris, wearing his sunglasses, storm across the courthouse patio, hit the crosswalk, and luckily have a walk sign. The photographer gets in front of them, snaps a few more pictures, and moves out of the way. Harris and the attorney never say a word.

GREEN MOUNTAIN GUNS INC.

ORDER# 4090   DATE: 12-18-7?

303-985-7240   PHONE #

NAME: Eric Harris

ADDRESS: ▓▓▓▓▓▓▓

STATE: CO

CITY: Littleton

ZIP 80123

ITEM TO ORDER: Hi-Point 9mm carbine magazines

9 mag @ $15.00 EA

H: ▓▓▓▓▓▓▓

W:

AMOUNT: 9 mags. 135.00

TAX: 8.51

TOTAL: 143.51

DEPOSIT:

TOTAL DUE:

* ALL SPECIAL ORDERS ARE NON-RETURNABLE*
DEPOSITS ARE NON-REFUNDABLE

JC-001-026360

FIFTEEN

A victim's tale

Isaiah Shoels, one of the few black students at Columbine, had a grand reputation. The eighteen-year-old was funny, kind-hearted, and always surrounded by others. "If you didn't like Isaiah, *you* had the problem," says his father, Michael Shoels.

As a child, Isaiah overcame heart surgery. As a teen, he lifted so many weights he was almost as wide as he was 4'11". Friends called him "Little Man."

A popular image of Isaiah is him in a football photo from Lakewood High School, which he attended before Columbine. Isaiah is posing on bended knee with a helmet tucked under his arm. He is wearing a dark blue football jersey with "Lakewood" and the number fifty-two printed across his chest in orange. He stares straight ahead in the photo, neither smiling, nor frowning. Maybe there is a hint of amusement in his face. It is the same photo that has been incorporated into his tombstone.

His family called him 'Saiah. He was a comedian who liked Eddie Murphy and performed skits poking fun at his parents, brothers and sisters. He made videos of himself mocking strippers and dancers. That humor helps his mother Vonda deal with his death. "I can hear Isaiah in my mind saying, 'Mom, why are you so down?'" she says.

Isaiah liked all kinds of music, except heavy metal and rock, and Michael says he was grooming him to take over the family music business, Notorious Records, which specialized in rap, R&B and funk. Michael had all the confidence in Isaiah's smarts. "If ever there should have been a black president, he would have been the one, because he could deal with anybody in the world. Not only in America, I'm talking about anywhere in the world," Michael says, in his trademark hyperbole.

Isaiah himself talked about death. "Just roll me out butt-naked" in a casket he would joke, saying his body looked too good to wear clothes. But even that was ended by a shotgun blast. "They couldn't roll him out butt naked," Michael says. "They messed his chest up."

On Saturday April 17, 1999, three days before the shootings, Isaiah and his parents were traveling in the family van. As the Shoels recount it, Isaiah asked them, "What would you do if someone shot down all your children?"

Michael and Vonda were taken aback. "I mean you know, no kid supposed to be asking their parents a question like that for no reason at all," Michael says.

The parents said they would not seek revenge. "Because God said, 'Let all vengeance be mine,'" Michael adds. But they said they would speak out against violence.

The families of other Columbine dead have recounted similar premonitions: Daniel Mauser asking his father about loopholes in the Brady bill two weeks before the shootings, and Lauren Townsend writing in her diary: "Unfortunately it usually takes a huge trauma to get people to realize what is important and I feel that is what is going to happen..."

In the mornings before school Isaiah would turn on the stereo, and every light in the house, to help wake up the family. He left the house on April 20, 1999 wearing a black polo shirt, dark green corduroy pants, and black and white Air Jordans. He had two gold earrings with clear stones in his left ear. His family would later retrieve his backpack and books from the sheriff's department. Michael cut the boys' hair, but Vonda says Isaiah planned on telling his father he wanted to let his hair grow out when he got home from school that day.

Michael was sleeping in after being up into the wee hours drawing up music contracts and didn't see Isaiah that morning. Notorious Records didn't register much on the music industry radar but Michael, forty-two at the time, says he was scheduled to leave the next day for Los Angeles to cut a deal. Thank God he wasn't airborne on April 20, he says. "I would have been trying to make that pilot turn around."

Michael was sitting at a large, dark wood desk in his basement office later that morning when the phone rang. Vonda, who was then thirty-four, picked up. It was a family friend, Patricia Metzer, calling to say there was gunfire at Columbine.

"Mike, they done killed Isaiah," Vonda said.

In truth, the outside world did not yet know who had been killed at Columbine, and who had pulled the trigger. Vonda had no proof Isaiah was dead. But she had a premonition because Isaiah had had run-ins at school, including a suspension for fighting the year before.

Michael, dressed in a robe, heard Vonda. He was 280 pounds back then—as big as Isaiah was small — but jumped up on his desk. He says he leapt up the five basement stairs, flying through the air, robe flapping, and touched down on the first floor landing. He still marvels at the feat. "That was adrenaline," he says.

Next came a call from the Shoels' daughter, Michelle, who also attended Columbine. She was safe. That left Isaiah and his brother Anthony, then fifteen. Vonda was already dressed and grabbed Michael's pants; he thinks it was some "joggers." "I got dressed in three or four seconds," he says, and threw on his sneakers as he ran out the door. "Good I had some clothes on at all."

Michael and Vonda didn't need to talk. They fixated on getting to Columbine and hopped in their brown van.

"I gave that van everything it had," says Michael, who estimates he hit 100 MPH on the suburban streets. "I was driving safely, of course. But I didn't spare no speed."

The lukewarm air of April 20, 1999 said spring, but Michael remembers mud and snow still on the grass surrounding the school where the sun had not yet reached. When Michael arrived at Columbine, he recalls only one reporter, and a handful of police officers "just browsing around." Vonda got on her knees and started screaming, "Isaiah's dead."

"That," Michael says, "made me lose my mind."

He tried to enter the school, and tussled with police. "Sir, you can't go up there," Michael says he was told by an officer.

Vonda added, screaming, "You can't go up there, they'll kill you too."

"That," Michael says, "brought me back."

The Shoels say they still heard guns and bombs going off. "It was almost like a nightmare, and you couldn't wake up," Michael adds.

Michael was in an anxiety-stricken holding pattern and cried as students were led out of the school. But still no Isaiah or Anthony. At 12:20 p.m., Michael couldn't bear any more, and walked up to the deputies. They told him that students who escaped were being transferred to Leawood Elementary School, just blocks away, and to the Columbine Public Library, across the park from the high school. Michael and Vonda hitched a ride to the elementary school with about eight other parents. They waited for forty-five minutes, eyeing the arriving buses for any sign of their children's faces. But short, stocky Isaiah and tall, lanky Anthony did not shimmy off any of them.

The Shoels then walked toward the public library, framed by the snowy Rocky Mountains–distant, yet still massive. Hundreds of police officers and a growing thicket of reporters buzzed about, although the hordes of journalists had not yet arrived on flights from Japan, Boston and New York that sent the message "Huge Story." That would happen the next morning with news trucks forming an exclamation mark to the news of the day that would drag on for years.

At the public library Michael and Vonda began another grim Columbine ritual, reading the lists of children who had safely escaped the school. Again, they came up empty-handed. They took the next painful step and called local hospitals. They were told their children were not there either. People, it seemed, had disappeared.

"I really started getting worried then," Michael says. "My blood pressure going up."

The Shoelses' cell phone had gone dead from so many calls to their house, and to Vonda's mother. They began crying. A woman offered her cell phone, but that also went out from being loaned out too many times. The woman suggested they walk to her house across the street and use a land line. On the walk, Michael noticed that the area was continuing to fill up with police officers and FBI agents. The first SWAT entered the school just after noon, but Michael didn't see the other officers going in.

Once the Shoels got to the phone, Vonda called Columbine, Leawood, and the sheriff's office. Still no information. They called home and checked messages. Nothing.

The Shoels got a ride to their van about one-half mile south of the school. They drove back toward Leawood Elementary but cars carrying police officers and frantic parents jammed the streets and forced them to park some four blocks away.

Parents waiting at Leawood and the library were an open mark for the media, and the reporters began to get on Michael's nerves. He was sick of being asked if he thought his kids would get out safely.

Around 4:00 p.m., "Things got to be lookin' real bad," Michael says. Then a bus pulled up with Anthony. The Shoels spotted him when he walked into the auditorium and they saw the tip of his five-foot, eleven-inch head. "I was mad," Michael says. "I was crying."

Yet still no Isaiah.

Isaiah was in fact in the library, his body leaning against another dead student. The same chest that had survived heart surgery was now bruised by a shotgun blast. Around 4:45 p.m. a doctor had entered the school and declared Isaiah and the other victims inside dead, but no formal death notifications to the families had occurred. Because the school still had to be checked for bombs, the coroner would not make it inside until the next day.

Michael and Vonda finally left Leawood around 8:30 p.m., nine hours after the shooting started. Calls to the hospital continued to draw blanks. "Our kids are trained to call us," Michael was thinking. He had a sense of how it would end, but says, "I was still in acute denial."

At home with their four other children and Vonda's mother, the Shoels went to bed at 3:30 a.m. "I heard guns and bombs in my sleep," Michael says.

Around 5:30 a.m., a steady stream of family, friends, and reporters began calling. Michael woke up to answer the phone. In conversation, Michael held out hope. "I told a reporter he [Isaiah] is still living. If anyone's still alive, it's Isaiah. He's smart, and he's fast."

But Michael really didn't want to talk to anyone except the sheriff and the coroner. They had the answers. When the sheriff's office did not call, Michael called them. He called so many times, he says, he was told to stop. That puzzled him. "I don't know how one man could interrupt their investigation," he says. "Only way I coulda see I was interruptin' is I was cuttin' in on that lie they was tryin' to get together."

***

Dave Thomas, who was then Jefferson County District Attorney, speaks fondly of the Shoels. He calls them a "fascinating study," and a family he respects. It would not seem an easy thing to do. His work — or lack of it — was among the many targets of the Shoels' post-Columbine wrath.

But Thomas easily recalls meeting the Shoels on the day after Columbine. He says he took it upon himself to give them the death notification. He did not know the family. But, he explained, "I took Isaiah Shoels because it was abundantly clear to me he was the only African-American. People had been talking about it."

He drove to the Shoels house that Wednesday, the day after Columbine, with then Denver District Attorney and fellow Democrat Bill Ritter. Thomas went to the door and met Michael Shoels. Both Michael and Thomas remember the time as around 1:30 p.m. Thomas says that in the first two to three weeks after Columbine, meeting Michael is the thing he remembers most. Michael was a man of business, Thomas says, and kept himself together. Thomas respected that.

"Is your wife here?" Thomas asked as Michael answered the door.

"She is," Michael answered, but she was in bed and in no condition to come down and meet with Thomas.

"Mr. Shoels," Thomas said, "I've met with the coroner and a detective this morning. I don't know how else to tell you this, but, your son Isaiah is in the school, he's dead, he was killed, and I just needed you to know that."

"My son is a tremendous kid, very imaginative, and I'll tell you, until two minutes ago, I thought he was alive," Michael said, according to Thomas. "I thought he was hiding."

Michael remembers the moment differently.

"I kind of lost it," he says. "I didn't know what to do, where to turn. Dave [Thomas] seen me getting weak, and he helped me up with the other guy. I didn't no longer have a reason to be in denial. He [Isaiah's] gone. Now somebody got to pay."

Michael sat on the stairwell and asked when the family could view Isaiah's body, but Thomas was not sure because the school was still a crime scene.

"Everything I was praying for and hoping for went down the tubes when that car pulled up" carrying Thomas, Michael says. "I started trying to investigate myself."

Vonda wondered about laying eyes on Isaiah. Her son's friends had alternately told her Isaiah was shot in the head, face, chest, back, and back of the head.

"I needed to know if he still had a face," she says.

Michael would check. It was three days after Columbine when he saw Isaiah's body at the mortuary. "I pulled the covers off of him," Michael recalled. "I looked at his face. That's all I was really concerned about was his facial area because I wanted to have an open casket funeral. And I just wanted to make sure his face wasn't messed up. But after I found out that wasn't messed up, we just lifted the cover off, you know of course, that was my baby. I had to hug him and I kissed him and his body was just frozen; cold. I thought I was doing pretty good till I walked off. When I walked off I passed out. That's all I remember; walkin' off."

Isaiah's funeral was one week later, the last of the Columbine funerals, and maybe the biggest. While Cassie Bernall's funeral drew an estimated 2,500, and Dave Sanders 3,000, some 5,000 packed the Heritage Christian Center in the suburb of Aurora for Isaiah. Televisions had to be set up in an overflow room.

Martin Luther King III spoke and noted that he himself had been a victim of violence: He was ten when his father was gunned down. The white, Republican governor Bill Owens, who had attended some of the other Columbine funerals, also made remarks. A video remembrance of Isaiah churned out photos and music.

Yet the funeral hardly helped Michael's grief. "Naw. I mean, there was so many people there to observe, I guess that was OK, but the point is that was my last time ever seeing him [Isaiah], laying eyes on him physically," he says. "And that was hard. That was very hard."

A man named William Collins Jr. also wanted to lay eyes on Isaiah. He said he was Isaiah's birth father. But security guards prevented him from entering, according to *The Denver Post*. The Shoels spokesman said Collins was being disruptive.

Michael remained incensed at the last words to fall upon Isaiah's ears. Words that still echoed in Michael's own head. "Could you imagine those words the last words you hearin', and you didn't have a prejudiced bone in your body? Can you imagine lyin', and knowin' you getting ready to go, and hearin,' 'There go that nigger?'"

Michael then adds: "You know, that's bad man, that's bad. A whole lot of people going to have to talk about that."

Their garage in Texas, where they have moved, holds four, red plastic crates with lids. The bottom one contains Isaiah's clothes. Michael and Vonda open it up. Inside are blue T-shirts, a Chaps Ralph Lauren blue polo shirt, and the size medium football jersey with number 52 on the front. The family used to wear each others' clothes, and Vonda at the moment has on Isaiah's white tennis shoes. "Every time I would look at my feet it would just break my heart," she says.

There is another place the Shoels can view Isaiah's football jersey. When Michael goes to Isaiah's grave in Denver his football photo, imprinted into the gravestone, stares back. It is a signal for Michael to begin his graveside ritual. He checks for weeds, gets down on his left knee, and tidies up flowers on the grave. He straightens a set of rocks, and places a coin under one of them. Michael's hat falls off as he kisses the ground. "That's just a deal we have," he explains. "Let him know I'm still thinkin' about him."

***

The path from victim to crusader is well-trodden, as if the individual and community response to school shootings has been scripted into the human DNA. A public execution such as Columbine grants a public platform to a victim's family. They are asked to show their grief, and are given the bully pulpit. Their opinions, politics, and culture are now newsworthy. They turn the dead, the injured, and the disappeared into lawsuits, foundations, and speeches to head off future tragedies. Charitable payouts are questioned, and authorities are taken to task for withholding information. It is painful, messy, controversial, intrusive, and long-lasting. It can also be good. Public policy improves — SWAT across America changed after Columbine to charge after gunmen rather than try to contain them. It's called the active shooter policy. Lawsuits unlock information - box loads in the case of Columbine.

Among the shootings before Columbine was West Paducah, Kentucky, where fourteen-year-old Michael Carneal killed three and wounded five on December 1, 1997 at Heath High School. The lawsuits that followed both predicted the Columbine lawsuits, and went beyond them. Those who were sued included, "students who had seen Carneal with a gun at school before the shooting; students who had heard that something was going to happen... [and] students who may have been involved in a conspiracy," along with the producers of the movie The Basketball Diaries and the Internet pornography sites Carneal visited, according to a study of that shooting.

Community backlash to the West Paducah lawsuits also forecast the post-Columbine reaction. According to the study called "No Exit" West Paducah victim families who brought suit "reported receiving some hate mail, being stared at in public, and being avoided by some of their old acquaintances. One of the teachers sued was still in his teacher training program at a local university at the time of the shooting and successfully countersued. This story was brought up by many as an example of the excess and carelessness of the handling of the suits. Some thought that the [victim] families were not actually interested in discovering the truth and were simply trying to win a large monetary judgment. Others felt betrayed because they felt they had reached out to the victims in their time of need, only to have them turn around and bring suit. A large majority felt that the suits were inhibiting the already very difficult healing process, making it impossible for the community to move forward. Although a fair number supported the entertainment industry suits, they thought that pointing fingers at others in the community was inappropriate.

"Michael Breen, the lawyer for the [victims] families, countered that it was exactly this unwillingness to pay attention to problems that had caused the tragedy in the first place. In Breen's view, 'accountability is always painful,' but by bringing attention to those at fault, schools, parents, and the entertainment industry will become aware of their responsibilities, which may help prevent future shootings."

"No Exit" said it was all part of the healing process: "Those who are farther removed from the epicenter heal more quickly and want to put the incident behind them faster. Not recognizing the differential rates of healing that people in the community go through, each side thinks the other is wrong. Those closer to the center feel that others are repressing their feelings and will never get through their trauma if they do not talk about it. Those on the periphery think those in the center are dwelling on the past and need to stop."

In his book *Gone Boy: A Walkabout*, author Gregory Gibson tracks how his son Galen died at the Simon's Rock College shooting in 1992. Gibson filed a lawsuit, but he also became a reporter, at least in his own mind, traveling the country and asking the fundamental questions that seem to arise after school shootings: What did school officials know? How were the guns obtained? What made the killer tick? "[My wife] Annie and I had a deep-seated need to learn all the facts surrounding Galen's murder," Gibson wrote. "Although we were very different people in many ways, we shared the same basic values. One of these was a belief in the redemptive power of truth. If the truth didn't always set us free, at least it kept us clean and made our lives less complicated.

"Part of our anger at Simon's Rock College, and one of the main reasons for the lawsuit, was our belief that they had failed to respect our need for the truth."

Some Columbine families, fighting the pull of this tragic gravity, chose silence. But many launched crusades, and the Shoels were no exception. Early on, they were among the victims families who spoke most loudly, and critically, from their new-found public platform. In turn, they were among the most criticized.

The Shoels undertook a traveling ministry that ranged across the country with a mix of gospel, grief and civics lesson. They armed themselves with a spokesman and an attorney, helpful tools in a modern American tragedy. They asked the questions on everyone's mind. They were the first to file a Columbine lawsuit, just over a month after the shootings, and went straight to Harrises and Klebolds charging that they had not properly controlled their sons. The Shoels were the first to sue the Jefferson County Sheriff. They alleged officers did not properly investigate the two teens before the shootings, and did not fully deploy the day of the shootings. "They might as well put they wings on and call themselves cluckers," Michael says of the police. "Chickens."

The Shoels sued the Columbine teachers for allegedly failing to piece together the violent class essays and videos that popped up in the classrooms, and again asked whether anyone could have predicted Columbine before the fact. The Shoels tried to take the gun accomplices to task for aiding and abetting; Michael figures Robyn Anderson knew what the guns would be used for, but wasn't prosecuted because she was white. "Now you know if that had been one of our daughters, we all woulda been in jail," he says. "We all woulda been lookin' for bondsmen, you know what I'm sayin'?"

Michael says he didn't sue for money, but answers. His pleadings seeking monetary damages were like the economic boycotts of civil rights era. "I just did the same thing," he says. "It's just in a modern way."

The injured, and other victim families, would also file lawsuits.

The Shoels appeared on radio and television, and two days after the shootings Michael took part in one of the most powerful moments in television history. On the "Today" show with Katie Couric he listened as student Craig Scott recounted seeing Isaiah get shot. Craig's own sister, Rachel Scott, had also been shot dead, and Michael held hands, healing and grieving, black and white, with Craig. Although looking back, Michael is almost amused by the scene. "When I went to see Katie Couric, it was to call all black men in America to help me fight the Klan," he says, "then something like the Holy Spirit struck me."

Leeza, Montel, Queen Latifah, Oprah, and The 700 Club also beamed the Shoels into America's living rooms, the couple recalls. But Vonda says, "I really would have rather go on for a different reason. Like maybe listenin' to other peoples' problems."

The Shoels have what might easily be called conspiracy theories. Michael and Vonda believe the whites who died at Columbine were killed because they liked black people. "We dealin' with the Aryan Nation or the Klan, and they hate to say it," Michael says at one point of the forces behind Columbine. "Instead of them sayin' a apple is a apple and a orange is a orange, they tryin' to make something; they tryin' to make those fruits be something else. You can't make a peach be a banana. How you gonna do it? They don't even look the same. You see what I'm sayin'? You can't turn a apple into a lemon. They too; they opposites. You might try, but you can't do it."

In fact, Michael at one point calls Eric and Dylan scapegoats. "If we really get down to it – I hope we can find out – but I don't think Dylan or Eric killed Isaiah," he says.

"Now I wouldn't say that," Vonda parries. "I don't trust that. I don't; [someone] would have to show me proof of that."

Yet Vonda has other conspiratorial thoughts. "Eric and Klebold I don't think shot theirselves," she says. "I think somebody else did it figurin' they was gonna snitch. They couldn't hold a secret. So they just got rid of them too. That's how I feel. Maybe not. That's how I really feel."

Michael adds: "This is the biggest cover-up in America."

The Shoels received their share of e-mails, phone calls, and hugs of support. They were also, as *The Denver Post* put it, "vilified," at least in Denver. "Are they victims or are they opportunists?" Denver talk show host Peter Boyles told the paper. "Clearly they're victims, but they've got the opportunism thing going pretty strong, too."

The media poked through the muck of Michael's rap sheet, almost as long as his list of complaints against the Columbine disaster. *The Denver Post* reported: "He served a three-year stint in a Texas prison from 1974 to 1977, according to the Texas Department of Corrections. He'd been on probation for burglarizing a pharmacy when police found him illegally in possession of a 12-gauge shotgun and .38-caliber revolver during a car accident, records show."

Michael told the paper he was seventeen at the time of the burglary when his friends did the break-in. He was just a bystander. "People are trying to pull up my history, something that wouldn't happen if I weren't black," Michael added. "I've proved myself to be a law-abiding citizen."

At one point he was behind on almost $7,000 worth of child support payments to his ex-wife.

After the Shoels sued the Harrises and Klebolds, the right-leaning *Rocky Mountain News* editorial page blasted their high profile attorney, Geoffrey Fieger: "It's about accountability, he [Fieger] promised. It's about responsibility. And who knows? Depending on what ultimately comes out at trial, he may even partly be right. But at his press conference

Thursday it was vibrantly clear that this first of the Columbine lawsuits is also very much about a loud, flamboyant attorney by the name of Geoffrey Fieger."

The father of slain student Dan Rohrbough and the Browns, all of whom are white, would later bear the brunt of the criticism for being the loudest Columbine critics. But Michael, a thundering black preacher in a quiet, white state, sees racism in the criticism directed at him. "We were the talk of the land," he says. "I'm just a mad, deranged black man."

He adds, "They treatin' us like we went in that school and pulled the trigger."

But the Shoels lived up to their own code, becoming the first and still only victim's family to release their loved one's full autopsy without a court order. They did it to emphasize the horror of Columbine, and the need to investigate it. Their spokesman called Colorado the "Rocky Mountains of Hate," and Michael moved his family to suburban Houston before Columbine's one-year anniversary. "Colorado is smothering with so much hate that black people like us cannot stay there," Michael says.

If the Shoels didn't seem intellectual, they made an intellectual argument. They said the derision they received was a version of the hatred that caused Isaiah's death in the first place. Columbine wasn't about tears and teddy bears, but finding meaning. That meant slogging through details to see what went wrong (and right) to head off future incidents. The Shoels believe that if the memories of Columbine are buried, the problems that caused it will rise again. Their protests against the sheriff and others were often justified.

Some people still wanted Columbine to just go away. But it would not. And neither would school shootings. And neither would the Shoels.

★★★

Michael says he was one of sixteen children. His father was a railroad worker, his mother a housewife. They could not read or write.

Born on October 1, 1956 Michael says he flirted with the idea of playing running back for the Denver Broncos, but never made tryouts because he hurt his back. Instead, he says he got an associate of arts degree, and a cosmetology license. He had his own barbershop in Texas.

In 1977, on his twenty-first birthday, records show, he married Renelda L. Westmoreland in Texas. She was nineteen.

Michael says he also worked for Discount Tire, became an ordained

Pentecostal minister, and was assistant pastor at True Pillar of Faith church in Denver. He got into the music business, and was director of Dankside Productions and Hit Room Productions – a couple of his record companies.

Michael is listed as the father on Isaiah's Colorado death certificate, and maintains he is Isaiah's father. The Shoels spokesman says Michael is "the only father Isaiah ever knew."

According to social security records Isaiah Eamon Moore was born August 4, 1980, and apparently took Vonda's last name. Vonda was only fifteen at the time and Michael was still married to Renelda. Michael married Vonda in 1983, six months after divorcing Renelda.

Vonda was born and raised in Denver. Petite and cute, she reads Stephen King, Harlequin romances, and pads around her house in brown clogs. She did not attend college, and her professional history boils down to working with Michael on various business projects.

If the Shoels did not have the background of world-class rabble-rousers, they had help from a pair of trained professionals.

***

In 1970 Sam Riddle was already making headlines at age at twenty-three. He became a member of the Associated Students of Michigan State University after beating out almost two dozen other petitioners, and an article in the *State News* noted he was also a member of the executive council of the Black Liberation Front. Riddle told the paper he saw no conflict of interest between the two organizations. He discussed race, decentralizing the Associated Students to make it more effective, and criticized a proposed "all-events building." "Physical fitness is a beautiful thing, but I seriously question the way priorities appear to be being set," he said, according a copy of the *News* provided by Riddle. A photo of Riddle shows him smiling and accented by an Afro, sunglasses, and what appears to be a jean jacket.

As a twenty-five-year-old senior he was already married, a father of two sons, and a U.S. Army veteran. On Feb. 26, 1972, Riddle and approximately 100 other blacks flooded onto the university basketball court during the national anthem of the MSU-Iowa game. They were protesting the suspension of two black University of Minnesota basketball players involved in a brawl during an Ohio State game. The MSU-Iowa game was delayed for forty-five minutes as Riddle struggled to read a statement that was nearly drowned out by "boos, jeers, catcalls and threats from the predominantly white audience," according to the *Lansing State Journal*.

Riddle said the audience outbursts mirrored the "true feelings" of white America toward blacks. He expressed the need to eliminate racism, but also "a restructuring of the present system of capitalism." Otherwise, he said, there would still be poor blacks and poor whites. "While the possibility of violent revolution is a real one, Riddle said he does not necessarily think it is an inevitable one," the *Journal* added.

More than a decade later Riddle had obtained a law degree, trimmed his afro, and looked comfortable in a suit and tie. A news clip (also provided by Riddle) from the April 3, 1988 *Detroit News* describes him as a key player in orchestrating Jesse Jackson's "stunning upset victory" over Michael Dukakis in the Michigan Democratic presidential caucuses. A thumbnail bio described Riddle as: "A Flint (Michigan) lawyer and former '60s militant, has worked for Jackson in 10 states and specialized in organizing standing room only rallies."

When the bullets started flying at Columbine Riddle was working for then Colorado Secretary of State Vikki Buckley. She was called the country's highest ranking African American Republican female to hold statewide office.

Riddle had been Buckley's campaign consultant when she was up for re-election, but under fire for how she ran the office and down in the polls. Buckley won and promptly retained Riddle as a seven-month consultant for $70,000. That came out to $250 an hour, according to press reports, and Buckley asked for an additional $22,500 near the end of the contract. Those numbers would later collide with Columbine.

Riddle and Buckley were eating breakfast when Michael Shoels emerged on the "Today" show. "The Secretary of State looked at me and wondered if the state should reach out to the Shoels," as Riddle recalls it. They headed out to Littleton, and the timing was right. A fight had just broken out in the Shoels home between the television shows "Hard Copy" and "Inside Edition" over who got to interview the Shoels first, Michael recalls. Fists were about to fly. Riddle restored order by sending the reporters out of the house and making them form a line. (Riddle doesn't exactly remember who the journalists were, but says they were "sensationalistic media.")

Riddle has been with the Shoels ever since, and the Shoels say they haven't paid him a dime. One of Riddle's observations is that people caught in the vortex of tragedy learn to "message," which is seizing a cause while in the media spotlight. He calls the Shoels the most messaged of the Columbine families.

★★★

Attorney Geoffrey Fieger not only wins multi-million-dollar judgments in cases fit for television — where he has appeared many a time — he has sued television. He won an approximately $25 million judgment against the Jenny Jones show for setting up a straight man (Jonathan Schmitz) with a gay man (Scott Amedure) who had a crush on him. Schmitz then killed Amedure. An appeals court later overturned the monetary judgment, but the case imbued Fieger with a certain power of attorney, and he ended up on the show called "Power of Attorney," and helmed a radio talk segment in Detroit called "Fieger Time." He has a web site devoted to him, fansoffieger.com, and a 2000 profile in *GQ* magazine called him the "lawyer of the moment." He was indicted in 2007 on federal charges of violating campaign finance laws, but acquitted by a jury.

His most famous client is probably assisted suicide doctor Jack Kevorkian, who Fieger kept free through nine years of courtroom battles before they split. Kevorkian ended up behind bars after a 1999 conviction for a lethal injection that was broadcast on "60 Minutes." Fieger, whose father was a civil rights attorney, has portrayed Kevorkian's cause in the same light.

One on one Fieger can be friendly and mellow but he also has a defining smirk and gleam in his eye. And while lawyering is his profession, politics is his hobby. Although his success at lambasting courtroom opponents has not always made for an even-keeled pol cultivating votes. In 1998, he ran as a Democrat for Michigan governor and lost to Republican incumbent John Engler. Among Fieger's more famous lines–and he has many–is accusing then Michigan Attorney General Jennifer Granholm of having all the loyalty of an alley cat.

Fieger is half Jewish, half Norwegian, and calls himself a "Jewegian," although he is also wildly popular in the black community. "Maybe they like my style. I'm outspoken," he says. "I challenge authority."

At federal court in downtown Detroit the city is gray in both color and character. But a couple years after Columbine Fieger provides the sunshine, and his courtroom appearance begins long before he handles the day's case. Wearing a blue suit and blue tie, Fieger comes across a beefy, black security guard in the hallway and shakes his hand like a politician. Someone else asks Fieger what it's like being a dad. It is Halloween, and as Fieger bides his turn in the courtroom, a snippet of conversation from two men floats into the air: "Dr. Kevorkian mask."

When Fieger picks up his deep blue metallic Volvo in the parking lot across from the courthouse, he knows the attendant. In the car on his cell phone Fieger is on the political hustle, talking about an upcoming mayoral race. That conversation is off the record, but he then turns and comments about his representation of the Shoels. He alludes to an offer the killers' parents made to settle. "To give up the opportunity to cross-examine the Klebolds and Harrises for $23,000?" he says. "Thank God Michael and Vonda wouldn't do it."

★★★

About one year before Columbine, Sam Riddle threw a phone at Fieger when he was running for governor and Riddle was his campaign manager. Riddle missed, but says he both quit, and was fired. Columbine, and a phone call, helped smooth things over as Riddle says he asked if Fieger would represent the Shoels. "I picked up the phone and Michael Shoels was on," Fieger remembers of the days after Columbine.

Fieger flew out to Denver a couple days later. Isaiah had not yet been buried, he recalls. Fieger walked through the Columbine parking lot, what he described as "a ground zero" and "a strange war zone." "Columbine had a lot of parallels to Sept. 11 in that nothing had ever happened like that in America," Fieger says. "That was a shock to the nation's nervous system."

Fieger's take no prisoner tactics were an aftershock to Colorado. But he figured if school shootings were going to be understood, Columbine was the "hot spot." He could take on the case and not expect to collect a dime. "And he [Michael] felt very strongly the only way you're going to get answers is with a lawyer," Fieger added, "and he's right."

★★★

The lawsuits would play out for years, and give rise to stacks and stacks and stacks of court files the size of telephone books. But they were not the only sabers the Columbine families, including the Shoels, would rattle.

Guns were among the first targets. And for the sake of controversy, the scripting couldn't have been better: The National Rifle Association was already scheduled to hold its national convention in Denver on May 1, barely two weeks after Columbine. Mayor Wellington Webb wanted it canceled. The NRA downsized it to a nub, but otherwise stood firm. Tom Mauser was among those who stood outside in protest. He held a sign with a photo of his son that read: "My son Daniel died at Columbine. He'd expect me to be here today."

Inside, Secretary of State Buckley welcomed the NRA with a speech and cited the Shoels. "I must agree with Isaiah's father Michael who has stated that guns are not the issue," she said. "Hate is what pulls the trigger of violence." The crowd went wild. Yet the Shoels soon showed up in Atlanta and Dayton, Ohio participating in gun buyback programs.

When the Shoels, like other victim families, met with President Bill Clinton and his wife Hillary at Light of the World Catholic Church in Littleton almost three weeks after the NRA meeting, Michael noted that dropping bombs over Kosovo and Yugoslavia may have set a violent example for Harris and Klebold. (Michael Moore, who knows Riddle, later made a similar reference in his film *Bowling for Columbine*.)

The Shoels did not only take on the high and mighty. On Denver's KHOW AM, two months after Columbine, Riddle was guest-hosting when the Shoels questioned injured Columbine art teacher Patti Nielson for crawling into a side room. "She got away," Michael said. "I'm not saying that to be mean. She could have had the kids to follow her, too." Nielson should have been a "mother duck," he added. "A duck knows you take the young with them."

Those and other words prompted a raft of angry calls against the Shoels. Nielson notes that she stayed in the library proper until Harris and Klebold left.

"The Shoels had the wrong information," she says. "They never talked to me."

By June the Colorado legislative audit committee was examining Riddle's contract with Buckley. "The very fact my contract is receiving scrutiny is because we're going around the country shedding light on the hate and racism that pulled the trigger and caused the carnage at Columbine," Riddle told the *Rocky Mountain News*. "We're making people uncomfortable."

The next month, on July 13, the *News* reported that the audit committee chair said Riddle's contract was "legal and proper." But that same day, Buckley suffered a massive heart attack. The next day, she died at age fifty-one.

Almost six months after Isaiah's death, on August 4, 1999, Michael and Vonda had not been eating well, and Michael was down to 220 pounds. But on the day Isaiah would have turned nineteen, Michael and Vonda cried, prayed, and looked at pictures. It was the first birthday they couldn't spend with their son. Soon it would be the first Christmas.

The Shoels juggernaut was saddened, but not stopped. By September, Michael and Vonda were in New York accompanied by Rev. Al Sharpton, presidential candidate, political activist, and for some a race-baiter. The Shoels spoke at a Brooklyn rally and took in donations, but also urged people to boycott the United Way given its handling of the Columbine Healing Fund. "We're calling on this nation to immediately stop giving money to the United Way until we have a complete accounting of what I refer to as the charity industry rip-off in Colorado," Riddle added. "They raised millions of dollars in Colorado, and less than twenty percent of those millions have gone to families."

The papers reported that about $2.8 million of the $4.4 million raised by United Way went to the families of the slain and injured; the organization felt some $1.6 million should go to counseling and violence prevention for the community at large. The families of the dead received $50,000 each, including the Shoels. Michael said his family used the money for general living expenses and to start up an anti-violence program in Isaiah's name, Let's Stomp Out Hate (which never did much fighting) but added that more money was necessary for a new home, private schools for his children, and counselors who specialized in black families. Michael and Vonda said the White House failed to follow through on a promise to move the family out of Jefferson County. They said they feared for their safety, and lived in motels while their children stayed with relatives.

The Shoels were hardly the only ones criticizing the memorial fund. "We've had our own disagreements with the way Mile High United Way has handled the Healing Fund set up to aid victims of the Columbine High School shootings," the *Rocky Mountain News* editorialized.

Although the paper added: "Yet somehow it never occurred to us to turn our quibbles into a nationwide boycott on giving to United Way.

"For a sweeping 'solution' like that, we had to await the inflamed imaginations of Michael Shoels and the people he lets manipulate him: political consultant Sam Riddle and the Rev. Al Sharpton, the charlatan and race-cardsharp from New York."

The Shoels were undaunted. When Attorney General Janet Reno visited the area in October, they handed her a letter requesting a federal grand jury to investigate the shootings. They said Isaiah was the victim "of a hate crime conspiracy" that local police could not handle. "Why would you get the home team to come in and investigate their kids?" Michael explains. "Bring the people in from out of state somewhere where they didn't have a reason to cover up anything. Why they didn't do that?"

Good question. At first, the Jefferson County Sheriff's Office may have appeared honest and competent. But looking back, with the Columbine investigation laced with cover-ups, one wonders if an outside review would have brokered more answers more quickly.

Leading up to the one-year anniversary many families of the murdered were immersed in a fund-raising campaign to build a new school library (the school district said insurance only covered repairs). At the same time, victim families were flooded with media requests. One solution was to invite select reporters to a closed meeting with families to discuss the tragedy along with library donations. The Shoels said they were not invited and when later told about it, didn't want to go. Michael called it "just another big gathering and hee-haw and la-dee-da."

But the Shoels were back in town for the one-year anniversary, still raging against the machine. They and Martin Luther King III were prevented from speaking at the Denver Public Schools campus named for King's father. The district said it was only abiding by the community's wishes and did not want to relive the tragedy. In fact, the one-year anniversary was a massive remembrance. How could it be anything else?

During that first year after Columbine the *Washington Post* had published a story, pivoting on the Shoels controversies, with the headline, "When Will The Healing Start?" In fact, it already had. It just would never end.

★★★

The Shoels, and other Columbine families, endured. Their lawsuits did not. While the court actions did bring forth information, not a one went to trial.

Criminal cases brought by the Jefferson County District Attorney were the first to resolve. Within six month Manes had pleaded guilty to supplying the underage Harris and Klebold with the TEC-DC9 handgun. He was sentenced at an emotional hearing attended by victim families on Nov. 12, 1999. He received six years for selling the TEC-DC9 and three for possessing an illegal, sawed off shotgun - essentially the act of firing it, as memorialized on the Rampart Range shooting video. Mane's terms were to be served concurrently, and he was moved to a halfway house in 2001. Two years later, he was paroled. Philip Duran, who introduced Eric and Dylan to Manes, pleaded guilty to the same charges as Duran and got four and half years. Manes' girlfriend, who also participated in the Rampart Range shooting spree, was given immunity for providing information to authorities. Yet a 2004 story in the *Rocky Mountain News* told of how she and Manes continued to date and were living together once he was living outside prison bars.

Robyn Anderson was never prosecuted because of a quirk in the law: She had purchased two rifles and a shotgun, or "long guns" for Eric and Dylan. In Colorado, it was not then illegal to transfer long guns to minors. After Columbine, the "Robyn Anderson Bill" made it illegal to do that without the consent of a juvenile's parent or guardian. In 2000, seventy-percent of Colorado voters approved Amendment 22, requiring background checks for all gun show buyers: Anderson said she would not have purchased the guns if she had to fill out any paperwork.

On April 19, 2001 an approximately $2.8 million lawsuit settlement was announced with thirty Columbine families. This had been civilian versus civilian or, as the lawsuits alleged, victim versus Columbine enabler. The Shoels were involved in all of them. Homeowners insurance would funnel the money that came from five sources, including $1.3 million from the Klebolds and $300,000 from the Harrises. The Manes family would come in at $720,000, with the Anderson and Duran family policies paying, respectively, $300,000 and $250,000. Families of the dead were to receive about $23,000, with at least some part of the payouts being divided among thirty-six victim families. But that was a squishy number. The settlement was to be continued.

In the meantime, it was Columbine victims versus the cops. Open Records lawsuits against the sheriff unleashed many of the documents and videos that are now public. But successfully suing police for allowing

Columbine to happen was another question. Families of victims and survivors, including the Shoels, alleged that the sheriff and school district missed numerous warning signs. Then they said the law enforcement response was flawed upon arrival. But in November 2001 a federal judge dismissed eight of the nine lawsuits filed against the sheriff or school district. U.S. District Judge Lewis Babcock said law enforcement officers had no duty to save the lives of the students and staff. The plaintiffs would have needed to show that police officers and teachers intended to harm the victims. Babcock made one exception in the case of a murder victim. He allowed Angela Sanders, the daughter of slain teacher Dave Sanders, to move forward with her lawsuit.

In the midst of appealing their dismissals the Shoels and other victim families who lost a child settled with the sheriff and the school district in June 2002. Each family, it was reported, would receive about $15,000 from each agency. Then in August Angela Sanders, negotiating with a different set of circumstances, settled for $1.5 million.

There were other legal battles - such as those against the drug company and video games - but the longest-running was parent versus parent. In 2003 five victim families who had refused to participate in the original agreement with the Harrises and Klebolds settled with the killers' families. They were the parents of Kelly Fleming, Matthew Kechter, Daniel Rohrbough, Lauren Townsend, and Kyle Velasquez. All died at Columbine.

"I did not take a penny from either one of those families," Lauren Townsend's mother, Dawn Anna, told the *Rocky Mountain News* as she discussed the settlement.

Victim parents were, however, privy to depositions with the Harrises and Klebolds. But they were to remain sealed, despite a lawsuit that would continue to twist nearly ten years after the shootings.

Then there were the Shoels. The Klebolds and Harrises said the Shoels had settled per the 2001 agreement. There was a letter from Fieger in the court file saying as much. Fieger countered that there was a mix-up and he was "falsely" told all the other families had originally agreed to settle. The Shoels took it to the U.S. Supreme Court, which declined the case in 2005.

Fieger had seen a trial as an event of historical proportions. "It was important to have the Nuremberg trial, the Scopes trial, the Kevorkian trials," he said. But now all the Shoels had to depend on were small accounts, like the slightly personalized victim letter they received from the Klebolds. "We read that Isaiah brought so much joy to those who knew him," according to the three paragraphs that appear handwritten by a female and signed by Tom and Sue. "He was a young man with self-respect, courage and love who was taken from you in a moment of madness." But they said they still didn't know why their son killed Isaiah.

★★★

Roanoke Regional Airport is the easiest way to fly into Blacksburg, Virginia. April 19, 2007 is three days after the deadliest mass shooting in U.S. history, and one day before Columbine's eighth anniversary. The clock is about to strike midnight as a bouquet of flowers sits on an airport table and Red Cross volunteers dot the halls offering assistance and comfort to those whose final destination is the Virginia Tech campus, about a half-hour's drive away. Thirty-three have just died there, including the killer. Since the world media has descended on Virginia Tech, it seems residents would have built up an immunity to reporters right quick.

But at the airport a lumbering figure still rustles up attention and turns heads: Michael Shoels. On their own dimes Michael and Sam Riddle have flown into Roanoke to bring the traveling Shoels gospel of civics lesson and grief counseling to the site of another school shooting. The dynamic duo wants to remind Blacksburg, and the world, about the lessons of Columbine. That secrecy hides information that can help stop school shooters. That schools must prepare for school shootings the same way they deal with tornadoes or fire drills. That the grief never ends.

But first, Michael moves through the airport dressed in a Hugo Boss anorak that reads "BOSS" in bold black letters across the front. Sam's son, twenty-eight-year-old Craig Riddle, films Michael for a DVD on how to prepare for violence in schools.

There is also the question of a hotel room. Sam, Craig, and Michael do not have a reservation in the small town of Blacksburg, which is now sold out given the crush of the shootings. Sam calls the Ramada Limited and feigns a reservation. Of course, they don't have one for him. "You have Kass, right?" Sam says. "Well, we're with Kass." The Ramada finds the "second room" for team Shoels. That's what you learn doing political advance work, Sam explains.

Michael says he doesn't want to be here. "Going to that college is like going back to Clement Park," he says, and adds, "The worst part of it is knowing what the families are going through. It's just like cutting a wound open and putting salt in it."

But this is also the place to seek answers. "Dylan and Eric is the same way" as the Virginia Tech killer, Michael says. "Something caused them to do that, and this is what we need to find." And if Michael himself cannot find it, at least he can give directions.

The next day is Friday, and reporters who have been covering Virginia Tech since Monday are on the downswing. They can only file so many stories of gunshots and mourning. The day's big event will be a noontime moment of silence, both powerful and canned, like a predictable Hollywood tearjerker.

But at 8:00 a.m. on the central, grassy quad known as Drillfield, Michael Shoels appears. He is wearing a black, double-breasted suit and a black Stetson hat. Black is his favorite color. "Him and Johnny Cash," Riddle quips. Only his cowboy boots are brown. Three fingers of each hand carry heavy gold rings, and Michael's necklace is a $10 Liberty gold coin. His beard is braided and threaded into black and clear beads. On most anyone else, it would be a heavy metal look.

Drillfield takes notice. And the media have their story: As if a dubious torch is being handed off from the once deadliest school shooting to the deadliest, the father of a Columbine victim is making a pilgrimage to Virginia Tech.

Like Columbine, and other American tragedies, a memorial has sprung up at Virginia Tech. Sam and Michael walk among the thirty-three square stones (including a potentially controversial one for the killer) set in a semi-circle on a sloping hill of Drillfield. The stones surround hundreds of flower bouquets and a clump of votive candles. It is an orderly rectangle of grief that contrasts with war-torn Clement Park and the massive, impromptu piles of teddy bears, candles, clothes, signs, and flowers that snaked across the grass at Columbine. But this grassy rise is Michael's new pulpit.

Some recognize him as "the Columbine guy" (maybe from the television moment with Katie Couric). Those who don't recognize him figure they should. Reporters sense it is their job to approach Michael and ask who he is. But first, Riddle has a question. "Ma'am, who are you with?" he asks, as he does of all the media who approach.

Associated Press, she answers, and five photographers suddenly surround Michael.

"This is Michael Shoels," Riddle explains. "S-H-O-E-L-S. His son Isaiah was killed at Columbine."

Click, click, click as the photographers get their fill.

Riddle tells reporters he and Michael will be meeting with the Virginia Tech administration, although they do not yet have an appointment confirmed. They have "messaged," in Riddle's parlance, with Blacksburg police about the lessons of Columbine, although that was by phone.

Michael takes a more emotional tack. "It's sad, it's really sad," he says to the small, assembling crowd. "All of these children dying so early for nothing. My heart is just bleeding right now."

In one hour, Michael and Sam will deal with more media than most people experience in a lifetime.

Michael walks to the center of Drillfield. Beneath white and maroon striped tent tops, plywood boards the size of refrigerator doors have been painted white and propped against each other to form an inverted 'V'. Felt pens are available for mourners to write messages on the boards, and many invoke the school nickname, Hokie, in their written messages: "Much Hokie Love. Never Forget." "Feel the love of a community and a nation in your hearts as you descend forth into heaven." Tissue boxes sit atop the boards.

Michael writes on a board as he bends his thick frame down: "Hearts goes out to you and we know the way and feeling. We Love You. God Bless and all of this is in memory of Isaiah E. Shoels 1980-1999."

Sam reminds Michael to date it, and Michael adds, "4/20/2007."

"Instead of vigils and candles, we're making this a working anniversary," Michael says.

Sam issues a caution, to no one in particular, about "media intoxication," when people "can be consumed with the lure of the cameras and microphones rather than real problem-solving."

The massive Drillfield is surrounded by school buildings made of the same pale stones laid out to commemorate the dead. It is called "Hokie stone," and makes even the newest buildings look aged and dignified. The reporters continue to throng, while Sam and Michael continue to move across the quad and "message." Sam and Michael attack the police for failing to shut down the Virginia Tech campus after the first report of shots fired. Reporters ask Michael what kind of boy Isaiah was. "Any man in America would have loved to call him his son," Michael says.

Michael walks up to a line of police tape. Eight years ago he was 1,500 miles away, but in the same place.

"I can't say it's going to get better, but I can say it's going to ease up," Michael says of the grieving process. "Just pray. No medicine, no doctors is going to pull this off because you lost your loved ones."

"We're from Peru," says one television reporter with an accent.

"Beirut?" Riddle asks.

"Peru," says the reporter, who explains that a twenty-one-year-old Peruvian student is among the Virginia Tech dead.

The camera rolls for Michael and Sam in Peru.

Sam is a mixture of casual and athletic that he pulls off as sophisticated. He has short, dark curly hair with touches of gray, jeans, running shoes, and a black zip fleece turtleneck. He tops it off with a herringbone sport coat and Detroit Tigers belt buckle with a tiger's head.

"The secrecy of Columbine–withholding the basement tapes–may have directly contributed to the deaths here," Sam says. He adds, "If the horror is not kept before the public, they'll never be any problem-solving."

"Let's call for world peace," Michael says.

"It's not the guns. It's the hate that's killing," Sam says. "If you lock up all the guns, they'll poison someone."

Michael walks into a small chapel on a hill alongside Drillfield, takes off his hat, and heads down the center aisle. In front of the altar he bends down on his left knee, bows his head, and prays. "Let these families see that there is a way... Let them heal... Protect them," he whispers.

Outside the chapel a woman is crying. "I'm Mike Shoels. My kid was killed eight years ago at Columbine."

The woman at first seems unsure of Michael, then gives him in a fierce bear hug. A man who is with her joins in. "I'm not going to say it gets better...," Michael intones.

The woman, who appears to be in her 30's or 40's, tells Michael she is a student and has friends who were killed. She then hurries off.

"I said there wasn't going to be no tears here today," Michael says, but adds, "I can't help it."

A girl and boy with a Christian organization walk by with an orange sign: "Free hugs and Hershey Kisses." Michael introduces himself, shakes hands with the boy, then briefly hugs him.

Michael walks onto Blacksburg's main street – literally, Main Street –

adjacent the campus and leans against a light pole that looks like an old-fashioned gas lamp. An orange and maroon ribbon – the school colors – is tied to the pole. A newspaper reporter senses a story just looking at Michael, and walks up and begins interviewing him. "Of course we need gun control," Michael says. "But it's not the guns that's killing. It's what's behinds the gun." A television reporter from the Washington ABC affiliate soon joins in.

If Michael and Sam have the media, they still don't have the university. No one has called them back to confirm an appointment. The president's office refers my inquiry about a possible meeting with Michael to the public relations office. The public relations office doesn't know anything.

At noon hundreds of students, staff, alumni, and others gather for the moment of silence. Television cameras, arrayed in a circle around the crowd, would film each other if they panned up at the same time. The quiet lasts a couple minutes; one moment is far too short for thirty-three dead.

Michael is on the front line of mourners, standing next to the semi-circle of memorial stones. To his left a tall, thin woman is sobbing. "I know where you coming from," he says, and gives her a bear hug. Two other women with her join in, making it a group hug. "I know the pain. I know the sorrow," Michael adds.

Michael turns to his right and as if by magic university president Charles W. Steger is there. Michael leans into him and talks softly. "Be real... I know for sure it's going to be alright," are Michael's words that can be overheard.

Michael then gets down on his left knee, head bowed. Steger picks up a flower and places it at a small mourning wall flanked by the memorial stones. Michael does the same. A handful of others in the crowd follow.

Sam is now ready to declare the trip a success: Michael has told the university president his concerns "in a brief face to face," and embraced those who are suffering "as only someone similarly situated could do."

At a late lunch on the second-floor patio of a Cajun restaurant Michael orders vegetarian, and Sam starts the meal with a piece of cheesecake. I ask whether they might be accused of playing to the cameras.

"Did you lose a son in Columbine?" Sam says, bothered but not bruised. "Then fuck you."

He adds: "We want to stop the killing. In America, if you're not techno-literate and you're not media-aware, you'll be a victim of those who are. Those haters should get over it and do something themselves."

Michael calmly interjects a reference to Isaiah's prophecy, seventy-two hours before Columbine, when he and Vonda said they would fight violence if he were killed.

"I'm honoring a promise I made," Michael says.

At lunch, Sam gets the call. The university wants Michael to speak to a meeting of counselors who will be working with victims' families. Within a half hour, an escort picks up Michael and Sam in a mini-van and drives them to the meeting. But inside the modern, Cook Counseling Center, they are informed it is the wrong location. The escort himself, a burly man fighting the heat and confusion, has made a mistake. He begins to hyperventilate. It is a bad omen: One wonders if the university employees can handle the waves of grief to come.

A meeting with another counselor is hastily arranged and Michael and Sam talk for fifteen minutes about what else the university can expect after the shooting: Fights over charity money, and the need to keep families from splitting apart.

"The university did finally reach out," Sam says. "That was the university deciding where the Shoels' experience best fit in. And you know what? They may not be too far off the mark."

Yet Sam stresses that Virginia Tech will have to move beyond the vigils and candles. Like an X-ray searching for disease, examining school shooters may be the only way to stop them. Tears and teddy bears won't do it.

But first a Japanese television crew is in the lobby. They have been waiting for Michael and Sam to finish the counseling meeting, and now film a segment with them on the sidewalk. (Columbine is big in Japan, a Japanese reporter explains.) After the interview Michael and Sam walk back towards Drillfield. A cameraman walks behind them, still filming.

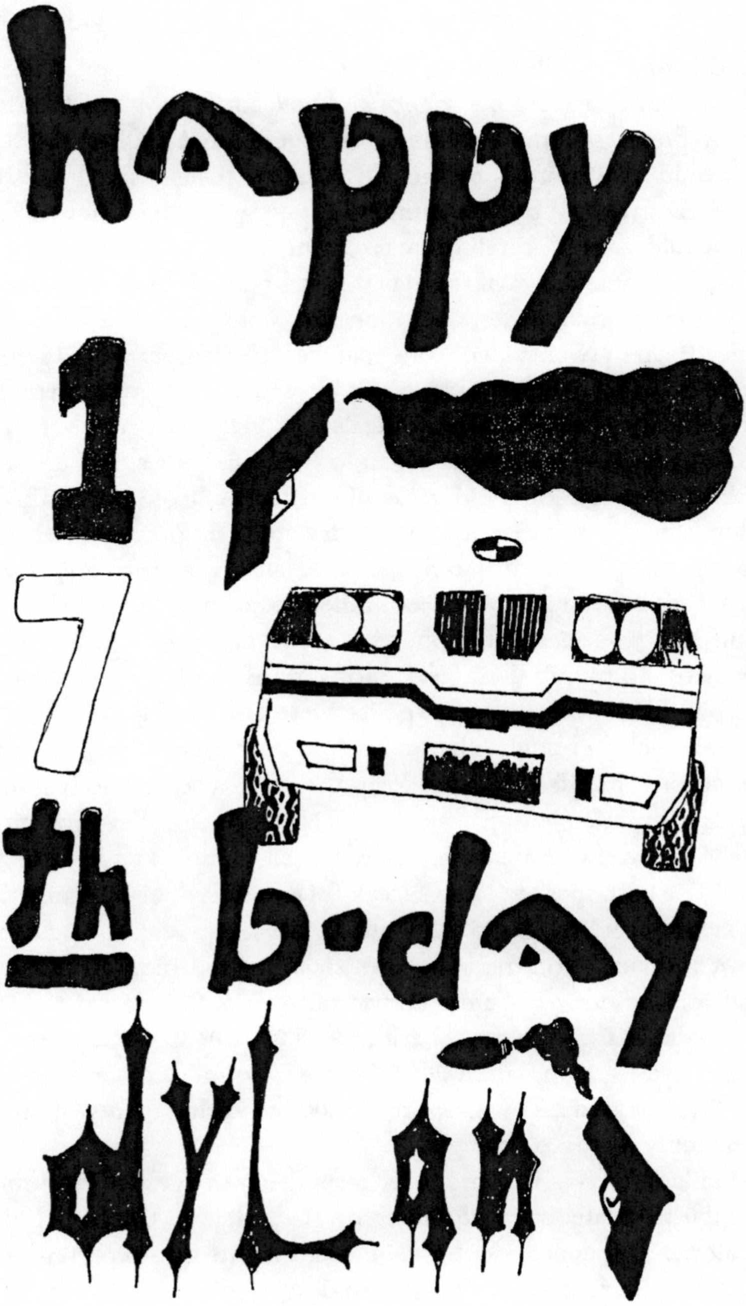
happy
17
th
b-day
dyLan

EPILOGUE

Police Report

On the day of Columbine, then Sheriff John Stone stood on the grass in Clement Park adjacent the school and held forth at one of the many makeshift press conferences. Stone, or silver-haired spokesman Steve Davis, would give updates to the media corps that was still relatively small, albeit growing by the minute. About every half hour sheriff officials would leave the briefing area to gather more information directly from investigators, although there was never enough time to answer all the questions from reporters. Among the many key questions: How many dead? Up to twenty-five Stone said. Yet the number would settle at fifteen. Did Harris and Klebold have any contact with law enforcement before Columbine? Maybe none, officials said. In fact, the number (at last count) was fifteen. The answers began to symbolize the character of the Columbine investigation: Nothing could be further from the truth.

Columbine was not meant to be a story about an otherwise obscure, suburban Colorado sheriff's office. It was, and is, a story about what motivated two teenage suburban killers and how to stop school shootings. But we needed the photos, videos, and documents amassed by the sheriff to plumb the killers' motivations. And almost as soon as they responded to the shootings, police were criticized for not entering the school quickly enough. That too would now have to be taken up.

But various sheriffs wanted to keep the truth a secret. So beginning on day one, an information war began. The media, other government agencies, and even victim families were forced to sue, prod and poke for answers. The fight sparked often successful lawsuits, publicly shamed the sheriff's office, and triggered five outside investigations: The 2000-2001 governor's review commission; the 2002 joint Colorado Attorney General and Jefferson County District Attorney task force; the 2002 review by the El Paso County Sheriff; the 2003-2004 Colorado Attorney General's investigation; and a 2004 Colorado grand jury investigation. (Sheriff Stone issued his own report in 2000, which has plenty of facts. It also has plenty of shortcomings.)

The tally, after eight years, was over 26,000 pages of documents reluctantly or belatedly made public by the Jefferson County Sheriff's Office alone. The department, meantime, kept its grip on a few select items, while others appear to have been destroyed or lost forever.

"It's amazing," Brian Rohrbough, whose son Dan died at Columbine, told the alternative Denver weekly *Westword*. "While we were planning a funeral, these guys were already planning a cover-up."

***

According to the official Columbine report, Jefferson County SWAT commander Lt. Terry Manwaring arrived at the school at 11:36 a.m., approximately seventeen minutes after the shooting started. Manwaring and other select officers saddled up more quickly than many realize. Around noon, an ad hoc SWAT team of Denver, Littleton, and Jefferson County officers had been lashed together. They commandeered a Littleton fire truck for cover, and as they approached the school, Manwaring split the officers up. Jefferson County Deputy Allen Simmons took a team of five others into the school around 12:06 p.m., about forty-five minutes after the shooting began. "They were immediately met by the deafening sound of Klaxon horns and the flashing lights of the fire alarm system," the official report says. But Harris and Klebold would kill themselves in about two minutes. Wounded teacher Dave Sanders would only be reached upon his dying breath.

In a rare view of the police response, Jefferson County Sheriff's Division Chief John Kiekbusch discussed the law enforcement tactics at Columbine in a video from the Federal Emergency Management Agency, obtained under the Freedom of Information Act. FEMA was involved in the talk over two years after Columbine, on August 29, 2001, as part of "Picking Up The Pieces: Responding to School Crises Conference."

Kiekbusch starts his approximately forty-five minute talk by saying he is not there to speak about Columbine. Yet he ends up discussing the police response, and is frank about some of the problems. Kiekbusch recounts his thoughts as the calls started coming in.

"Oddly enough, we had a new sheriff, a new undersheriff," he told the small, classroom-sized conference room. "We knew that the office was going to go through a reorganization. And the odd thought that went through was maybe this is some kind of a really bizarre, super-complicated exercise that they're putting the organization through just to see if we're suitable to hang around, get promoted, or what have you. Unfortunately, that wasn't the case either."

Kiekbusch touched on what was apparently the ad hoc SWAT team. "At the time, our people were willing to do something completely contrary to the policies in which they were trained," he said. "We didn't have time to assemble a full SWAT team. We didn't have time to plan our tactics to make sure that we knew where everything was inside that building."

He adds that "the only information that they [the ad hoc SWAT team] would have would be to go to the sound of the gunfire."

Yet dispatchers had information from Patti Nielson's 911 call. Those with Dave Sanders would also call. Information from fleeing students was conflicting and confusing, but coming in. And the parents who lost children in the library - who were told to stay down and that help was on the way - might find themselves angrily agreeing with what else Kiekbusch said at the FEMA conference: "I can tell you any number of police officers that I've spoken with who were involved in one way or another with Columbine went home and told their children, 'If you hear gunshots, you run. You run as fast as you can, you run in the direction away from those, and you keep running until you don't hear gunshots anymore.'" He added, "And there's a very strong element of truth in that."

He did not give details, but Kiekbusch made a generalized statement of contrition to his audience: "No one would ever say that everything we did was absolutely correct at Columbine. That would be foolish."

He talked of preserving the scene, and how important it was to solving the crime. "If it gets messed up from the get to, you're going to be out of luck," Kiekbusch said. "It's very, very difficult, if not impossible, to go back and put that sort of thing together." The same could be said of the Columbine investigation itself.

***

Within three days after the shootings, the information war was kicking up. On April 23, Randy Brown was quoted anonymously in the *Rocky Mountain News* as a "Columbine father" and he talked of how he gave police printouts of Eric's Web site in 1998. (The Brown family does not have a memory of Aaron Brown's 1997 report.)

"Sheriff's Sgt. Jim Parr said he knew nothing about the complaint," the *News* story added. "District Attorney Dave Thomas said he never received it."

All the while, the Jefferson County Sheriff's Office was using the Browns' report to bolster search warrants for the homes of Eric and Dylan. On the day of Columbine, investigator Cheryl Zimmerman wrote to a judge: "Your affiant discovered a report made to the Jefferson County Sheriff's Office on March 18, 1998, [case number] 98-5504, by Randy Brown. Randy Brown stated that Eric Harris was making death threats towards his son, Brooks Brown."

The search warrants were granted. But sealed.

The Denver Post argued they were public and filed a motion with the court the day after Columbine. At an April 23 hearing, the Post was met by two Jefferson County deputy district attorneys, whose office opposed unsealing the warrants. They said it would compromise public safety and jeopardize the investigation. Jefferson County District Judge Henry Nieto, who had signed the warrants, agreed to keep them sealed.

But the scramble was on. Numerous Open Records Act requests were made seeking "any and all" types of information related to the Browns' report, and police contact with Eric and Dylan.

Deputy Guerra, who had done his own investigation into the Browns' report a year earlier, had been busy at the school gathering the bombs he had meant to uncover before Columbine. A few days into the investigation — no one can pinpoint the exact date — Guerra was still at the school when he was summonsed to the internal affairs office. Detective Dennis Gerlach told Guerra he was wanted at a meeting regarding his draft affidavit. Some dubbed it the "Open Space meeting" because it took place at the government building dedicated to Jefferson County's trademark parklands. When the meeting's existence was finally revealed five years later, as the police themselves were being investigated, a grand jury raised a critical eye and called it a "private meeting." The media and others were less diplomatic, although arguably no less accurate. They called it a "secret meeting."

Now, in the early stages, Guerra seems to have innocently grabbed his file. Gerlach looked it over, and off they went. Recollections vary as to who was at the meeting. But those named include Sheriff John Stone, Undersheriff John Dunaway, Kiekbusch, District Attorney Dave Thomas, Assistant District Attorney Kathy Sasak, County Attorney Frank Huftless, and Assistant County Attorney Lily Oeffler. Stone has said he did not attend which, if true, may not be an issue of ethics on his part, but rather because no one invited him.

"The meeting was called to discuss the Guerra draft affidavit; the potential liabilities of the document, and how to handle press inquiries that may arise concerning the document," according to the grand jury report, which added, "Based on discussions at the open space meeting the JCSO proceeded with the approach to not disclose the existence of the affidavit at a press conference."

The grand jury noted that "as a result of the meeting" sheriff's Lt. Jeff Shrader drew up a press release but did not mention the draft affidavit. A smokescreen was now placed around events before, during, and after Columbine.

Spokesman Steve Davis read the press release to the world's media, which was now in full force at Columbine, ten days after the shootings on April 30, 1999. The two-page statement also was handed out on plain paper—no official logo, letterhead, or other identifying characteristic. Kiekbusch handled the questions.

The release now confirmed that Randy Brown made a report concerning Eric's threats, and Web pages. A background check, according to the press release, was done on Eric on April 2, 1998 (when he would have been entering the diversion program). It doesn't state the outcome. And while the department did investigate, with the crown jewel being Guerra's draft affidavit, the press release focused on why sheriff's deputies allegedly didn't investigate. The department argued it could not confirm that the violent words came from Eric and fully pursue the case because Investigator John Healy could not access Eric's Web site. But no mention is made of Healy accessing the Web profile of Eric Harris wanting to join the marines.

The department said it could not conduct a full-fledged investigation because Randy Brown wanted anonymity. The actual report says Randy was "interested in remaining anonymous" - and anonymous tips are standard in police work. Not an excuse to let an alleged crime slip by. The Browns indeed wanted investigators to pursue the case - why the heck else would they report it - just leave their name out of it.

There was no mention of Aaron Brown's 1997 report. And of course, zilch on the secret meeting. Maybe the biggest whopper was not mentioning Guerra's investigation and draft affidavit. The sheriff's office even added that no other pipe bombs could be linked to the Brown's 1998 report, although Guerra pursued a possible match from a previous case.

The press release says the Browns' report "was forwarded to the Jefferson County Sheriff's Office Investigations Division for follow-up" and maintained "as a [sic] 'open lead' since it was originally reported." Yet police records show the Brown's case was closed out the same month it was reported.

The press release also noted that Guerra briefed the Columbine High resource officer, sheriff's deputy Neil Gardner, about the Browns' information. "Deputy Gardner, with this knowledge occasionally engaged Harris, and Klebold, along with several of their friends and associates in light conversation. Deputy Gardner made no observations of inappropriate behavior and has stated that both Harris and Klebold treated him with appropriate respect," the release stated.

Following standard procedure Gardner, like other officers who fired weapons at Columbine, was debriefed the day of the shootings. Yet he did not recognize a photo of Eric Harris shown to him at the command post. "So you really don't know this kid at all?" the interviewer asked. "I had never dealt, I had never dealt with Eric Harris," said Gardner, who at one point called him "Scott."

In the confusing aftermath, maybe Gardner forgot he had checked on Harris and Klebold. Yet no one seems to have reconciled this discrepancy.

In yet another twist *The Denver Post* published an article on Gardner one week after Columbine. He said he knew of Harris and Klebold, but didn't know them personally. "They had never been disrespectful to him," the *Post* reported.

"There are certainly kids in the school that scare me more than he [Eric] would have," Gardner added.

On May 1, 1999 the *Rocky Mountain News* reported that Gardner had discussed the Browns' report with a Columbine High dean. But Kiekbusch would not give a name. The next day, the *News* wrote that Gardner shared limited details with the two deans, but they were not given a copy of the police report. "Academically, these were two very good students, so it didn't raise a lot of red flags," said Jeffco Public Schools spokesman Rick Kaufman.

Jefferson County turned to other agencies throughout Columbine for extra manpower. But Guerra was taken off the case. And he wasn't the only one. The others included Hicks and Grove, who had also been brought in on the Browns' report back in 1998. That prompted Guerra to wonder why the bomb experts – in a crime involving dozens of bombs – were removed. "I was told it was a shooting, not a bombing," he said.

Hicks says Kiekbusch told him not to respond to the school. Instead, he "watched the events on television and took notes." It was one or two days after the shootings that Hicks realized he had crossed paths, so to speak, with Eric Harris before Columbine.

Jefferson County Sheriff's Deputy Cheryl Zimmerman tells yet another story. According to her report Hicks helped execute a search warrant on Klebold's home. Hicks checked two computers on the main floor, and seized three from Dylan's room. A notation on Zimmerman's report reads: "See Sgt. Hicks' report for details." Another report says that three days after Columbine, on April 23, Hicks helped interview Harris and Klebold buddy Zach Heckler. But there are no reports from Hicks.

***

As the one year anniversary approached, along with the deadline to sue the sheriff's department, victims' families asked police if they could view the official report on the shootings, which was still unreleased. The sheriff said no, and gave any number of reasons: It wasn't done. A case against a gun supplier was pending.

The families then filed an Open Records Act lawsuit. They won, and the first 11,000 pages of raw police reports were made public in November 2000. Another 15,000-plus would come in the following years. But no one, at least outside the sheriff's department, knew exactly what was in the evidence vault. The sheriff was engaged in a game of public records charades.

In April 2001, nearly two years to the day after Columbine, CBS News (doing a segment for 60 Minutes II) and victims families knocked loose Guerra's draft affidavit after joining forces in a lawsuit. The sheriff department's response showed that they would just never get it.

The department claimed that the draft had not been kept secret, and was openly discussed in the days after Columbine. Spokesman Mike Julian specifically said the sheriff revealed the existence of the draft in a late April 1999 news conference - he was probably referring to April 30.

In fact, few knew the draft even existed, and no newspaper in America had ever reported on it because it had never before been disclosed. The official report released on May 15, 2000 gives only a possible - and even then inaccurate - reference to the draft when it says, "Further investigation [of the Browns' report] was initiated but no additional information was developed." The same criticisms of the April 30 press release could be leveled against that sentence.

The draft also confirmed that the Browns actually met with Hicks

- in a dig at them, the sheriff had long denied a face to face meeting occurred.

Jefferson County District Attorney Dave Thomas was now on the hook too for keeping silent about the affidavit. He had at least a few reasons as to why he had never mentioned it. He alternately said he thought it had been publicly revealed, or was up to the sheriff's department to release because it was their investigation. He also said the draft was too weak to convince a judge to approve a search warrant. It was an attempt at good PR for the cops. They didn't do anything bad because they didn't have enough info to search Eric's home in the first place and prevent Columbine.

In fact, Eric's Web pages threatened two crimes: Possessing pipe bombs and going after Brooks Brown. That alone could justify a judge's signature. The probable cause was admittedly thin, but close.

And a little more investigative elbow grease might have shored up the draft. Investigators could have added more Web site information - something Eric had provided plenty of. Or they could have indicated the distance between the Harris home and the pipe bomb found in the field.

Not a lot of work to get a search warrant, especially once the affidavit was already drafted. Not a lot of work to prevent Columbine.

***

The draft affidavit had been flushed out. But on July 24, 2001 I filed a five-page open records act request (Colorado's equivalent of the Freedom of Information Act) for "Documents or other material from deputies John Hicks, John Healy, Mike Guerra, Deputy [Neil] Gardner and any others on the complaints by Randy and Judy Brown regarding Eric Harris."

I also requested "Videotapes, writings, photos, cassette recordings, newspaper articles, and computer files created, or related to Dylan Klebold and Eric Harris taken from their homes, Columbine High School, cars, and any other locations (emphasis added). Also, any transcripts, summaries, or photos of the videotapes, recordings, writings and computer information." The idea was that if some items themselves were not releasable, for whatever reason, at least a summary might be available.

The request also sought, "Any and all Jefferson County e-mails regarding the Columbine shooting, including e-mails surrounding the investigation, and other post-shooting events."

Assistant county attorney Lily Oeffler, who was at the secret meeting and later went on to become a Colorado state judge, wrote back representing the sheriff. In months of letters back and forth Oeffler said a judge had already declined to release documents seized from the homes of the killers but she did not cite any specific orders. Regarding the Browns, she wrote, "Reports and related documents regarding the Browns' complaint against Eric Harris regarding the internet have been released."

Oeffler also stated that, "Many items to include videotapes, writings, photos, cassette recordings, and computer files have been returned to their owners. Some materials responsive to your requests have already been released in the materials."

She made it seem like case closed. But in 2003, under scrutiny from the attorney general's office and the command of Ted Mink, a new, more open sheriff, the department released the Rampart Range target practice video. More videos came in 2004, including the "hitmen for hire" tape. In 2006 nearly 1,000 documents that provide some of the most intimate portraits of the killers – their diaries – and Wayne Harris' journal, were released in response to a lawsuit by *The Denver Post*. Much of it was taken from the homes of Eric and Dylan.

And there were even more documents related to the Browns. They were in the county attorney's office.

***

Any Columbine e-mails from the sheriff's office remain secret. Or maybe destroyed. Oeffler said it would be "virtually impossible" and might take "thousands of hours" to retrieve them.

When the *Rocky Mountain News* requested them, the county said it would cost over $1 million to find the e-mails and even then, there was no guarantee any would be released. The *News* declined to pay the fee.

***

On June 28, 2000 investigator John Hicks, denied promotion and shaken by the handling of the Columbine investigation, left the department and gave a binder to fellow investigator John Healy. Healy actually says he got the binder in 1999 and ended up putting it in his home office. Then in October 2003 the self-described pack rat was ordered by his wife to clean out some of his "old junk" because guests were coming over in three days. He found the binder. Inside was the "missing" 1997 report that Aaron Brown had filed at the Southwest Plaza regarding Eric.

Then Attorney General Ken Salazar was already helming the Columbine Task Force when Sheriff Mink asked him to investigate what happened with the 1997 report. It led to the most honest investigation to date concerning the events surrounding Columbine, and prompted the grand jury proceeding. Guerra, Grove, Hicks, and a host of other police finally opened up through the remarks they made to attorney general investigators.

The most uncooperative (and least helpful) witness appears to be former sheriff John Stone. Investigators met with him at 9:00 a.m. on February 11, 2004 in the office of his new employer, the private investigations firm Business Controls Inc. Stone told investigators that he was not sheriff when Guerra undertook his draft affidavit for a search warrant, which was true. But he also said he "has no knowledge about it." A stunning admission, if true, given that its public disclosure came when Stone was sheriff and that it was a key part of whether Columbine could have been prevented.

Stone, a Republican, also claimed Attorney General Ken Salazar, a Democrat, was only after him for partisan reasons. "He [Stone] expressed the opinion that our investigation was politically motivated, and he was visibly angry about this investigation and the way he was treated by the press regarding Columbine," the investigators wrote.

Stone stood out among the other interviewees for not allowing his interview to be taped. "We were unable to ask Stone any questions or have any meaningful dialogue regarding our investigation due [to] his apparent state of agitation," investigators added. Stone declined comment for the *Rocky Mountain News*, calling this reporter a "horse's ass."

Shortly after the attorney general's investigation wrapped up, *News* gossip columnist Penny Parker did a piece mentioning that the Browns had spotted Stone working in the bakery department at a Costco. Parker contacted Stone. "I'm working a holiday job, what's the big deal?" he told her. "I just want to be left alone."

★★★

Something else was missing: The sparse summaries of how officers spend their time and known as DaFR's (pronounced "daffers"), or Daily Field Activity Reports. Daily Supervisors Reports, or DaSRs, serve the same purpose for supervisors. The county had failed to turn any of them up under numerous open records act requests filed by me and other media.

But attorney general investigators, writing five years after Columbine, noted that, "Copies of some DaFRs and DaSRs for the year 1998 had been sent to the Jefferson County Attorney's office by the Jefferson County Sheriff's office in mid-1999. These included DaFRs and DaSRs for Investigator Michael Guerra, John Hicks, Glenn Grove, Randy West and Jim Pritchett." The investigators added that "these documents had been kept at the offices of the County Attorney and had not been released to the public."

The sheriff's department retained its own copies of the documents – but had never before released them. The sheriff also purged the originals, although investigators concluded that they had been properly destroyed under the records retention policy. But why would the sheriff withhold, then destroy, such key documents related to the state's biggest criminal investigation?

One report survived. Sgt. Jim Prichett's DaSR from May 1, 1998 indicated that Guerra worked on the Harris affidavit that day. It is also the last recorded day Guerra worked on it.

But investigators could not find Guerra's DaFR for May 1 and his entire "investigative file" containing his work on the search warrant was also missing. That's when investigators took the Columbine case to a statewide grand jury. It convened on August 6, 2004. In September 2004 the grand jury released its decision not to indict, noting it did not have enough evidence of a crime. But it did release its findings.

Kiekbusch, the grand jury noted, had asked his assistant to locate the Guerra file and a related file by checking the computer network and physical records. The assistant thought the logical thing would be to contact the officers involved. Yet Kiekbusch told her to keep the query secret from them. When the assistant told him she could not locate the files, he seemed "somewhat relieved."

Kiekbusch told the grand jury he had nothing to do with any missing files or documents and "cannot specifically respond to the conclusory statement that for some unknown reason an assistant thought he appeared 'somewhat relieved.'"

But the grand jury concluded, "the absence of these particular files is troubling... because the open space meeting focused on these documents and at the press conference there was no mention of them. The absence of any file that should have been located in Records, the working file and the associated electronic files is also troubling."

★ ★ ★

The feds, many of whom assisted in the Columbine investigation, had their own disclosure difficulties. The Secret Service, dedicated to protecting the U.S. president and other national and international leaders, wanted to transfer its method of "threat assessment" to school shooters after Columbine. But its May 2002 "Safe School Initiative" is vague, and the Secret Service concluded it could draw no profile of school shooters.

The Secret Service was also secretive about its research. The agency issued an interim report on school violence in October 2000 that noted, "For each incident, researchers reviewed primary source materials, such as investigative, school, court, and mental health records and answered several hundred questions about the case." The following month, on November 10, 2000, I sent a four-page Freedom of Information Act request seeking the research related to Columbine.

Money was the first obstacle. The Secret Service denied a fee waiver, saying that the information requested would not significantly help the public understand how the agency conducted its investigation. The Secret Service added that I could not prove the information was not primarily in my commercial interest (although journalists are often given that exemption). The agency noted I was still entitled to two hours of free search time, and 100 free pages of documents. After that, we would have to reopen discussions. That letter was dated April 2, 2001. I was almost five months into the process.

In December 2001, eight months later, I was still paperless and contacted the Secret Service. The agency said they had sent out a letter in August, which I never received, but then faxed it to me. "A search for files responsive to your request is being conducted," the letter said. "When the results of the search are known, you will be notified." I had now been waiting one year and one month.

In January 2002, the Secret Service told me, "Your files have been assigned to a processor for review." After numerous follow up calls, I was asked to clarify my request. So in a letter dated September 6, 2002 I told the Secret Service I did not want any newspaper articles they might have used in their research. I figured I could find relevant articles myself (if I hadn't already), and striking them would speed things along.

The next month, on Nov. 27, 2002, I spoke with Secret Service liaison Reginald Hudson. He said he thought I only wanted court documents related to the Secret Service work on school shootings, and that I never clarified that I wanted all supporting documents (except newspaper clippings). Two years out, the Secret Service had now failed to understand the basic request, let alone fulfill it.

On December 16, the Secret Service wrote back saying they indeed understood the full scope of my request. But they still hadn't produced any documents.

A March 19, 2003 letter finally brought documents relating to my original request, after two and a half years. As originally stated, I received 100 pages. They were from a variety of court cases, some with names blocked out, and mostly provided boilerplate information such as the defendant "knowingly caused the death" of the victim.

The Secret Service also said it had expended 24 hours of search time looking for documents; it had taken two and a half years to squeeze in three full work days. The first two hours of search time were free, as originally noted. But the letter, signed by Secret Service liaison Latita Huff, noted that the other twenty-two hours were charged at the hourly rate of the employee making the search, plus sixteen percent. I owed $774.62. Federal rules require, as pointed out in Huff's letter, that the agency inform a requestor when the fees exceed $250. At that point, the requestor must pay up front to complete the processing. So I informed Huff that I should have been told of the fees when they hit $250, or before, not slapped with a bill after the fact. I never heard from Huff, nor the Secret Service again. Admittedly, I never got anything useful out of them either.

★★★

The U.S. Bureau of Alcohol, Tobacco and Firearms played a significant, direct role in the Columbine investigation, and much of their work was referenced in the first 11,000 pages released by the sheriff's office. I sent the agency a FOIA request on February 3, 2001. With no word as of May 14, I spoke with "disclosure specialist" Marilyn LaBrie. The agency's reply, she said, had been sent to the wrong address. It was then faxed to me. The letter indicated that nothing could be released because any information "could reasonably be expected to interfere with law enforcement proceedings." I wrote back to them noting that the Columbine investigation had already been "exceptionally cleared." And the two criminal cases – Manes and Duran – had been resolved.

I then spoke with Associate Chief Counsel for Disclosure and Forfeiture Richard Isen on July 10, 2001. He himself was bothered about how his agency had handled the FOIA. "Not that this hasn't happened before," he said, "but I don't want it to happen again."

He added: "They never really did the search," and acknowledged, "It just was not their finest hour with that." He suggested I re-file the FOIA, which I did on July 12.

I also sent a check for $400 to cover potential costs. (They promptly lost, then found, the check.)

By now it was no surprise, yet still infuriating and disappointing, that documents were not released for another seven months, in February 2002. After a one-year wait, the 454 pages did contain some new information, such as photos of the bombs used by the killers, and an indication Klebold had harassed someone at Columbine before the shootings. The final charge was $58 in copying costs.

The list of agencies continues. The FBI was arguably the easiest to deal with, and the most forthcoming. The U.S. Department of Education released hundreds of documents, but was difficult about it.

★★★

It is no leap to expect that thousands of Columbine documents remain locked in government file cabinets.

END NOTES

Columbine documents released to the public by the Jefferson County Sheriff's Office begin with JC-001. The actual page numbers follow in six-digit sequence, so page one is JC-001-000001. The final page so far released is JC-001-026859. To avoid unneeded numbers, those pages are referred to here as JC and then the page number, so page one would be JC-1.

I used a PDF file for the latest round of documents - nearly 1,000 - released by the sheriff's office in 2006, so for those documents I have included the PDF page, which provides for much easier searches. The final page (JC-001-026859), for example, would be listed as JC-26859 (PDF 946).

When generally referring to someone's interview with police, I cite the first page of the interview.

Misspellings, poor grammar, lack of capital letters, all capital letters, bold, etc. were left intact in the diaries as much as possible given any formatting limitations such as translating handwriting to print.

The drawings interspersed throughout this book come from Harris and Klebold documents released in 2006 from locations including their diaries, day planners, and computer files.

The Jefferson County Sheriff's 2000 report has officially been called the "Sheriff's Office Final Report on the Columbine High School shootings." It is, in fact, anything but final, and is referred to here as the official report.

I have attempted to make the endnotes as extensive, and formal, as possible, although many documents and reports may be found on the Internet.

One: Day One
Evan Todd tells police Dylan looks like a clown. JC-173.

Official report and Dylan's autopsy describe his clothes and facial hair the day of Columbine.

The official report notes, "Based on comments Klebold and Harris made in their homemade videotapes, the investigation determined the two planned to shoot any surviving students able to escape from the cafeteria after the bombs exploded."
"Klebold and Harris also have bombs constructed with timers in their cars, set to go off once they go back into the school."

Peter Horvath set to be on lunch duty that day comes from interview with him at the school on 10 Jan. 2007.

Eric and Dylan saying as the shooting starts, "This is what we always wanted to do" is from official report as is Gardner being told, "I need you in the back lot!" Gardner actions come from official report.

Lance Kirklin himself recalls Dylan standing over him and shooting him. The Klebold-Lance Kirklin exchange comes from Kevin Vaughan and Lynn Bartels, "Brutal Klebold Emerges in Accounts Survivors Say Teen Was No Meek Follower as He Methodically and Sadistically Killed," *Rocky Mountain News*, Sunday, 6 June 1999 .

Patti Nielson information comes from official report, police interviews with her, and my interview with her in 2008. Some of her information slightly contradicts the police accounts or appears to logically fill in blanks. Given the tradition of errors and lack of clarity in the police reports, I defer to this interview done directly with Nielson.

What happened to Brian Anderson includes information from the official report, other police reports, Nielson interview, and Norm Clarke, "Bullet Just Bounced Off," *Rocky Mountain News*, Friday, 23 April 1999.

Official report says Smoker fired three rounds at Harris. A newspaper report indicates confusion on that, and the number may be four: Kevin Vaughan, "Questions Linger Concerning Columbine Ballistics Reports - Origin of Some Bullets Remains a Mystery as Weapon They

Were Fired From Cannot be Identified," *Rocky Mountain News*, Friday, 28 Dec. 2001.

Jon Curtis and Jay Gallatine actions come from official report.

Number of people in library from official report.

Harris kills five in the library, and Klebold two. Together, they kill an additional three at JC-11141.

Peggy Dodd and Carol Weld information comes from their police interviews, JC-322 and JC-596, respectively.

Accounts of what Eric and Dylan in the library come from official report, the "Columbine Task Force Library Team Executive Summary" (JC-11139), and individual reports of those in the library, including Peter Ball, Patricia Blair, Jennifer Doyle, Lindsay Elmore, Andrew Fair, Makai Hall, Sara Houy, Heather Jacobson, Heidi Johnson, Byron Kirkland, Lisa Kreutz, Joshua Lapp, Nicole Nowlen, Kathy Park, Rebecca Parker, Bree Pasquale, Diwata Perez, Kacey Ruegsegger, John Savage, Valeen Schnurr, Dan Steepleton, Evan Todd, and Aaron Welsh.

The official report appears to have depended on the "Executive Summary," which is far more detailed.

Evan Todd says it appears Eric Harris had a broken nose; his face was also bloody and he was dizzy and wobbly. JC-173. According to the official report, "Investigators believe Harris broke his nose as a result of the 'kick' from the shotgun when he bent to fire under the table." (After killing Cassie Bernall.) Official report also says Bree Pasqual thought Harris was disoriented.

Official report talks of shotgun pellet grazing Tomlin's chest.

Evan Todd, and the official report talk of Dylan shooting the television before leaving the library.

Circumstances of how Sanders is shot comes from official report,

Sanders autopsy, and daughter Angela Sanders' lawsuit.

"Ballistics cannot positively identify the bullets or the weapon used to shoot Sanders," according to the sheriff's official report. "Evidence indicates that both Klebold and Harris at some point fired their weapons south down the library hallway." Yet JC-11869 says Harris shot Sanders with his carbine rifle.

"We are here for the living and the walking" comes from Sanders lawsuit. See also Jeff Kass, "Teacher Struggled to Live - Sanders was Shot Early During Attack, Survived for Hours," *Rocky Mountain News*, Wednesday, 21 Aug. 2002.

After the library, "The gunmen did not appear to witnesses to be overly intent on gaining access to any of the rooms," the official report says. "Their behavior now seemed directionless."

11:44 a.m. cafeteria movements come from sheriff report. At 11:46 a.m., the sheriff concludes that a fiery explosion that fills the screen is a partial detonation of the propane bomb.

I recalculated the number of shots the official report says Eric and Dylan each fired because the El Paso County Sheriff investigation into Dan Rohrbough's killing later found that Eric, not Dylan, shot Rohrbough.

"A thorough investigation by a CBI arson investigator determined that there was evidence on the table and around the gunmen's bodies indicating that the gunmen took their own lives before the fire occurred on the table," according to the sheriff's final report.

Guerra's comments the day of Columbine come from State of Colorado Department of Law Office of the Attorney General [Ken Salazar], *Report of the Investigation into Missing Daily Field Activity and Daily Supervisor Reports Related to Columbine High School Shootings*, 16 Sept. 2004. Guerra follow-up interview, 2. That is actually the second report filed by Salazar when he was attorney general. The first is *Report of the Investigation into the 1997 Directed Report and Related Matters Concerning the Columbine High School Shootings in April 1999*, 26 Feb. 2004.

Two: The Wild West
Devon Adams, Dylan's parents via their police interview, and some news clips are among the accounts that say what was in Dylan's room.

U.S. Census puts the county's residents at 87% white.

Lack of crime centers in the suburbs comes from Mark Baldassare, *Trouble in Paradise* (New York: Columbia University Press, 1986), 13.

Dylan's University of Colorado application being incomplete comes from author's interview with University of Colorado spokeswoman Bobbi Barrow on 6 Sept. 2000.

Some of the information on Buffalo Bill comes from the PBS Web site, http://www.pbs.org/weta/thewest/people/a_c/cody.htm.

Also, "William Frederick Cody" by Paul Fees, Former Curator Buffalo Bill Museum at http://www.bbhc.org/edu/readyReference_01.cfm. Buffalo Bill Museum and Grave, at http://www.buffalobill.org/history.htm.

Youth suicide and firearms:
http://www.pbs.org/thesilentepidemic/riskfactors/guns.html.

http://www.safeyouth.org/scripts/facts/suicide.asp.

http://www.medicalnewstoday.com/articles/81868.php.

Chivington information comes from Robert G. Athearn, *The Coloradans* (Albuquerque: University of New Mexico Press, 1976), 74-75.

Also, http://www.pbs.org/weta/thewest/people/a_c/chivington.htm.

Joe B. Frantz, "The Frontier Tradition: An Invitation to Violence," in

The History of Violence in America, ed. Hugh Davis Graham and Ted Robert Gurr. (New York: Frederick A. Praeger, 1969), 148.

Chivington funeral comes from Alan Dumas, "The Agony and the Infamy Historians Re-evaluate the Civil War Hero Who Led The Bloody Raid on Sand Creek," *Rocky Mountain News*, Sunday, 12 Oct. 1997.

Warring religions in Athearn, *The Coloradans*, 48-49.

Information on the Harris home when it was up for sale comes from the author's walk-thru and copy of the buyer's brochure.

Also, Lynn Bartels, "Harris Home Up For Sale – Two Agents Critical of Family Can't Show It," *Rocky Mountain News*, Wednesday, 25 Aug. 2004.

And, Kieran Nicholson, "Family home of Columbine killer on market Agent's daughter was in school library," *The Denver Post*, Thursday, 26 Aug. 2004.

The daughter of Harris real estate agent Jay Holliday, Jessica, is also the girl clutching her head in the famous *Rocky Mountain News* "Heartbreak" front page photo.

Three: Family
Information on discrimination against Leo as he grew up is from Mary Hoover, "Leo Yassenoff and the Yassenoff Foundation," in *Columbus Unforgettables*, ed Robert D. Thomas. (Columbus: Robert D. Thomas, 1983), 39-40.

Leo's activities in college and some other Yassenoff family history comes from Solly Leo Yassenoff, "The Family of Abraham Yassenoff" (A family history distributed to extended Yassenoff family members, dedication dated August 1999), 22-27.

Milton Yassenoff military information comes from U.S. military records.

"Sandra" comes from W. Hugh Missildine, M.D. and Lawrence Galton, *Your Inner Conflicts-How to Solve Them* (New York: Simon and Schuster, 1974), 24-26.

Author's telephone conversation with Susan Klebold is 17 Dec. 2002.

Susan Klebold's work in college, and beyond, is outlined in her resumes, employment applications, and other school information. Because she often worked for public universities in Wisconsin and Colorado, the material was obtainable through open records laws.

Information on death phobia, phobias in general, and personality disorders comes from: Diagnostic and Statistical Manual, 4th ed. TR, s.v. "personality disorders."

The Encyclopedia of Phobias, Fears, and Anxieties, 2 Rev Sub edition (June 2000), s.v. "death, fear of."

The Gale Encyclopedia of Medicine. 2nd ed., s.v. "Phobias."

Tom Klebold's Wittenberg photo is undated, but is from 1967, according to a university researcher.

Tom Klebold's employment with Conoco comes from the company.

Four: Growing Up
Dylan Candyland incident comes from Cornell professor James Garbarino on the Web site mothersofamerica.com ("April 2001 - News Archive"), and author's 4 Sept. 2002 e-mail exchange with Garbarino.

Brooks Brown, *no easy answers: the truth behind death at columbine* (New York: Lantern Books, 2002) talks of Dylan growing up and playing with Lego and crawdads. School transcripts show Dylan enrolls at Governor's Ranch from August 1989 to June 1993.

Columbine student Nathan Vanderau spoke for *Investigative Reports: Columbine: Understanding Why*. New York: A&E Television Networks,

2002. Television documentary.

Susan Klebold interview with police talks of Brooks and Dylan discussing writing a play in the year before Columbine.

Richard Pool's military background comes from U.S. military records.

Background on Wayne and Kathy Harris comes from their high school yearbooks, Wayne Harris military records, and Lynn Bartels with Carla Crowder, "Goal of Harris' Dad: 'Raise 2 Good Sons' '66 Englewood High Grad Mentioned Kids in Form for 20-year Reunion," *Rocky Mountain News*, Friday, 4 June 1999.

Also, Carla Crowder with Dan Luzadder and Lynn Bartels, "Harrises Didn't See a Monster in Their Midst Friends Believe the Family Taught Kids Right and Wrong, Respect for Others," *Rocky Mountain News*, Monday, 21 June 1999.

Wayne Harris driving the kids to Columbine football games comes from Lynn Bartels and Carla Crowder, "Fatal Friendship How two suburban boys traded baseball and bowling for murder and madness," *Rocky Mountain News*, Sunday, 22 Aug. 1999.

The lack of sibling rivalry between Eric and Kevin comes from *no easy answers* and Eric's AOL profile. JC-26859 (PDF 946).

Information on Katherine Harris from Robyn Anderson comes from Anderson's deposition, p. 214.

Regarding Eric growing up:

Nora Boreaux in Lynn Bartels and Ann Imse, "Friendly Faces Hid Kid Killers Social, Normal Teens Eventually Harbored Dark, Sinister Attitudes," *Rocky Mountain News*, Thursday, 22 April 1999.

Pam Belluck and Jodi Wilgoren, "Shattered Lives–A special report; Caring Parents, No Answers, In Columbine Killers' Pasts," *New York Times*, Tuesday, 29 June 1999.

Kris Otten in Betsy Streisand and Angie Cannon with Joannie M. Schrof, Jeff Kass, Ben Wildavsky and Susan Gregory Thomas, "Exorcising the Pain Littleton buries its dead and tries to understand," *U.S. News & World Report*, 10 May 1999. (Otten's first name is spelled "Chris" in the story).

Alisa Owen in *Investigative Reports: Columbine: Understanding Why.*

Terry Condo in "Fatal Friendship."

Eric's memories of Oscoda come from his essay found on page on JC-26772, (PDF 858).

Oscoda population in 1990 comes from http://www.state.mi.us/msp/cjic/ucr/ucr_h03.htm

Official report says the Harrises moved from Plattsburgh to Littleton in July 1993; in his 1997 class essay Eric recalls Independence Day at Plattsburgh before the move.

Plattsburgh closing in 1995 comes from http://www.strategic-air-command.com/bases/Plattsburgh_AFB.htm

Eric enrolled at Ken Caryl Middle School in Littleton comes from summary of Wayne and Kathy Harris interview in the official Columbine report.

Michelle Hartsough, who worked at Blackjack Pizza with Eric, says his parents were "always grounding him." JC-10150.

Blackjack employee Angel Pytlinski said, "Harris was upset with his dad, because his dad accused him of using LSD." JC-10193.

Obfuscation on the Harris meeting with police is exemplified by author's e-mail exchange with lead Columbine investigator Kate Battan on 29 Dec. 2004. She was asked if she could say when Wayne and Katherine Harris gave the information quoted in the official report to investigators. "No," she said.

My follow-up question was, "'No' meaning you don't know? Or you know, but can't say?"

"It just means no," Battan wrote back in an e-mail.

In the same e-mail exchange about the Klebolds I asked:

"The Klebolds had a well-publicized interview with law enforcement, and the 11,000 pages contain a report on the meeting. They also spoke with detectives the day of Columbine. But were there other meetings with the Klebolds? Two cites lead me to that question. A Sept. 14, 1999 article in *The Denver Post* notes that, 'Klebold's parents, Tom and Susan, have spoken several times with detectives.' And a Sept. 23, 1999 Salon.com article quotes Kate saying: 'It really does begin with the family. But I'm here to tell you, I sat down and I've spent a lot of time with the Klebolds, and they're nice people. It's not like they're these monsters that raised a monster. I mean, they truly are clueless about any warning signs that this was going to happen.'" Battan wrote back: "All reports of interviews have been released."

I asked, "Are there other interviews that did not result in reports? If so, what were the circumstances of them?"

Battan: "I've provided the best answer I can."

Various accounts put the high school renovation at $13.4 million, including Lori Tobias "School Has History of Excellence Columbine Academics, Athletics Win Praise," *Rocky Mountain News*, Wednesday, 21 April 1999.

Eric and Dylan as freshmen comes in part from author's interviews with Rich Long in 2007 and 2008.

Tom Klebold's comments on Dylan in the days before Columbine come from what he told an officer who came to their house the day of Columbine (JC-10522) and in the police interview ten days after the shootings (JC-10507).

"Shattered Lives" reported that Kevin had an A-average and varsity letter, although it is unclear if it was in football. "Shattered Lives" and

Eric's diversion file say he saw his brother often after Kevin started at the University of Colorado.

The recounting of Eric's sports comes from his own paper JC-26567 (PDF 653). In the diversion file, he says he played for the Columbine Rush.

Eric calling Littleton hell and wanting to live on *Doom's* Phobos and believing in aliens comes from his AOL profile.

"Both didn't have a whole lot of friends, but people liked them," as freshmen, according to classmate Kevin Hofstra in "Fatal Friendship."

Rich Long says Eric did the Web pages for physics and science departments.

Five: Rebels
Byron Klebold information comes from a Regis school document, Dylan's diversion file, and news accounts including Lynn Bartels, "Klebold's Brother Stunned When News Broke, He Rushed Home to Check on Dylan," *Rocky Mountain News*, Saturday, 1 May 1999 .

Klebold interview with police talks about Byron's living situation at time of Columbine. JC-10507.

Six: Summer Dreams
People being shoved into lockers comes from *no easy answers* and Robert Perry interview at JC-10852

Doom which "was an escape for him into a world he understood; it was a reality far preferable to the miserable existence of school," according to *no easy answers*. "Eric found himself truly at home there."

no easy answers talks of the different versions of *Doom* Eric created.

Various press accounts talk of the Wiesenthal investigation into *Doom* including Burt Hubbard with Lynn Bartels, "Researchers Say Harris Reconfigured Video Game Boy Turned '*Doom*' into School Massacre,

Investigators Claim," *Rocky Mountain News*, Monday, 3 May 1999.

Robyn Anderson told police Eric's parents were conservative and he wanted them to leave him alone. JC-10619.`

The windshield story and aftermath comes from *no easy answers*, various accounts the Browns have given, and *Report of the Investigation into the 1997 Directed Report and Related Matters Concerning the Columbine High School Shootings in April 1999.*

Some description of the skits where Eric plays a teacher comes from Eric Veik at JC-10908.

Aaron Brown and his parents don't remember the August 1997 report, but there does not appear to be any reason to doubt the chain of events based on the thoroughness and honesty of the Colorado Attorney General investigation. The investigators were Attorney General investigator Michael Jones and Adams County Sheriff's Lt. Michael McIntosh.

Eric says in his diversion file he got along better with men.

Eric's assessment of his own writing comes from JC-26548 (PDF 634-5).

According to Eric's diversion file when there was a family fight, the parents would, "Discuss the conflict, reasons. Usually wait a few days to impose punishment." The fight was over "when we discuss the incident or situation and agree on the facts and punishment. Then he [Eric] has to accept responsibility for his actions and complete his punishment."

Eric himself said he got punished for "anger, not doing chores." When the family has a feud, "Dad yells (at me), or me and my brother yell at each other." An argument was over "When my parents say so."

Eric's taste in music comes from JC-26189 (PDF 272) and his hatred of some bands comes from JC-26784 (PDF 870). His talk of the KMFDM song comes for JC-26552 (PDF 638).

no easy answers indicates Brooks Brown and his friends "got to know" the Trench Coat Mafia in their sophomore year. The key point was that the Mafia "had chosen to take a stand against the bullying at Columbine." "For the first time, [Eric and Dylan] were seeing a group of outcasts who weren't taking the bullying lying down. For once they were seeing kids who dished it right back. Neither of them would forget that lesson."

Eric and Dylan began wearing trench coats about one year before Columbine, Chris Morris believed, for self-protection. Harris' relatively small frame made him susceptible to getting picked on, and he wore the coat to make himself feel tougher. Chris Morris police interview at JC-10796.

Accounts of the Trench Coat Mafia come from police interviews of Thaddeus Boles (JC-10649) and Robert Perry (JC-10852).

Tom Klebold interview with police talks about Dylan and Trench Coat Mafia.

See also Regina Huerter, "The Culture of Columbine" (Submitted to governor's Columbine Review Commission 1 Dec. 2000).

Anne Marie Hochhalter's thoughts about Eric and Dylan comes from Lynn Bartels, "A Story of Healing and Hope - Faith and Friends Helped Paralyzed Student Overcome a 'Very Dark Place'," *Rocky Mountain News* Tuesday, 20 April 2004.

Reports of bullying and especially Eric getting bullied come from "Fatal Friendship," police and media interviews with at least a half-dozen students, Tom Klebold and Kristi Epling police interviews, and *no easy answers*.

Also, Holly Kurtz with Carla Crowder and Lynn Bartels, "Columbine Like a Hologram Life at School Depends on Angle of One's View," *Rocky Mountain News*, Sunday, 25 July 1999.

DeAngelis' rebuttal of "rampant bullying" comes from Holly Kurtz, "Investigating Columbine Principal Questions Notion that Killers Felt Alienated from School Environment," *Rocky Mountain News*, Friday, 25 August 2000.

Robyn Anderson information on bullying comes from police interviews and her deposition.

Joe Stair information comes from his police interview at JC-10889 and various *Rocky Mountain News* stories, including "Like a Hologram."

Eric Dutro information comes from police interview at JC-10684.

Rich Long in 2007 interviews with author says he noticed Dylan wearing a trench coat by his senior year. Dylan saw it as a solution, Long believes. "It was a way for Dylan to say, 'I'm attached. I'm not this follower. I'm involved [in a group].'"

Kim Carlin police interview at JC-5238 and "Fatal Friendship" talk about Dylan being busted for pipe bomb at Blackjack.

Dylan not a morning person comes from Robyn Anderson police interview.

Seven: Junior Criminals
Harris suspension information comes from author's interview with Horvath, Horvath's police interview, and the document at JC-26336 (PDF 420). Dylan's diversion file indicates he got a five-day suspension.

Devon Adams 2007 interview with author talks about her part in being suspended for hacking into lockers.
Eric Harris essay "Guns in School" is from JC-26150 (PDF 232).

Information on the van break-in and what the boys said comes from Deputy Walsh's report at JC-10561.

Trauma of the van break-in on Eric comes from his diversion file. Information on Eric's medication and visit to the psychologist comes from Peter Breggin Oct. 21, 2002 memo in the Solvay court file (1:01-cv-02076-LTB-PAC).

According to Eric's diversion file, "After this incident [the van break-in] occurred, Eric expressed his feelings concerning the above items to a psychologist," the parents wrote. "The doctor recommended antidepressant medication which seems to have helped. His mood is more upbeat. Eric seems to suppress his anger, then 'blow up' and hit something or verbally lash out. He hasn't done this at home but has done it at school and work." Counselor Andrea Sanchez indicated Eric had been on the antidepressant Zoloft for six weeks, and was feeling better. He saw his psychologist once every three weeks, and the family occasionally met with him too. Eric's early diagnosis of his psychological treatment as "nice" comes from his diversion file.

Eric's visit to Kevin Albert comes from Robert Kriegshauser deposition, Eric's diversion file, and Breggin October 21, 2002 memo.

Diversion file indicates the van break-in was the most traumatic experience for Dylan. As to when Dylan got suspended for scratching the locker, it is possibly Sue Klebold who notes in the van break-in diversion file "He [Dylan] recently (within last month) received a one-day in-school suspension for scratching a locker belonging to a student he was mad at. He had to pay $70 to repair the locker." Horvath remembers the incident as occurring in the spring of 1998.
Horvath thinks the design may have been a swastika. A page from Dylan's day planner is a reminder to talk to one of the school deans: "Talk to Mikesell Buying locker front & moving fag away." JC-26456 (PDF541).

The number of times JeffCo investigators called back Randy and Judy Brown comes from Lynn Bartels, "A Trail of Frustration," *Rocky Mountain News*, Monday, 26 April 1999.

The year in Dylan's diary entry regarding a killing spree is not legible, but following the order of the pages it would be November 3, 1997.

Brooks Brown being alerted to Eric's Web pages in March 1998 by Dylan comes in part from *no easy answers*.

Diversion counselor Andrea Sanchez reported that Eric went to the after prom for the (junior) prom and had a good time.

Nate Dykeman friendship with Eric and Dylan and bomb information comes from Nate Dykeman interviews with police JC-8191 and JC-10693.

Zach Heckler at JC-10753.

On the basement tapes Eric says his parents found pipe bombs and took them away: Dan Luzadder, Kevin Vaughan and Karen Abbott with Lynn Bartels, "Killers Taped Chilling Goodbye Harris, Klebold Apologize, Brag in Videos Made Days, Minutes Before Attack on Columbine," *Rocky Mountain News*, Monday, 13 Dec. 1999.

According to JC-10379 it was one bomb.

Eric's talk of turning over his weapons to his parents in his class paper "Good to be bad, bad to be good" is dated September 21, 1998 on JC-26199 (PDF 282). After Columbine Eric Veik told police Harris' mom had found the bomb named "Atlanta" within the last year.

Accounts of deputies Mike Guerra, John Healy, and John Hicks, and Mark Miller and the Browns' report come from the Browns themselves, Report of the *Investigation into Missing Daily Field Activity and Daily Supervisor Reports Related to Columbine High School Shootings*, and *Report of the Investigation into the 1997 Directed Report and Related Matters Concerning the Columbine High School Shootings in April 1999*.

It also appears that Eric's site was unavailable, at least temporarily, after the Browns' 1998 Web report. Aaron Brown said he contacted AOL to report the site, then noticed it had been taken down, according to the attorney general's report.

Eric and Dylan's appearances before Magistrate Jack DeVita come in part from Howard Pankratz, "Youths claimed theft from van was their first crime Jeffco magistrate questioned two during '98 plea," *The Denver Post*, Wednesday, 28 April 28, 1999.

Eight: Diversion
The diversion files of Eric Harris and Dylan Klebold are publicly available.

In the diversion file counselor Andrea Sanchez notes that Eric had brought in a "new" apology letter to her May 14.

Link records show Eric and Dylan only worked together one day at Link and Dave Kirchoff noted the final review for Eric at Link.

The director of diversion, Bobbi Spicer, said the MADD panel is not always a drinking issue but meant to channel a victim's pain.

Nine: Gun Show
"My wrath for January's incident" comes from JC-26237 (PDF 321).

The official report says Eric put X's over the faces of many in his yearbook.

Eric's references for Tortilla Wraps comes from "Fatal Friendship."

Eric at Tortilla Wraps comes from shift manager David Cave at JC-10217 and Jennifer Laufenberg's interview with police. JC-13306.

Dylan's diversion file and the police interview with his parents talk about the Computer Renaissance job at JC-10508.

Eric's research paper on the Nazis is October 1998 at JC-26134. There also appear to be various versions of the paper in the files released in 2006. Eric's other school essays and diary entries here also come from the 2006 files.

Robyn Anderson and her thoughts on Dylan come from her deposition, news stories, and her interviews with police. The account of the purchases comes from Anderson police interviews, news clips, and police reports of interviews with gun dealers James Washington and Ronald Hartmann beginning at JC-8245.

The two shotguns date to at least 1969; the rifle to 1998: JC-8203.

Robyn Anderson told ABC News and the Colorado legislature that Eric and Dylan did not say what they wanted the guns for but she assumed they might go hunting. She said in her deposition the boys might also use the guns for target shooting. She said some people, like her father, only use them for gun collections.

Wayne Harris taking the call from Green Mountain Guns and saying he didn't order any clips comes from the basement tapes.

Billy Dao (JC-10146), Mathew Paul Jackson (JC-10153), and other Blackjack employee interviews say Eric and Dylan tried a classmate and other Blackjack employees to get guns. Phil Duran information comes from his police interview JC-8213.

Manes information comes from his police (ATF) interview: Begins on JC-8237.

Info on Rampart Range camera comes from Jeff Kass and Kevin Vaughan, "Harris-Klebold Video Released - Tape Made 6 Weeks Before Teens' Bloody Columbine Rampage," *Rocky Mountain News*, Thursday, 23 Oct. 2003.

Ten: The Basement Tapes
Except for the intro to the chapter on the basement tapes, I tried to hew as closely as possible to the chronological order but total accuracy is near impossible. I have not seen the tapes, but viewing them would probably not solve the entire problem. Several studied viewings would be needed for a full transcript.

It appears newspapers and *TIME* magazine often take selective basement tape quotes out of chronological sequence to tell a story - i.e. small, focused highlights to discuss, for example, their arsenal. It is still honest and completely understandable, and not necessarily the media's job to give the official transcript.

The sheriff's office has declined to make the tapes fully public, and lead investigator Kate Battan, while helpful at some points, declined to help fill in holes during a latter round of fact-checking. My method was to generally use the sheriff's summary (beginning at JC-10374) as a guide for the chronological order. The summary sometimes gives full quotes from the tapes but often fails to specify who is speaking and just says something to the effect of "they said." I used specific quotes and more details from media accounts to try and fill in the timeline outlined by the sheriff. The first part of the chapter, however, is an amalgam and not meant to represent chronological order.

The basement tapes, according to the sheriff's official report, appear to consist of three different tapes: "One of the tapes was almost two hours long and taped on three separate occasions in March 1999. The second tape, about 22 minutes in length, was shot on two separate occasions on April 11 and 12, 1999. The third tape, 40 minutes long, was taped on eight separate occasions from early April 1999 to the morning of April 20, 1999. Harris and Klebold taped a tour of Harris's bedroom and showed off their weapons and bombs. They recorded each other conducting dress rehearsals and they taped the drive in Harris's car to buy supplies needed for their plans."

A major article on the tapes that also says there are "five secret videos" is Nancy Gibbs and Timothy Roche with Andrew Goldstein, Maureen Harrington and Richard Woodbury, "The Columbine Tapes," TIME, 20 Dec. 1999, 40-57.

Most tapes appear to have been made in Harris' home. In writing that one session was filmed on April 17 at Dylan's house the day of prom, I relied on Peggy Lowe, "Killers' hatred shows in vitriolic "film festival'," The Denver Post, Tuesday, 14 Dec. 1999.

The tapes being called visual suicide notes comes from Howard Pankratz, "Police reveal videos made by Columbine High killers," The Denver Post, Thursday, 11 Nov. 1999.

For parts of the first basement tapes read at the Manes sentencing, where Eric and Dylan thank the gun suppliers, a detailed account comes from Karen Abbott, "Video Message from 2 Killers," *Rocky Mountain News*, Saturday, 13 Nov. 1999.

Battan says all the excerpts she read at the sentencing were from the basement tapes.

Another story is "Killers Taped Chilling Goodbye."

The sheriff trying to downplay the tapes comes from Jeff Kass, "Court to Hear Excerpt From Columbine Killers' Video," *Chicago Tribune*, Friday, 12 Nov. 1999.

One story on Mink not wanting to show the tapes comes from Jeff Kass and Kevin Vaughan with Lynn Bartels and Charlie Brennan, "Sheriff won't release Columbine recordings - But Mink planning to make public 936 pages of documents," *Rocky Mountain News*, Tuesday, 20 June 2006.

Judy Brown recalls the part where Eric angrily reacts to Dylan being Jewish. Dwayne Fuselier recalls the same scene, but in his mind, Eric was surprised rather than angry.

Placing the various bombs and keeping the fire department busy comes from the official report.

Eleven: Senior Projects
Eric considering a two-year college and majoring in computer graphics comes from JC-26631 (PDF 717). In his diversion file Eric talked of majoring in computer science and joining the marines. His dream of being a "marine or something" at JC-26632 (PDF 718).

Author's interview with Gonzales occurred on 19 Sept. 2000.

The summary of Gonzales' interview with police comes at JC-10085. It says that after learning of the Luvox, Gonzales said he would call

Eric back about his eligibility to join the Marines because Gonzales wasn't sure. The summary adds that Gonzales called back Friday or Saturday and left a message for Eric to call him. Gonzales never got a call back, and so never told Eric he was ineligible.

Rather than rely on that second-hand summary, I defer to my direct interview with Gonzales. Gonzales may not have fully known what Luvox was, or have given Eric an official rejection, but based on what Gonzales heard of the drug that night at the Harrises', he figured it would disqualify Eric. That message seems to have been made clear, and Eric reportedly mentioned the rejection to his friends the next day (see *no easy answers* page 121, and Lynn Bartels, "Parents Found Bomb in Room Harris' Pal Tells FBI, Paper That Dad Detonated Explosive With His Son, Didn't Report It," *Rocky Mountain News*, Saturday, 29 May 1999.). Gonzales also says he called his boss immediately after leaving the Harris home to say Eric was no longer a candidate.

"Fatal Friendship" gives account of Rock N' Bowl on Eric's last birthday, as do the police reports with those who were there.

Blackjack owner Christopher Lau talks about Eric ad Dylan's work at JC-10176.

Dylan essay on avenger in a trench coat is on page JC-10467.

Eric's dream essay comes from JC- 26753 (PDF 839).

Official report says Dylan was going to University of Arizona for dorm room. The conversation between Sue Klebold and Judy Brown after Arizona comes from various accounts the Browns have given and *no easy answers*. Dylan's discussion with Horvath about Arizona comes from this author's interview with Horvath.

Dylan's exchange with Peggy Dodd comes from this author's interviews with Rich Long in 2007 and 2008.

Susan DeWitt told police about her date with Eric at JC-10207.

Dylan's behavior before, during and after prom comes from "Fatal Friendship," and Robyn Anderson, Kelli Brown, Nate Dykeman, and Sue Klebold police interviews. Also, Devon Adams interviews with author. The description of Eric's clothing at after prom comes from Kristi Epling. Prom at Denver Design Center comes from JC 8194.

The "26.5 hours" Columbine diary entry for Dylan is from official report.

Police reports with Robyn Anderson, Eric Jackson (JC-10769), and Dustin Gorton (JC-3157 and JC-10733) discuss Eric and Dylan on the day before Columbine. The video may have been released after the shootings: Rock music blares on the stereo as the boys order orange soda, and "cinnamonies." Someone jokes about getting ketchup for the cinnamonies.

Manes' dealings with Eric the night before Columbine comes from his police statement.

A statement from a KMFDM member opposing Eric's actions and beliefs was released after Columbine.

"To do" lists are at JC-026022 to 26025 (PDF 103-106).

Dylan saying "I just wanted to apologize..." on the final segment of the basement tapes comes from *no easy answers* page 207. Some other parts come from "Killers Taped Chilling Goodbye."

Twelve: Violent Profiles
Fuselier hesitates to definitively say Harris was a psychopath, but notes that he acts like one. Information from Fuselier comes from numerous interviews with him from 2004-2008.

Diagnostic and Statistical Manual, 4th ed. TR, s.v., "Antisocial Personality Disorder."

Robert D. Hare, *Without Conscience: The Disturbing World of the Psychopaths Among Us* (New York: The Guilford Press, 1999).

Other cites on causes of antisocial personality disorder:
http://www.mayoclinic.com/health/antisocial-personality-disorder/DS00829/DSECTION=3
http://www.psych.ucsb.edu/~kopeikin/103lec7.htm
Aubrey Immelman information from numerous interviews with him from 2004-2008.

Immelman approvingly quotes psychologist Theodore Millon that the "malevolent psychopath" is "the least attractive of the antisocial variants because it includes individuals who are especially vindictive and hostile." Millon also talks of the "cold-blooded ruthlessness."

Eric's "sadistic"diary entry at JC-26016 (PDF 97).

Mayo Clinic gives causes of depression at mayoclinic.com.

Depressives more likley to commit suicide: http://www.nimh.nih.gov/health/publications/older-adults-depression-and-suicide-facts.shtml#role

On Eric and Dylan committing suicide:
"Who are we to tell Eric what he should or should not do?" is the thought process, Fuselier says.

Immelman says, "That's the ultimate control. You're not going to let them kill you. You will take your own life when you're ready to do it."

Jeremy Coid, "The epidemiology of abnormal homicide and murder followed by suicide," *Psychological Medicine* (Great Britain), 1983, 13, 855-860.

And, James Selkin, "Rescue Fantasies in Homicide-Suicide," *Suicide and Life-Threatening Behavior, Vol. 6 (2)*, Summer 1976, 79-85.

Anthony Barbaro comes from Bill Dedman, "Bullying, tormenting often led to revenge in cases studied," *Chicago Sun-Times*, Sunday, 15

Oct. 2000.
Also, "Upstate Youth in Sniper Trial a Suicide," *New York Times*, Sunday, 2 Nov. 1975.

And, Ford Fessenden with Fox Butterfield, William Glaberson and Laurie Goodstein, "They Threaten, Seethe and Unhinge, Then Kill in Quantity," *New York Times,* Sunday, 9 April 2000.
James P. McGee and Caren R. DeBernardo, "The Classroom Avenger," Sheppard Pratt Health System, originally published in *The Forensic Examiner,* Volume 8, Nos. 5 and 6, May-June, 1999.

Mayo Clinic on atypical depression: http://www.mayoclinic.com/health/atypical-depression/AN01363

Readings and quotations on Southern and Western violence (in chronological order of when studies were published):

Richard E. Nisbett, "Violence and U.S. Regional Culture," *American Psychologist*, 1993. Vol. 48 No. 4, 441-449.

Dov Cohen, Richard E. Nisbett, "Self-Protection and the Culture of Honor: Explaining Southern Violence," Personality and Social Psychology Bulletin (PSPB), October 1994, Vol. 20 No. 5, 551-567.

Dov Cohen, Richard E. Nisbett, Brian F. Bowdle, Norbert Schwarz, "Insult, Aggression, and the Southern Culture of Honor: An 'Experimental Ethnography,'" *Journal of Personality and Social Psychology*, 1996. Vol. 70 No. 5, 945-960.

Dov Cohen, "Law, Social Policy, and Violence: The Impact of Regional Cultures," *Journal of Personality and Social Psychology*, 1996, Vol. 70 No. 5, 961-978.

Dov Cohen, Richard E. Nisbett, "Field Experiments Examining the Culture of Honor: The Role of Institutions in Perpetuating Norms About Violence," *Personality and Social Psychology Bulletin* (PSPB), November 1997, Vol. 23 No. 11, 1188-1199.
Dov Cohen, "Culture, Social Organization, and Patterns of Violence,"

Journal of Personality and Social Psychology, 1998, Vol. 75 No. 2, 408-419.

Dov Cohen, Joseph Vandello, Sylvia Puente, Adrian Rantilla, "'When You Call Me That, Smile!' How Norms for Politeness, Interaction Styles, and Aggression Work Together in Southern Culture," *Social Psychology Quarterly*, 1999, Vol. 62 No. 3, 257-275.

Stephanie Verlinden, Michel Hersen, and Jay Thomas, "Risk Factors in School Shootings," *Clinical Psychology Review*, 2000, Vol. 20 No. 1, 3-56.

National Research Council and Institute of Medicine (2002) Deadly Lessons: Understanding Lethal School Violence. Case Studies of School Violence Committee. Mark H. Moore, Carol V. Petrie, Anthony A. Braga, and Brenda L. McLaughlin, Editors. Division of Behavioral and Social Sciences and Education. Washington, D.C: National Academy Press.

Readings on suicide in the West include:
Karen Auge, "State's high suicide rate slowly getting some care," *The Denver Post*, Saturday, 6 May 2000.

Todd S. Purdum, "Bleak Statistics Tarnish Nevada's Glitter," *New York Times*, Saturday, 19 May 2001.

Bill Scanlon, "Injury deaths down statewide," *Rocky Mountain News*, Friday, 7 June 2002.

Electra Draper, "State's suicide rate eighth-highest," *The Denver Post*, Thursday, 29 Nov. 2007.
On suicide see also Madelyn S. Gould, Sylvan Wallenstein, and Marjorie Kleinman, "Time-Space Clustering of Teenage Suicide," *American Journal of Epidemiology*, Vol. 131, No. 1. 71-78.

Thirteen: The Klebolds: Searching
Those present at the April 10, 1999 interview with Klebolds comes from police report.

Dylan's undated diary entry on society appears to be a couple months before Columbine if you assume the entries are in chronological order; an entry a couple pages before that is dated January 1999. JC-26416 (PDF 501).

The Klebolds the day of Columbine comes from Rollie Inskeep police report (JC-10522) and Inskeep interview with author 29 May 2002.

Robyn Anderson gave this account in her deposition, as she recalled a post-Columbine visit with Tom and Sue Klebold at their home. "They said that he [Dylan] acted kind of weird that morning when he was leaving, that he was just kind of like—when he closed the door to leave, he just said, 'Bye,' you know, like—like he was in a bad mood," Anderson said. "And his mom said that she had planned on asking him what was wrong when he got home from school."

Dykeman's information comes from police interviews. Also, Tom Klebold and Dykeman interviews with police pretty much agree on what was said in their conversation the day of Columbine.

Don Marxhausen interviews with author include 27 Sept. 2000; 5 Oct. 2000; 11 Oct. 2002; and 17 Jan. 2007.

Dee Grant interview with author 31 May 2002. See also J. R. Moehringer, "No One Really Knew Them –Not Even Their Parents," *Los Angeles Times*, Sunday, 25 April 1999.

Klebolds fighting autopsy in Kevin Vaughan, "Klebold Parents Release Autopsy - Decision Ends Long Legal Battle to Keep It Sealed," *Rocky Mountain News*, Saturday, 11 Jan. 2003.

First Klebold statement comes from media reports on Thursday, 22 April 1999.

Klebold funeral includes author interview with Marxhausen, Kornfeld interview with author 25 June 2002, media accounts, and "Exorcising the Pain."

Edgar Berg says Klebolds were prepped for a television appearance.

Klebold letter to Brian Rohrbough in Beth DeFalco and Evan Dreyer, "Klebolds saw no hint of son's rage, letter says," *The Denver Post*, Saturday, 19 June 1999.

Robyn Anderson was deposed on 16 Aug. 2001.

Marxhausen and Adams attest to Klebolds planning scrapbook.

Lawsuit settlements include Karen Abbott and Hector Gutierrez, "Settlement Announced Insurance Companies to Pay $2.5 Million to Families of Columbine Shooting Victims," *Rocky Mountain News*, Friday, 20 April 2001.

Fourteen: The Harrises: Immunity
Harris and Pools immediately after Columbine comes from author interviews with the Fergusons on 30 Jan. 2003 and David Olinger and Peggy Lowe, "Parents try to cope with killers' legacy Pain of own loss, others' lingers after Columbine," *The Denver Post*, Monday, 18 Oct. 1999.

Harris parents reaction day of shootings comes from author interview with Connally 18 Jan. 2001 and his report (JC- 10242).

On the day of Columbine movie in VCR and books in basement at Harris home (JC-9058); a possible bomb and explosive levels of gas (JC-7963); when the house was cleared and what was taken from the home comes from search warrant returns and JC-9088.

Harrises statement comes from "Parents try to cope with killers' legacy."

Author interviews with Dave Thomas on 22 Feb. 2001, and 17 Aug. 2001.

Harris letter issue comes from various news reports including Lisa Levitt

Ryckman, "Columbine Killer's Mom Irate Letters Weren't Delivered Sheriff's Office Has Notes Harris Wrote Expressing Condolence to Families of Victims," *Rocky Mountain News*, Friday, 16 July 1999.

John Masson remarks in Jeff Kass, "No Report of Interview With Harrises 'Nothing of Substance' came from Meeting with Killer's Parents, County Official Says," *Rocky Mountain News*, Thursday, 23 Nov. 2000

Fifteen: The Shoels
The Carneal lawsuits come from Deadly Lessons, "No Exit: Mental Illness, Marginality, and School Violence in West Paducah, Kentucky."

Michael Shoels remarks on Patti Nielson come from Kevin Vaughan, "Calls Swamp Radio Station After Shoelses Criticize Wounded Teacher," *Rocky Mountain News*, Thursday, 1 July 1999.

Nielson's reaction to that radio show comes from author's 2008 e-mail correspondence with Nielson.

United Way in Andrew Guy Jr., "Shoelses decry fund decisions," *The Denver Post*, Wednesday, 15 Sept. 1999.

Riddle remarks on releasing Isaiah's autopsy in April M. Washington, "Shoelses Want Columbine Autopsies Unsealed Judge Blocks Release, Including Killers' Reports," *Rocky Mountain News*, Friday, 18 June 1999.

Peter Boyles remarks comes from Andrew Guy Jr., "Shoelses see love, hate after Columbine Parents fighting charges of opportunism," *The Denver Post*, Sunday 26 Sept. 1999.

Dankside and Hit Room have business filings with the Colorado Secretary of State.

Author traveled to Virginia Tech with the Shoels as a reporter for the *Rocky Mountain News*: "Voice of comfort, insight - Father of Columbine victim goes to Virginia Tech to honor 'promise'," *Rocky Mountain News*,

Saturday, 21 April 2007.

Epilogue
See, *Report of the Investigation into Missing Daily Field Activity and Daily Supervisor Reports Related to Columbine High School Shootings*, and *Report of the Investigation into the 1997 Directed Report and Related Matters Concerning the Columbine High School Shootings in April 1999.*

"Grand Jury Report: Investigation of Missing Guerra Files," In Re: State Grand Jury 2003-2004 Term, Case No.03CR0002, District Court, City and County of Denver, Colorado.

A Sampling of Author's Letters

Aug. 29, 2000

Dear Mr. and Mrs. Harris:

I am writing a book on the Columbine shooting, and recently sent you a packet of newspaper articles I have written to familiarize you with my work.

(Again, I am a former Los Angeles Times reporter now on staff at the Rocky Mountain News. I am also a regular contributor to *US News&World Report*, *The Boston Globe*, *The Christian Science Monitor*, and (New York) *Newsday*.)

I am still interested in speaking with you, and hope that you have had time to look at the articles.

The grieving process, I understand, continues. But I would very much appreciate any insight you could provide that would help explain Columbine, and even other school shootings. The general interest book will examine the many factors that may influence such shootings.

As I have said before, people portray you as good parents, shuttling children to soccer games and attending awards banquets. But you are in a unique position to tell your family's story.

Thank you for your time, and I hope we can begin a dialog.

Sincerely,

Jeff Kass

June 5, 2001

Dear Mr. and Mrs. Harris:

It has been almost one year since I first corresponded with you about the book I am writing on Columbine.

As all of us have come to recognize, Columbine is an ever-changing case. New revelations, such as extra pages of sheriff's documents, continue to alter our perceptions of what happened.

At the same time, some things never change, or change very little. After attending the governor's commission and anniversary observances, it is clear that the pain for many victims' families remains just below the surface. Sometimes it begins to fade, then jumps back as if the shooting happened yesterday. Others say they are only now beginning to grieve after first helping other family members, or spending the past years in anger and civic crusades.

I can only imagine that you are experiencing the same roller coaster of emotions that have yet to show signs of ebbing.

There is another thing that has not changed. The theories I have come to rely upon to make sense of school shootings continue to resonate, despite new developments in Columbine, and copycat school shootings across the country. One part of those theories, for example, is the suicidal element behind many school shootings.

As I continue to research my book, I would hope that you would consider speaking with me. I believe my experience in covering Columbine from day one provides me with the understanding to fully and properly convey your feelings. I also believe I am the only journalist/author who is pursuing a systematic study of why school shootings occur and by extension, how to recognize warning signs and prevent them. That work can greatly benefit from your thoughts and experiences.

I appreciate any help you can provide.

Sincerely,

Jeff Kass

Nov. 21, 2008

Mr. and Mrs. Harris:

We have corresponded many times over the years and I wanted to inform you that the book I have been researching on Columbine and other school shootings will be published in April by Ghost Road Press near the ten-year anniversary.

I have endeavored to find the common denominators among school shooters across the country, and also to paint as full a picture as possible of Eric, Dylan and their families. I have gone beyond the people who have already been quoted in the media.

But your stories have yet to be fully told, and I view your help as an issue of historical significance. In ten years, there have been no major, mainstream books on Columbine. This will be the first, and it may be the only one. This book will be placed in libraries and tell your stories to the world, but only through the eyes of various documents and other people. I have no doubt it will be difficult for you to talk about, but your perspective and understanding would be invaluable.

And this is not just about telling your stories. It is about trying to find answers behind school shootings that continue to wrack the world since Columbine: Conyers, Georgia; Santee, California; Red Lake, Minnesota; Erfurt, Germany; and now the worst of all, Virginia Tech.

If we could speak by Dec. 15, I can still make changes to the book. Thank you for your time.

Sincerely,

Jeff Kass

June 27, 2000

Dear Mr. and Mrs. Klebold:

A newspaper article near the one-year anniversary of Columbine wrote about you, and Dylan's parents. "Four of the saddest people in America," it began.

I know you are still grieving for Dylan, Eric and all those who lost their lives at Columbine. And I'm sure you are still searching for answers.

I am also searching for answers; I wrote to you about three months ago regarding the book I am preparing on Columbine, and other school shootings.

For months, I have been reading books, newspapers, magazines and scholarly papers to understand why school shootings have swept across the country over the past few years, and on April 20. There is probably no one answer, but a number of different causes in each case.

But in order to fully understand the phenomenon, and possibly prevent others from occurring, I need to speak with those closest to the tragedies. You can help.

Your friends and others have portrayed you as good people, and good parents. I remember interviewing Ed Berg when he mentioned Tom's sharp wit during debates on politics, and how he landed on his feet after the state's oil bust. The fact that Sue's job entails helping the disabled speaks to compassion.

But I also need to hear from you. You are in a unique position to tell your stories, Dylan's story, and the story of Columbine. No one can convey the emotions and provide the insight quite like you can. You are key in the search for answers.

Again, as for my credentials, I am a former Los Angeles Times reporter now on staff at the Rocky Mountain News. I am also a regular contributor to US News&World Report, The Boston Globe, The Christian Science Monitor, and (New York) Newsday on national stories out of Colorado and Wyoming. Enclosed are some of my clips on Columbine and other topics to familiarize you with my writing and reporting.

Thank you for your time, and I will plan on contacting you in the coming weeks.

Sincerely,

Jeff Kass

Sept. 28, 2000

Dear Mr. and Mrs. Klebold:

We have, in a manner, corresponded on the issue of teen suicide, and I assume you received the last packet I mailed with some of the studies I had come across.

It would be helpful to know your reaction to the studies, and if you feel they are relevant to understanding Columbine.

      Also, the Education Week articles on teen suicide discuss measures at schools that may help suicidal students. The measures range from smaller classes to training staffers to spot trouble signs. Do you think this should have been done at Columbine High? Would it have helped?

In talking to you about this, I think back to your statement near the one-year anniversary of Columbine. "We are convinced that the only way to truly honor all the victims of this and other related tragedies is to move clearly and methodically toward an understanding of why they occur, so that we may try to prevent this kind of madness from ever happening again."

I believe my book approaches Columbine and other school shootings in a systematic, and in-depth manner, and would again ask for your help.

If you want to begin a dialog, maybe by talking about these questions, we could go through an intermediary. Some of the people who come to mind that I have spoken with at various times are Lisa Simon and/or Gary Lozow, Don Marxhausen, and the Browns.

Thanks again for your time.

Sincerely,

Jeff Kass

Nov. 21, 2008

Mr. and Mrs. Klebold:

We have corresponded many times over the years and I wanted to inform you that the book I have been researching on Columbine and other school shootings will be published in April by Ghost Road Press near the ten-year anniversary.

I have endeavored to find the common denominators among school shooters across the country, and also to paint as full a picture as possible of Eric, Dylan and their families. I have gone beyond the people who have already been quoted in the media, from visiting Bexley and Waldmar Road, to reading a Yassenoff family history and the Sylvania High yearbook.

But your stories have yet to be fully told, and I view your help as an issue of historical significance. In ten years, there have been no major, mainstream books on Columbine. This will be the first, and it may be the only one. This book will be placed in libraries and tell your stories to the world, but only through the eyes of various documents and other people. I have no doubt it will be difficult for you to talk about, but your perspective and understanding would be invaluable.

And this is not just about telling your stories. It is about trying to find answers behind school shootings that continue to wrack the world since Columbine: Conyers, Georgia; Santee, California; Red Lake, Minnesota; Erfurt, Germany; and now the worst of all, Virginia Tech.

If we could speak by Dec. 15, I can still make changes to the book. Thank you for your time.

Sincerely,

Jeff Kass

Carolyn Thomas Christy
Columbus School for Girls
56 S. Columbia Ave.
Columbus, OH., 43209

Oct. 29, 2001

Ms. Christy:

We spoke on the phone last week about conducting research in your archives, and you indicated that they were not organized, and it would not be possible to look through them.

I wanted to make clear that I am not seeking any confidential or private information. Rather, I am looking for past yearbooks and student publications such as TOPKNOT. As you know, such items are publicly available, but are sometimes hard to find and not in a centralized location.

I am asking for your assistance because I am writing a book on Columbine, and other school shootings. It is to be a general interest, nonfiction publication.

Columbine is the deadliest school shooting in U.S. history. It left 15 dead, and has become part of a puzzling, and troubling trend among students throughout the country. Dozens have been killed and injured in various shootings.

My book looks at the common denominators among school shooters to help spot trends and head off future shootings. One place we look for answers, and a way to tell the story, is to follow the lives of the shooters. As you may know, Susan Yassenoff Klebold, the parent of Columbine shooter Dylan Klebold, attended Columbus School for Girls in the 1960's.

In order to better understand the motivation of school shooters, it is important to trace their families. I do not know if the parents of the Columbine shooters played any role in their delinquent behavior. But it is an important avenue of research—if for no other reason than to rule out the family and focus on other factors.

Research in your archives can help illuminate the Klebold family by noting their interests and achievements.

The issue here is not the Columbus School for Girls. But I am appealing to your unique status as an institution of learning. Your school has an excellent reputation. I am sure that comes from asking students to tackle difficult social issues through debate, research, and writing. I have no doubt that your library brims with books on history, politics and society that are respected, in large part, because of their dedicated research and insights.

I hope your institution can now help me with this important endeavor.

Thank you for your time, and I hope to speak with you soon. Enclosed is a copy of my resume.

Sincerely,

Jeff Kass

Nov. 10, 2000

Gary Edwards
FOI Request, U.S. Secret Service
950 H. St., N.W., Suite 3000
Washington, D.C., 20001

Mr. Edwards:

Pursuant to the Federal Freedom of Information Act, 5 U.S.C. Sec. 552, I request access to and copies of:

Secret Service files and information on the Columbine High School shooting in Jefferson County, Colorado on April 20, 1999.

According to the Secret Service's "Safe School Initiative, An Interim Report on the Prevention of Targeted Violence in Schools," the agency studied 37 school shootings. "For each incident, researchers reviewed primary source materials, such as investigative, school, court, and mental health records and answered several hundred questions about the case. Teams of investigators and social science researchers coded each of the cases, with at least two raters assigned to each case. Each rater independently answered questions about the incident in a codebook, then discussed their ratings with the other team member and produced a single 'reconciled' scoring for the case. Information gathered about each case included facts about the attacker's development of an idea and plan to harm the target, selection of the target, motivation for the incident, communications about their ideas and intent, acquisition of weapons, as well as demographic and background information about each attacker." The report was prepared by the Secret Service National Threat Assessment Center.

According to various press reports, I believe some of the information and items in possession of the Secret Service—and also used by the Federal Bureau of Investigation—may be:

1) The FBI interview with Columbine High School Student Nate Dykeman.   According to a May 29, 1999 article in the Denver Rocky Mountain News, Dykeman gave the FBI information about Eric Harris and his father detonating a homemade bomb. Records of the interview may be in the National Center for the Analysis of Violent Crime.

2)   The surveillance videotape recorded in Columbine High School's cafeteria on April 20, 1999—or a copy of it. Also, any notes, analysis, or other information relating to the tape.   A June 17, 1999 article in the Denver Post says that the video was enhanced by the FBI and apparently did not indicate the presence of a third gunman at the shooting. The tape was enhanced by the FBI lab in Quantico, Va., according to the article. Also, the FBI/ the National Center for the Analysis of Violent Crime monograph titled "The School Shooter: A Threat Assessment Perspective," states that the agency requested crime scene photographs and videos from school shootings it studied.

3)   A list of the 18 school shootings studied for "The School Shooter" monograph

COLUMBINE: A TRUE CRIME STORY

and any explanation as to why those 18 cases were used. Also, the minutes and/or summary of the meeting convened by the FBI in Leesburg, Va. to discuss school shootings. A list of those who attended, and what role they may have had; what they may have said, what speeches they may have given, and the text of the speeches. And the accounts of the different topics discussed and events held.

More than 300 educators and law enforcement officials from around the country gathered for a four-day symposium beginning on or around July 12, 1999, according to the July 13, 1999 edition of the Denver Post. The Post reported that author James Garbarino was among the speakers, and the National Education Assn. and U.S. Dept. of Education were among those invited. Rick Kaufman, spokesman for Jefferson County schools where the Columbine shooting occurred, also was in attendance, according to the Post.
"The School Shooter" monograph states that at least 160 were invited to the symposium. The monograph also states that the symposium included expert panels, breakout groups, and conclusions that were presented.

4)   The FBI's structural model of the Columbine High School library in relation to the April 20, 1999 shooting at the school, and a photo, videotape, or other description of the model.   The July 14, 1999 Denver Post reported on the FBI model.

5)   Letters threatening violence like the April 20, 1999 Columbine High School shooting and sent to Arvada West, Bear Creek, Dakota Ridge, Pomona, Standley Lake and any other high schools in Jefferson County, Colorado following the Columbine shootings. Also, similar letters sent to the Denver Rocky Mountain News and Denver Post. Also, any other notes, conclusions, and documents relating to the FBI-led team that investigated hundreds of school threats after the Columbine shooting.
The Sept. 2, 1999 Denver Rocky Mountain News reported on the work of the FBI team.

6)   Documents, interviews or other information relating to Tom and Susan Klebold and Wayne and Kathy Harris, the respective parents of Columbine High school shooters Dylan Klebold and Eric Harris. Also, any documents, interviews or other information relating to other relatives of the two shooters.
The FBI's school shooter monograph states that on the cases studied, the agency requested "Interviews with persons who knew the students and families and provided information about offenders' background."

7)   What have been called the "home videos" made by Columbine shooters Eric Harris and Dylan Klebold, and any other materials produced by Harris and Klebold.
The "home videos" were found in Harris' home the day of the shootings, and made in Harris' home, according to the Dec. 13, 1999 Denver Rocky Mountain News. The FBI school shooter monograph states that the agency requested "Examples of the shooter's writings, drawings, doodles, essays, letters, poems, songs, videotapes and audiotapes," along with "school records and any class work that would provide insight into the shooter and his relationships with teachers and other students," and "other pertinent case materials."

8)   The America Online Internet writings, and any other Internet materials, of former Columbine High School students Dylan Klebold and Eric Harris, who participated in the April 20, 1999 shootings at the school. Any FBI analysis of Internet materials related to

the shooters.

An April 22, 1999 article in the Denver Rocky Mountain News states that America Online pulled and preserved Harris' Internet writings in anticipation of a subpoena to turn them over to the FBI. In the article, America Online did not indicate whether Klebold had an account. And the FBI "School Shooter" monograph states that the FBI requested the "writings and drawings" of school shooters.

9)   Psychiatric, or other medical records and/or information, relating to Eric Harris and Dylan Klebold.
It has been widely reported that Harris was taking the prescription drug Luvox at the time of the April 20, 1999 shooting. According to the FBI monograph, the agency requested "counseling and psychiatric reports and evaluations" of the shooters in the cases it studied.

10)   Disciplinary records concerning Eric Harris and Dylan Klebold from the Jefferson County School District, and police records prior to April 20, 1999 concerning Harris and Klebold. Harris and Klebold were in a Jefferson County District Attorney diversion program; their case numbers are 000336 and 000337, respectively.
                              The FBI monograph states that in cases it studied, school records were requested, along with "a summary of the incident, as described in investigation reports."

11)   Search warrants for the homes of Eric Harris and Dylan Klebold on or after April 20, 1999. The FBI monograph states that it requested "a summary of the incident, as described in investigation reports."

12)   A 1997 videotape made by Columbine students that depicts trenchcoat-wearing students armed with weapons moving through the school halls. The film ends with the school exploding. The son of Denver FBI agent Dwayne Fuselier was involved in the making of the tape, according to the May 8, 1999 Denver Rocky Mountain News.

13) Any attempts to rescue Columbine teacher Dave Sanders, who was shot early on at Columbine on April 20, 1999 and later died.

Please waive any applicable fees. Release of the information is in the public interest because it will significantly contribute to public understanding of government operations and activities. Also, the information will be used for a book I am writing, tentatively titled "Columbine Family: The search for answers among a victim's family, and the killers' families." I am currently a staff writer at the Denver Rocky Mountain News, and regular contributor to US News and World Report, The Boston Globe, The Christian Science Monitor and (New York) Newsday. Because subsequent requesters may also want copies of these documents, I do not consider it fair that as the first requester, I should bear the full cost of the initial search for this material.

I would also ask that the information released be relayed to me in chronological order, as it becomes available.

If my request is denied in whole or part, I ask that you justify all deletions by reference to the specific exemptions of the act. I will also expect you to release all segregable portions of otherwise exempt material. I, of course, reserve the right to appeal your decision to withhold any information or to deny a waiver of fees.

I would appreciate your communicating with me by telephone, rather than by mail, if you have questions regarding this request. I look forward to your reply within 20 business days (excluding Saturdays, Sundays and legal holidays), as the statute requires.

Thank you for your assistance. Enclosed are the various newspaper clips I have cited.

Jeff Kass

June 9, 2002

Co-Director
Office of Information and Privacy
U.S. Dept. of Justice
Flag Building, Suite 570   FOIPA No. 934,178-001
Washington, DC 20530-0001   Freedom of Information Appeal

Dear Sir or Madam:

I am a Denver-based reporter writing a book on Columbine, and other school shootings.

Thank you for your May 14, 2002 response, and fee waiver, to my Nov. 10, 2000 FOIA
request.

I would like to appeal deletions and pages withheld regarding documents on the Columbine
High School shooting, in Jefferson County, CO. on April 20, 1999.

The names of every FBI agent among the 320 pages were deleted. I appeal that because
law enforcement documents generally reveal the names of officers involved. This is basic,
factual information. FOIA is meant to illustrate the workings of government, and that work
is hidden if the names of officers are blocked out. While violent threats, nationwide, arose
out of Columbine, I do not believe FBI officers involved in the Columbine investigation
were dealing with matters of national security. The role was more as assistance to Jefferson
County. Huge quantities of information on Columbine have emerged in the three years
since the shooting. Follow-up with FBI agents to double check information, fill in missing
information, and fully evaluate their work is near impossible without their names. Revealing
the names does not relate to the internal rules and practices of the agency, and would not in
itself reveal confidential, investigatory techniques or procedures.

Names of FBI agents involved in Columbine have already been released through the Jefferson County Sheriff's Office. Jefferson County, the lead investigative agency, has released
approximately 17,000 documents under court order. Those documents include reports from
other law enforcement agencies, such as FBI. Jefferson County did not block out the names
of law enforcement officers. This produces the odd situation of FBI not confirming the
names of its own officers that are already public in the same exact documents. See enclosed
Dykeman interview FBI agents involved in the Columbine investigation have also been interviewed by the media, and their names placed in newspapers. See enclosed

On a practical level, some FBI documents have so many redactions, which I believe are un-
necessary, they make no sense.

The public interest in these records derives from Columbine being the deadliest school
shooting in U.S. history. Fully documenting the multi-agency response, and the activities of
perpetrators and accomplices, can help improve law enforcement tactics and prevent future
school shootings. (Your own agency has said as much given its request for Columbine-relat-
ed materials to prepare for a monograph and symposium on school violence) See enclosed

FBI document

I would also appeal the redactions of the names of those interviewed. Often, documents only indicate a contact was made. But there is no evidence of any follow-up or conclusions. Providing the names would allow for such follow-up research. These names also have been revealed in previously released documents. See enclosed Dykeman interview

In addition, I would appeal on the basis of an inadequate search. For example, there is no mention of an FBI interview with the University of Arizona, where Columbine killer Dylan Klebold was planning on attending college. See enclosed FBI document

Finally, if redactions were made to prevent interference with law enforcement activity, the Jefferson County Sheriff's Office says the case was closed and "exceptionally cleared" on Feb. 8, 2001, because suspects Eric Harris and Dylan Klebold are dead, and there can be no filing of charges against them. There were no other shooters, according to the sheriff. Those who improperly supplied guns to Harris and Klebold have been prosecuted.

My appeals would include the following, specific issues based on the 320 pages released:

Page 33: There is a fax cover sheet, but it is unclear if any pages follow due to a deletion, inadequate search, or other reason.

Pages 45-56: Names on FBI surveillance logs and automobile documents are deleted. Yet the Jefferson County Sheriff's Office, the lead investigative agency on Columbine, has already released the names of the gun suppliers, and the "associates" of the two killers.

Pages 76-77: The pages include no printout or inventory of the messages, essays, etc. of what was found on the computers of the Columbine shooters.

Page 81: Referencs an internet chat on a floppy disk, but there is no reproduction of what was contained on the disk.

Page 83: Reference to another computer disk containing an internet chat room conversation, but no reproduction of the disk contents is included.

Page 92: References an e-mail that is not included.

Page 98: References assistance from the FBI Structural Design Unit for a 3-D model of Columbine High. But no other mention or information exists. I had originally requested any photo, videotape, or other description of the model.

Pages 99-100: Two computer CD's containing Columbine shooter Eric Harris' account with America Online are referenced, but there are no copies or inventories of their contents.

Pages 109-110: Reference a subpoena served on America Online; again there is no record of what was found, and no copy of the search warrant.

Page 111: A surveillance videotape is mentioned, but there is no copy of the tape.
Page 136: Mentions America Online profiles, but no formal request or search warrant to

obtain the materials is included.

Page 149: Faxes of America Online profiles regarding the Columbine shooters are mentioned, but not included.

Page 154: References certain e-mails from Colorado State Patrol, but none are included.

Page 155: E-mail addresses are referenced, but not included.

Page 163: Mentions a written statement regarding an encounter with Dylan Klebold, but the statement is not included.

Pages 175-81: Mention computer evidence and audiotapes, but no transcripts or inventories of the materials are included. (A Columbine 911 tape enhanced by the FBI concerning the call of art teacher Patty Nielson from inside the school library on April 20, 1999 was among my original requests, along with any FBI conclusions, or analysis of the tape. A June 12, 1999 article in the Denver Rocky Mountain News said the FBI was enhancing the tape.)

Page 184: Mentions handwriting samples, but none are included.

Page 202: A male subject was guaranteed anonymity for use of his name and information on a search warrant affidavit until charges were filed. There are no pending, criminal cases regarding the Columbine shootings, so I would request that the name be released.

Pages 211-213; and 239-241: Indicate analysis of computer evidence, but includes no summary, transcript of contents, etc.

Page 248: References aerial photographs of Columbine taken 4/28/99, but no photos are included.

Pages 262-265: Concern 'consent to search' forms, but no results of those searches are included.

Page 284: An evidence report gives no indication of the evidence seized.

Page 291: References an America Online chat log and two copies of a profile, but nothing is attached.

Page 297-299: Medical release documents. I would appeal the deletion of the name or names. The names of those injured and killed at Columbine have been widely disseminated and officially released. Indicating the name(s) on the medical records sought would not reveal the medical records themselves, but rather provide a better view of exactly what parts of the Columbine investigation the FBI participated in. There appears to be one or two medical release forms among these three pages, so releasing the names would clear up any confusion.

Page 307: References photos of Columbine High on 5/6/99, but none are attached.

Also, the following items listed in my original request do not appear to be referenced at all, even to deny them. If these items were overlooked as part of my FOIA response, I would ask that they be searched for, and that they not be treated as an appeal at this point:

1) The actions of FBI SWAT officers at the Columbine High School shooting on April 20, 1999, including any shots fired by the SWAT officers. The Rocky Mountain News reported on July 20, 2000 that the head of the Denver FBI office, Mark Mershon, told the governor's Columbine Review Commission that an FBI SWAT team waited an hour to enter the high school to be briefed on available intelligence.

2) The surveillance tape recorded in Columbine High School's cafeteria on April 20, 1999—or a copy of it. Also, any notes, analysis, or other information relating to the tape. A June 17, 1999 article in the Denver Post says that the video was enhanced by the FBI and apparently did not indicate the presence of a third gunman at the shooting. The tape was enhanced by the FBI lab in Quantico, Va., according to the article.

3) Any other letters (than those enclosed in the response) threatening violence like the April 20, 1999 Columbine High School shooting and sent to Arvada West, Bear Creek, Dakota Ridge, Pomona, Standley Lake and any other high schools in Jefferson County, Colorado following the Columbine shootings. Also, similar letters sent to the Denver Rocky Mountain News and Denver Post. Also, any other notes, conclusions, and documents relating to the FBI-led team that investigated hundreds of school threats after the Columbine shooting.

4) A 1997 videotape made by Columbine students that depicts trenchcoat-wearing students armed with weapons moving through the school halls. The film ends with the school exploding. The son of Denver FBI agent Dwayne Fuselier was involved in the making of the tape, according to the May 8, 1999 (Denver) Rocky Mountain News.

5) Any records or discussion of a conflict of interest regarding Denver FBI agency Dwayne Fuselier, the lead FBI investigation on the Columbine case whose son once attended the school. According to the May 8, 1999 Rocky Mountain News, the FBI did not see a conflict of interest.

6) FBI knowledge of any attempts to rescue Columbine teacher Dave Sanders, who was shot early on at Columbine on April 20, 1999 and later died.

Any other information, conclusions or analysis of the FBI regarding the Columbine shooting.

Thank you for your time. I look forward to hearing from you shortly.

Sincerely,

Jeff Kass

June 15, 2001

Assistant Director, Liason and Public Information
Department of Treasury
Bureau of Alcohol, Tobacco and Firearms, Disclosure Division
650 Massachusetts Ave., N.W., Room 8290
Attn: Disclosure Branch
Washington, DC 20226
FOIA Appeal

Dear Sir or Madam:

I am appealing the denial of my FOIA request, number 122000-MRL 01-820, regarding the
Columbine High School shooting in Jefferson County, Colo. on April 20, 1999.

The request was denied on May 14, 2001 because "these records could reasonably be
expected to interfere with law enforcement proceedings." (see enclosed) I am appealing
because the Jefferson County Sheriff's Department that has jurisdiction over the shooting
and that has been the lead agency, has closed its investigation. The case was "exceptionally
cleared" on Feb. 8, 2001, according to the sheriff's department, because suspects Eric Harris
and Dylan Klebold are dead, and there can be no filing of charges against them.

As stated in my previous request, I am a Denver-based reporter writing a book on the
Columbine High School shooting with the working title "Columbine Family: A victim, the
killers, and the families' search for answers." Pursuant to the Federal Freedom of Information Act, 5 U.S.C. Sec. 552, I request access to and copies of Bureau of Alcohol, Tobacco and
Firearms information and involvement related to the Columbine High School shooting.

Some of the ATF's role is covered in the Jefferson County Sheriff's Department "investigative files" on the Columbine shooting comprising 11,000 pages. There was no index of these
pages made available to the general public. But one reading of the files indicates that at least
some of the ATF's role is covered in the following pages of the Columbine investigative files:

-JC-001-7724, to 7726, inclusive; (and continuing using only the last four numbers to prevent
redundancy);
-7780 to 7784, inclusive;
-7804 and 7805;
-8135 to 8145, inclusive;
-8150 to 8191, inclusive;

-8201 to 8258, inclusive.

I would therefore not request copies of those documents, which are mostly summaries of
interviews. But I am requesting any other documents or materials in possession of the ATF
relating to the Columbine shooting.

Documents and/or other material that may be in the possession of ATF in relation to Columbine may be those used in the creation of the Mosaic-2000, and those used in conjunction

with the U.S. Dept. of Education to help school officials deal with homemade explosives in schools.

As for documents and information on ATF analysis of pipe bombs and fragments from Columbine, at least part of the work was done at the ATF lab in Walnut Creek, California. The ATF may also have a map of where bomb fragments—and possibly whole bombs—were located inside Columbine High School.

I am also requesting videotapes that may be in possession of the ATF. They include a videotaped interview with Robyn Anderson, one of the Columbine gun suppliers. According to Jefferson County investigative report page JC-001-008219, that videotape was in the ATF evidence vault in Denver, Colorado as of 4/25/99.

I would also request videotapes of interviews with Mark Manes and Philip Duran, two others also involved in supplying guns to the Columbine shooters. In addition, I am requesting a videotape showing Columbine shooters Eric Harris and Dylan Klebold firing weapons. The videotapes are mentioned in ATF interviews in Jefferson County investigative report pages JC-001-008176 and 8240. According to ATF interviews, the video was made on March 6, 1999 by Philip Duran and Mark Manes using a camera from Columbine High School. It was in the possession, at one point, of Mark Manes' attorney. There is already public disclosure as summaries of these, and the interview videotapes, are in the investigative reports.

Supporting documentation for the newspaper articles and police reports cited above was included in the original request.

Another request I am making is for any index the ATF has for the 11,000 pages of investigative reports from the Jefferson County Sheriff's Dept.

I am not interested in any documents available through the ATF Web site. I do not wish to inspect the records at an ATF office; please send them to the above address.

My user category is news media. The book "Columbine Family" is a general interest, nonfiction publication to be distributed through standard outlets such as book stores and the Internet. Cost per book is as yet undetermined, but is expected to be commensurate with the industry standard for hardcover and/or paperback books.

Please waive any applicable fees. Release of the information is in the public interest because it will significantly contribute to public understanding of government operations and activities. Also, subsequent requesters may request copies of these documents or other information given the high profile nature of Columbine and other school shootings across the country. I do not consider it fair that as the first requester, I should bear the full cost of the initial search for this material.

I would also ask that the information released be relayed to me in chronological order, as it becomes available.

If my request is denied in whole or part, I ask that you justify all deletions by reference to the specific exemptions of the act. I will also expect you to release all segregable portions of otherwise exempt material. I, of course, reserve the right to appeal your decision to withhold any information or to deny a waiver of fees.

I would appreciate your communicating with me by telephone, rather than by mail, if you have questions regarding this request.

Thank you for your assistance.

Sincerely,

Jeff Kass

Printed in the United States
138542LV00002B/101/P

9 780981 652566